WAR & MIL

D0816542

THE WILD GEESE

Other books by the author

THE CONGO
AFRICA UNDER MY HEART
I'LL COME BACK IN THE SPRINGTIME
THE RAJAH FROM TIPPERARY

with Edwin Sauter, Jr:

A CROWN FOR THOMAS PETERS
SWORD OF THE HAUSAS
SOLDIER OF AFRICA

The *Wild Geese*

The Irish Soldier in Exile

MAURICE HENNESSY

THE DEVIN-ADAIR COMPANY
OLD GREENWICH

Copyright © 1973 by Maurice N. Hennessy
Permission to reprint material from this book
must be obtained in writing from the publishers
For information, address
The Devin-Adair Company,
Old Greenwich, Connecticut 06870

Library of Congress Catalog Number 74-13747
ISBN 0 283 97953 4
Printed in Great Britain

Contents

Acknowledgements

It is not easy to express my full gratitude for the very considerable help I have received from so many interested people and sources in the writing of this book.

I owe special mention to Padraig O Maidin, the Cork County librarian, both for his constant advice and help in obtaining the necessary source material, but also for the opportunity to discuss frequently with him and our mutual friend, William Declan O'Connell, M.A., Literary Editor of the *Cork Examiner,* so many of the Wild Geese historical personalities and events. I was particularly fortunate in finding two men, so well-informed and so close to authentic sources, who were interested and willing to volunteer all their information about the Wild Geese.

Professor John A. Murphy of University College, Cork, both in discussion and by a gift of his book *Justin MacCarthy Lord Mountcashel,* was most helpful in clarifying the actual account of the exchange of armies.

Walter McGrath's intensive research into Irish Brigades in the Boer War was invaluable, as was Walter's personal advice given to me during our discussions.

To Daniel O'Keefe and William Cahill of the University College, Cork, library I also express my thanks for their kind assistance.

Without constant reference to Jennings's and O'Callaghan's wonderful works and various volumes of *The Irish Sword,* this book could not have been written. The latter publication is, in my humble opinion, one of the finest research documents published in the English language today and as an historical record is invaluable in the world of military history.

For assistance on the American side, I am particularly grateful to Thomas J. Mullen from New Jersey and the Sons of St

Patrick, whose excellent volume, *The History of the Friendly Sons of St Patrick in the City of New York,* contains an abundance of information. Both the chapter references and the bibliography contain a list of the many reference works consulted. If I have failed to pay tribute to any authors or sources, I do so unwittingly and hope that they will accept my sincere gratitude for the very scholarly material which was available.

My gratitude must also be extended to Patrick Cockburn, whose advice during the early chapters of the book was both constructive and helpful; to John de Courcy Ireland for his help on the naval side and to Micheline Walsh for her remarkable work on the Women Wild Geese.

To Anne Stewart of the National Gallery and Oliver Snoddy of the National Museum I am greatly indebted for their help and co-operation in finding suitable illustrations.

Lastly, but by no means least, my profound gratitude is due to Mary Hennessy who, under the most arduous circumstances, combined her outstanding skills as an editor and typist with those of a mother.

Publisher's acknowledgements

We are grateful to the following for permission to reproduce extracts from their books: to Curtis Brown for Jon Manchip White's *The Life and Times of Maurice Comte de Saxe,* to Edward Arnold for H. A. L. Fisher's *A History of Europe,* to Chatto and Windus and Christopher Duffy for *The Wild Goose and the Eagle,* to Rupert Hart-Davis for Stephen Clissold's *Bernardo O'Higgins and the Independence of Chile,* and to Mrs. I. Wise, the Macmillan Company of Canada and Macmillan, London and Basingstoke for James Stephens' *Collected Poems.*

Illustrations

We are grateful to the National Museum of Ireland for permission to reproduce plates 7, 8, 9, 10, 11, 14, 15, 18, 19 and 21; to the National Gallery of Ireland for plates 1, 2, 3, 4, 5, 6, 13 and 22; and to the National Library of Ireland for plate 20.

Dedication

In devoted friendship to William Declan O'Connell and Padraig O Maidin, with whom I have so pleasantly and often winged with the Wild Geese the world over, mourned for their exile, gloried in their triumphs, and drunk with pride to their magnificent achievements.

Note

In an effort to clarify the political complexity of Europe with its resultant wars and battles during the seventeenth and eighteenth centuries, a military chronology will be found on p. 212. This will enable the reader to put the battles mentioned in the text in their proper historical perspective.

Introduction

INIS FAL

Now may we turn aside and dry our tears!
And comfort us! And lay aside our fears,
For all is gone!

All comely quality!
All gentleness and hospitality!
All courtesy and merriment

Is gone!
Our virtues, all, are withered every one!
Our music vanished, and our skill to sing!

Now may we quiet us and quit our moan!
Nothing is whole that could be broke! No thing
Remains to us of all that was our own.

James Stephens, *Collected Poems*

A political wag is reputed to have said of the British Empire:
'The Irish fought for it, the Scottish and the Welsh ran it,
but the English kept the profits.' Like so many such statements,
apocryphal or not, it contains an element of truth. This book
will, I hope, substantiate any such truth with reference to the
Irish, but it will do something else also: it will confirm that
during the days of empire-building, British or other, Irish emigrants played a dominant role even though their influence was
felt far from their native soil.

It was inevitable that a people who helped to found five
navies, who contributed largely to the liberation of numerous
nations and who participated in conflicts in practically every
part of the world before and since the days of Louis XIV of
France, should have had a major effect on world events.

A prime purpose of this work is to give a concise account of this effect and to show that despite the good and bad characteristics attributed to the Irish people, they must have had a unique inherent greatness, which survived despite years of injustice and subservience to alien rule.

The name 'Wild Geese' was given to the wandering Irish emigrants who, either freely or as victims of political strife, left their homeland during the seventeenth and eighteenth centuries. It is with these that this book concerns itself, especially since those who remained at home rarely measured up in terms of military achievement to their nomadic kinsmen.

As an Irishman I am, naturally, open to charges of chauvinism and hagiography. My defence is that an attitude of mind derived from a life lived in four continents and exhaustive research should be sufficient protection against the subjective.

It was inevitable that the series of events which forced the leading clansmen of a nation to leave their home and people would have dramatic effects. For the basic cause of the Irish emigration in the seventeenth century was that two foreign kings faced each other across a river on Irish soil to fight for the British crown—a crown that for centuries had, as one of its primary objectives, the suppression of Irish freedom.

The Irish river was the fateful Boyne; the battle between the kings became the prelude to the partition of a country and to a sectarian struggle between two fanatical denominations.

Those who study the events in these pages will, I hope, be compelled to ask themselves the following questions and answer them according to their varying viewpoints : why, after 300 years, must a large part of the British Army still be forced to stand between these two 'Christian' peoples engaged in a conflict that still divides one of the smallest countries in Europe? How can a people who have brought to the world such courage and humanity and excellence still be wallowing deep down in the petty muck of sectarianism and bigotry, and be so apparently indifferent to the judgment of the world to which they have contributed so much?

Maurice N. Hennessy
Youghal, County Cork, 1973

CHAPTER I

The Departure

*These men are leaving all that is most dear in life for a
strange land in which they will have to endure much, to
serve in an army that hardly knows our people; but they
are true to Ireland and have still hopes for her cause; we
will make another Ireland in the armies of the great king
of France.'*

—Patrick Sarsfield, as he
watched his Irish Army
embark for France in 1691,
quoted by William O'Connor Morris
in *Memoirs of Gerald O'Connor*

In the spring of 1690 one of the strangest transactions in military history took place in Ireland : two countries exchanged
armies. In Cork harbour a brigade of Irish soldiers, two-thirds
of whom were young recruits, embarked for France under the
command of Justin MacCarthy, Lord Mountcashel, on ships
which had just landed 6,000 veteran French troops. The ragged, unarmed, and inexperienced Irish force was a major
migration of the Wild Geese — a name that has lasted through
the centuries and identifies the forerunners of 'great hosts of
Irishmen who were to die under the French flag'.[1] On the face
of it, the bargain seemed to be one-sided; later events proved
that the real benefactors of the exchange were to be the French,
whose army was commanded by the effeminate Count de
Lauzun.

In the year 1690 Ireland held the key which was to open
the door leading to the throne of England. Two kings were on
her soil and were preparing to face each other in the most vital
struggle of the Jacobite War. It was natural that James II of
England should pin his faith on the Catholic heart of Ireland
in order to retain his throne; it was equally understandable
that William of Orange should find his support in Protestant

Ulster — the counties of Armagh, Tyrone, Donegal, Fermanagh and Caban — which had been so expertly settled by Protestant authority in 1641. Not only did the conflict between Protestant William and Catholic James II almost create civil war in England, but it also spilled over into Ireland.

Louis XIV of France, while he distrusted James II, nevertheless gave him his support, some of it quite practical. Louis was prepared to go to any lengths to bring about the downfall of William of Orange. It was the latter who in 1686 had engineered the League of Augsburg which had as its objectives the destruction of the hegemony of France, the appropriation of the English throne and its recognition as the arbiter of all European quarrels. The House of Orange, the Hapsburgs, the Brandenburgs, the Duke of Lorraine and later the King of Spain and the Duke of Savoy were signatories of the Treaty. The Pope, on the surface, sat on the fence but for some devious reason urged on members of the League to defeat Louis.

The Royal combatants fought at the Battle of the Boyne where the forces of Catholicism were defeated. Similar defeats were repeated at Aughrim and Galway; then the battle zone moved to Limerick. As a result, Limerick city was the scene of two sieges. In one of them so stubbornly did the Irish resist that King William went home to England — that is, of course, if one is justified in referring to England as his home at that time. James II, fearful of the outcome of the conflict, had already fled to France leaving behind him a commander whose name has become the symbol of love and pride and Irish romance. He was Patrick Sarsfield, the first Earl of Lucan.

In 1691 the second siege of Limerick was fought and resulted in a treaty between the Irish and the English besiegers. Even the more charitable of historians agree that this so-called 'treaty' was one of the less honourable in the annals of British Imperial conquest. Not only was it signed by the English with the knowledge that it could never be kept, but it was followed by penal laws which for all time — no matter what the future relationship between the two countries — must remain a blot on the record of British justice.

General Ginkel, who was William's leader in Ireland, on 27 September 1691 signed a series of proposals which were the foundation of the treaty : 1. An Act of Indemnity for all past crimes and offences. 2. All Catholics to be restored to their estates, of which they had previously been deprived because of their support for James. 3. They were to be allowed freedom of worship and permitted to have a priest in every parish and town in Ireland. 4. Catholics to be given employment in any capacity and all civil and military professions were to be open to them. 5. The Irish army was to be kept as part of the British Army for all those who wished to transfer. 6. Catholics were to be allowed to live as and how they wished in all towns and cities; they could exercise all trades and have equal privileges with their Protestant neighbours. 7. An Act of Parliament was to be passed ratifying all these decisions.

The negotiations for the treaty took place between 26 September and 3 October. On 24 February 1692 these articles, with minor alterations, were ratified by William and Mary of England. No attempt was made to adhere to them; instead, a penal code, which had already been set up after the settlement of Northern Ireland in 1641, was exercised with renewed ferocity. The essentials of these Penal Laws were as follows:

1. No Catholic could represent his people in the Irish Parliament.

2. All Catholics were excluded from the army, the navy, and from all the important professions.

3. No Catholics could possess firearms; if they were found guilty of doing so, they were either whipped, pilloried, or had their property confiscated.

4. No Catholic could own a horse worth more than five pounds; any Protestant offering him that sum could compel him to part with the animal.

5. All education was barred to Catholics.

6. The purchase of land by Irish Catholics was forbidden; a Protestant, aware that a Catholic owned land, could become the proprietor of it by notifying the authorities.

7. By becoming a Protestant, the eldest son of a Catholic could seize his father's estate.

8. A wife, renouncing the Catholic faith, could automatically defy her husband and be freed from any responsibility towards him.

9. There was no redress for the seduction of a Catholic woman by a Protestant.

Although the Treaty of Limerick promised emancipation from all these, there were many who still suspected the English of treachery and, having little faith in the king for whom they had fought so valiantly, they decided to emigrate. It was a condition of the treaty that soldiers serving in the Irish army could volunteer to leave the country with all the honours of war and join the army in France. Although a considerable effort was made by William and his government to induce the Irish to remain in order to strengthen the British army, most of the soldiers who fought with Sarsfield elected to leave their country. Roughly some 2,000 of them left the army and went home; approximately a thousand joined Ginkel's army and, to the chagrin of the Protestant community, some 11,000 decided to go with Sarsfield to France. Most of them took transport from Limerick while others left from Cork.

Sarsfield had promised that the exiled soldiers could take with them their families but those who embarked from Cork found that the ships had no room. Gerald O'Connor, who was one of Sarsfield's aides, gives a harrowing description of this leavetaking: 'Loud cries and lamentation broke from the wives and children who had been left behind; some dashed into the stream and perished in its depths; some clung to the boats that were making off from the shore; many of the men, husbands and fathers, plunged into the waters.'[2]

But of all the descriptions of the departure of the Irish, few are more poignant than that of Colonel Charles O'Kelly who went with them. Later, he wrote in his book *The Destruction of Cyprus*: 'And now, alas! the saddest Day is come, that ever appeared above the Horizon of Ireland. The sun was darkened, and covered over with a black cloud, as if unwilling to behold such a wofull spectacle: there needed noe Rain to bedew the Earth, for the Tears of the disconsolate Irish did abundantly moisten their native Soile to which they were that Day, to bid the last Farewell. Those who resolved to leave it never hoped to see it again; and those who made the unfortunate Choise to continue therein, could at the same Time have Nothing in Prospect but Contempt and Poverty, Chains and Imprisonment, and, in a Word all the Miserys that a conquered Nation could nationally expect from Power and Malice. . . .'³

Seán O'Faoláin paints an even blacker picture in his beautiful prose : 'The Wild Geese come in their thousands with the October moon. They blacken the sky and they cry the coming of autumn. Where there are low marshlands, or sloblands, they settle down, and then the cabins are cooking them with much butter or grease in the bastables all the Winter. About the estuary of the Shannon, and all up the river into Limerick, they must have whizzed and moaned, that Winter of 1691, when Ginkel offered the terms that ended the Jacobite War, and started bitter quarrels among the tired and tattered Irish. The flying Irish, down the Shannon or down the Lee with Sarsfield, looked up at the skies, and took the name, The Wild Geese. It was the end of a period. It was all but the end of a race.'⁴

1. John A. Murphy, M.A., *Justin MacCarthy, Lord Mountcashel*. An O'Donnell Memorial lecture delivered at University College, Cork, in May 1958, and published by Cork University Press, p. 32.
2. William O'Connor Morris, *Memoirs of Gerald O'Connor*, p. 81.
3. Quoted by James Carty in *Ireland From the Flight of the Earls*, p. 98.
4. Seán O'Faoláin, *King of the Beggars*, p. 11.

CHAPTER II

The First Flight

This was a distinguished crew for one ship; for it is indeed certain that the sea had not supported, and the winds had not wafted from Ireland, in modern times, a party of one ship who would have been more illustrious, or noble in point of genealogy, or more renowned for deeds, valour, prowess, or high achievements than they, if God had permitted them to remain in their patrimonies until their children should have reached the age of manhood. Woe to the heart that meditated, woe to the mind that conceived, woe to the counsel that decided on, the project of their setting out on this voyage, without knowing whether they should ever return to their native principalities or patrimonies to the end of the world.

—The Four Masters,[1] *Annals of the Kingdom of Ireland*

Before pursuing the fate of the two Irish armies which went into France it is necessary to take a brief look at the Irish military background at home and abroad at that time.

Irish soldiers of fortune went into Europe in organized units as far back as the thirteenth century; prior to that most Irish expeditions had been designed to bring and disseminate high standards of learning and culture to the known western world. As early as 1243 Irish soldiers went to help the English in a war with the Welsh; later they insulted the Scots in the same way. They also took the winning side in the War of the Roses in 1485 and helped in the suppression of the rebellions of Perkin Warbeck and Lambert Simnel. Most of this military junketing ceased when Henry VII became firmly established, when the tendency was to keep the Irish soldiers at home to meet the political demands of a country becoming more and more divided.

An interesting anecdote illustrates this division. After the

War of the Roses, Gerald Fitzgerald, 'The Great Earl of Kildare,' one of Ireland's more renowned leaders, was sent for by Henry VII to answer a charge of traitorous behaviour in Ireland. When he was questioned by Henry, the latter asked him whether he was provided with sufficiently able counsel to defend himself against the various charges of disloyalty. He replied ' "Yea, the ablest in the realm; your Highness I take for my counsel against these false knaves" '.[2] The monarch immediately leant towards the Irishman who, when accused of burning down the Archbishop's Cathedral, replied : ' "Sure, I would not have done it if I had not been told that the Archbishop was inside." '[3] Henry is reputed to have laughed long and loudly and even though he had been warned that 'all Ireland cannot keep this Earl of Kildare in order,' retorted : ' "Then let this Earl keep all Ireland in order. It is my will." '[4]

Had matters between the Irish and the English been capable of resolution with such ease and humour, the fate of Ireland might have been different. But by the end of a century, in 1595, another decisive phase broke out in Ireland between the English and the Irish. It was really the culmination of a game of religious seesaw which was very similar to what went on in England during the Tudor period. There was much right and wrong on both sides; injustice and anomaly were everywhere. But the quick-tempered Irish were far too sensitive to past injustice to be very easily won to the English cause.

O'Rourke, the chief of Brefni, one of Ireland's more colourful personalities, was invited by Queen Elizabeth to London, though under the displeasure of the Lord President Bingham. The Queen made him 'warm professions of honours and service, intending by this invitation to lead him into a kind of exile, in order to secure his obedience. O'Rourke confided and obeyed her summons; but before his departure he assembled his vassals and friends in the great hall of his castle, and entertained them with all the splendour of the times. (Such was the parting feast which gave rise to the song of the bard in afterdays.)'[5]

On the arrival of the Irish chief in Whitehall, the Queen was ready to receive him. The elegant symmetry of his person and his noble aspect struck Her Majesty and he was soon ranked among her choicest favourites. The authenticity of the sequel

to the visit has been disputed, but, as the action attributed to
Elizabeth is consistent with her character, one can assume that
there is in it at least an element of truth. Walker[6] says, 'One
night a person tapped at O'Rourke's door and was admitted —
it was a woman. The visit continued to be repeated, the lady
always retiring before daybreak. The Chief's curiosity became
urgent; he pressed the mysterious lady to reveal herself, but
she refused; a straggling moonbeam, however, discovered to
him a ring that glittered on her fiinger; he examined it unob-
served by the wearer. The next day he saw it upon the Queen's
finger at Court, and had the impudence to hint his suspicion
to Her Majesty. His fatal curiosity (adds the tradition) was
punished with secret death — he was executed for treason
on a trumped-up charge that night.'[7]

Two great chieftains, Hugh O'Neill and Rory O'Donnell, the
respective Earls of Tyrone and Tyrconnell, were in the tradition of O'Rourke but before their defeat at the Battle of Kinsale in 1601 there were many who saw that Ireland was destined for a period of rigorous repression and savagery based on
religious bigotry.

The flight of these two Earls in 1607 marked the beginning
of a new era of military emigration. They too were called Wild
Geese; the term had originated with the export of wool from
Ireland and the illegal transactions which resulted from the
English attempt to suppress the wool trade. The illicit contra-
band was linked with the recruitment and surreptitious departure of Irishmen for European armies. The Earls fled from
Ireland in 1607 but were determined to assemble armies in
Spain, Holland and in France — in fact, anywhere they could
get them — and to return one day to take their own country
back from the English invaders. It is one of the many sorrows
of Irish history that neither of them ever returned to his native
land again although their offspring did; their stories form a later
part of this volume. The Earls themselves went to Rome where
they died.

One of the Wild Geese, Hugh O'Neill, had a son in Spain
at the time of his flight from Ireland in 1607. In 1605 the son,
Henry, was given by Philip III the command of a regiment of
Irishmen in Flanders; this unit was recognized officially by
the Spanish crown, full authority being given to its commander

to recruit Irish mercenaries already serving in Flanders in any capacity. Henry O'Neill remained in command of his regiment until 1610; apparently, he was able to recruit Irishmen with the authority of the English. In 1605 the Baron of Hoboken reported from London that on 30 April he had spent the whole evening negotiating a levy of 500 Irish. The actual document, dated 2 April 1605, which originated in Brussels, states in one section of it : 'Commission as captain of a company of 200 men to William Wals, Irish gentleman, who has come to this country with 60 men recruited by him in Ireland at his own cost.'[8]

Many documents for recruiting during the year 1605 are extant; for example, one such record notes that a grant of twelve crowns monthly to Thomas Preston was paid for service in the Irish infantry; another refers to Maurice MacMortagh to serve in the Irish infantry and cites his previous service in the defence of the Catholic cause in his own country. These references are numerous and provide useful information such as rates of pay given for service at the time. For example, one record shows that Thomas Preston was to be raised later to the rank of Major-General and command all the Irish regiments in the Low Countries. It is recorded that at the time his was the highest rank bestowed on an Irishman; he received the highest rate of pay — 300 crowns monthly — of any Irish officer. There seems to have been very little equality in the rates of pay especially for those above that of an Irish private soldier who was paid four crowns monthly and got four pence a day for billeting.

A somewhat incongruous aspect of the pay system was that a disbanded officer usually received half of his active pay. It is difficult to ascertain what the word 'disbanded' meant, whether it was a system similar to what is commonly known in these days as 'half pay' or whether it was, in fact, a pension paid for services rendered. There is abundant evidence to show that captains on active service were paid eighty crowns a month but on disbandment received forty. An ensign usually received twenty crowns a month and half that on disbandment. A sergeant obtained twelve crowns a month. One of the apparent anomalies was that at the same period a chief surgeon received only five crowns monthly. This was in the year 1606, and the actual document states that 'a grant of five crowns monthly to Murgan Colan, Irishman; to serve as chief surgeon of the regiment of Colonel Henry O'Neill.'[9]

The pay for surgeons increased later; a chief surgeon's rate in 1623 had risen to fifteen crowns a month. It is difficult to understand why a surgeon should be paid less than a sergeant in the same way it is easy to understand that a chaplain was paid twelve crowns. Incidentally, someone called the Preacher of the Regiment was paid twenty-five crowns monthly. One document dated 1627 stated :

> Whereas Father Hugh Cavello, Guardian of the Irish Franciscan Convent at Louvain, held the post of head chaplain of the regiment of Irish infantry of Colonel the Earl of Tyrone through a substitute, as he was not able to act in person on account of the duties of his office; and whereas on account of his death his pay has ceased; consequently, because it is becoming for His Majesty's service that the soldiers of that regiment should receive the administration of the Sacraments, and of all else which is necessary, as they have up to the present, we have thought well to assign, as we do by these present, the pay of twenty-five crowns monthly to the said Convent; that the Superior may provide a person of ability and learning, approved by the Archbishop of Malines, and the Vicar-General of the Army, to serve as head chaplain to the said regiment.[10]

This reference is of particular interest because not only does it indicate that most of the chaplains were drawn from the religious orders but one can assume that the superior of the order received the pay of the chaplain. What it does not do, however, it to throw any light on the preacher. One conclusion could be that a member of the order of preachers (the Dominicans) was attached to each unit.

The reference to the Colonel the Earl of Tyrone through a substitute can be explained by the fact that when Henry O'Neill died his son, John O'Neill, the younger brother of Henry, took over the regiment although at the time he was too young to take over actual command. Consequently, a Major Edward Geraldin was appointed to the command. Later this was the regiment which was to be commanded by the famous Owen

Roe O'Neill. Incidentally, many of the available documents show that the 'O apostrophe' had ceased to exist when many of the Irish regiments were formed on the Continent during this period.

So much for the O'Neill regiment. On the Earl of Tyrconnell's side Hugh O'Donnell, the son of the Earl, was also an infant when he came to the Low Countries where he was handed over to the care of the Irish Franciscans. He went to Louvain University and remained there until he reached military service age. Although at the time of his leaving the university on 11 September 1629, Philip IV of Spain was requested to give him the command, it was denied him. The blame for the refusal was laid at the feet of the Archduchess Isabella who was then governor of the Spanish Low Countries. Two years later he was commissioned as a Captain in a Spanish regiment where he held command of a cavalry troop until 1632. Then somebody had a change of heart and he was commissioned as a colonel of a regiment of Irish infantry to consist of fifteen companies with Spanish rights. The latter reference is of particular importance because one of the major problems which faced so many of the Wild Geese in later years was the effort made by many nations to look upon them as second class citizens despite the fact that they were recognized as amongst the finest fighting soldiers.

Although the reasons are quite obscure, there is no evidence to substantiate that the O'Neill and O'Donnell regiments of this period made a noteworthy contribution to history. They did not. Indeed, in 1636 Don Ferdinand, then governor of the Low Countries, recommended to Philip IV that the Irish Regiments should be handed over to more able commanders; both the regiments had between them at this period only 800 men. While there is no absolute proof it is probable that both the regiments were sent from the Low Countries to Spain in 1638 because of inefficiency.

Of this particular force only one very eminent figure comes to the fore. He was Colonel Owen Roe O'Neill. Apparently he had been twenty-five years in the Low Countries; the first reference to him was in 1606 when he had received a commission as a captain of a company of Irish infantry in the O'Neill regiment. So important was the career of Owen Roe that he must be made the subject of a special chapter. In the meantime, it is worthwhile looking at some of the other regiments that came into being about the time.

Colonel John Barry formed one in 1636; he also recruited in Ireland. Colonel Patrick Fitzgerald formed another in 1639 and a Colonel Philip O'Reilly grouped his in 1655 to be followed five years later by Colonel James Dempsy's. The famous Taffe regiment came into being in 1672. The intricacies of the formation and disbandment of these fighting units are many; one thing is certain: there was a great deal of coming and going between the Low Countries and Ireland.

Brendan Jennings gives an interesting quotation: 'I would let you understand that Preston of Gormanston his sonne is going over instantly . . . Know you what good he would doe you or me; doe what you can with ye Deputy (Wentworth) that noe body that did promise either to you or me, shall goe to him. And knowe you it is uppon the licence I gott that he seems to bringe over his men.' A month later, on 27 September, de Necolalde, the Spanish ambassador at London, to whom all arrangements for recruiting had been committed, reports for his part that in virtue of a licence he had obtained, 'with little noise, and in small parties, 6,000 men have passed over to Flanders; this on account of my friendship with the Lord Deputy.' He also remarks incidentally that for the 6,000 men referred to he had not expended 2,000 crowns, whereas to an Irish colonel lately sent over to recruit, 5,000 crowns had been allotted, "which will send up the price accordingly." The colonel here referred to is undoubtedly Preston, who was in Ireland on 2 October, and perhaps earlier, and remained there until April 1635, on the 15th of which month he was reported back again in Flanders where two months later he took an important part in the defence of Louvain against the combined armies of the French and Dutch.[11]

In retrospect it is possible to understand the varied and conflicting relationships between Ireland and England at this period. Obviously the Cromwellian and Restoration periods had so muddled the political issues that few really understood them; those who did were quick to see that Ireland was about to become the cockpit for the opening rounds of the Jacobite Wars. According to Lord Macaulay, quoted by O'Callaghan:

'The Irish were considered foreigners in England; and of all foreigners they were the most hated.'[12]

This is in direct conflict with the fact that King James was recruiting 'a more trustworthy and respectable class of officers' as well as 'a superior or native Irish soldiery, remarkable for their stature.'[13]

So it all amounted to the fact that the First Flight of the Wild Geese was swinging to and from Europe and the circumstances which were to send the Second Flight on its way were being created by religious bigotry, the belief in the Divine Right of Kings, and the financial demands of a corrupt Court.

1. 'While the Plantation of Ulster, according to official reports, was being successfully completed, a group of poor scholars of the Order of St Francis were gathering up the threads of Ulster history as far back as writing or tradition could reach, and compiling the *Annals of the Kingdom of Ireland,* better known as the *Annals of the Four Masters.* The collection of the material occupied many years; the work is said to have been written in the neighbourhood of the ruined Franciscan monastery of Donegal.

'The chief compiler was Brother Michael O'Clerigh, member of a family which for generations had been professional historians to the princely house of O'Donnell. A lay brother in the Irish Franciscan monastery at Louvain, he was sent by his superiors to Ireland at a time of comparative peace, when the persecution of Catholics was not intense, to collect, transcribe, and synchronize the annals of Ireland, with special reference to the province of Ulster. "In all Irish history," says his modern biographer, Father Brendan Jennings, O.F.M., "there is no more wonderful and touching figure than the humble and learned Brother, wandering through the length and breadth of our land, gathering up and transcribing the precious fragments of Ireland's sacred and profane history, that the glories of her past might live."

'Brother Michael's three colleagues, according to Father John Colgan (1645), were Fearfeasa O Mulconry, Peregrine O Clerigh and Peregrine O Duigenan. Maurice O Mulconry and Conaire O Clerigh also gave some help.'
James Carty, *Ireland From the Flight of the Earls to Grattan's Parliament, 1607-1782,* p. 53.
2. Elliott O'Donnell, *The Irish Abroad,* p. 7.
3. *Ibid.*
4. *Ibid.*
5. *Ibid.,* p. 12.

6. Walker was the author of *Irish Bards*. He published the above incident as an editorial note to Lady Morgan's *O'Donnel*.
7. Quoted by O'Donnell, *The Irish Abroad*, pp. 12-13.
8. *Wild Geese in Spanish Flanders, 1582-1700*, edited by Brendan Jennings. Document   143.
9. *Ibid.*, Document   214.
10. *Ibid.*, Document   1009.
11. *Ibid.*, p. 29.
12. John Cornelius O'Callaghan, *History of the Irish Brigades in the Service of France*, p. 4.
13. *Ibid.*

CHAPTER III

Patrick Sarsfield and the Second Flight

Farewell O Patrick Sarsfield, may luck be on your path!
Your camp is broken up, your work is marred for years;
But you go to kindle into flame the King of France's wrath,
Though you leave sick Eire in tears——

—James Clarence Mangan

The one Irish name, above all others, associated with the Wild Geese is Patrick Sarsfield who led the Second Flight after the Treaty of Limerick. That he was the vital Irish figure in the final scene of that tragedy no one questions, but various and many opinions have been voiced about his character both as a leader and as a man. His courage, his daring, and his striking personality have never been doubted. Yet the Duke of Berwick wrote: 'He was no general but merely a dashing cavalry officer; a handsome fellow if you like, a fine, good-natured, generous, irascible Irish giant, exceeding even his own dragoons, so much admired by the French in strength and stature.'[1]

The controversy surrounding him is reminiscent of that which coloured the performance of General Custer at the Battle of the Little Big Horn. There is a strange similarity expressed in the views of their military critics. Accusations have been levelled at both leaders that they were 'brave without brains'; Sarsfield's successes, however, were certainly deserving of more praise than those of the American General, and to all Irishmen south of the Boyne Sarsfield was, is and always will be considered a poignant figure and a dedicated, courageous patriot.

Sarsfield came of a family which combined the blood of the Normans with ancient Irish stock. The Sarsfields had a long record of military service dating back to 1180 when one of his ancestors was a standard-bearer to King Henry II. Others fought in 1302 under King Edward I and some thirty years later under Edward III.

There is no acceptable record of the date or place of his

birth although it was probably about 1650. As a young man he went to a French military college and served in France as an ensign. It is likely that he took part in Louis XIV's campaign against the Dutch in 1672. It was not until the 1680s that Sarsfield put in an appearance in Irish military circles where he was something of a stormy petrel. One reads that on 14 September 1681, 'Captain Sarsfield, who challenged the Lord Gray, was taken into custody, but hath since made his escape out of the messenger's hands.'[2]

There is little further information on this incident, but a few months later there is a further entry about his life, dated 9 December, which states : 'There was a duell fought the 6th, between the lord Newburgh and the lord Kinsale, as principalls (two striplings under twenty), and Mr. Kirk and Captain Sarsfield, seconds; the principalls had no hurt; but Captain Sarsfield was run through the body, near the shoulder, very dangerously.'[3] Nothing further is available on how or why the seconds became involved in the fight when neither of the two principal contestants was injured. One can assume that as Lord Kinsale was an Irishman his protagonist was an Englishman and the whole thing was the result of a nationalistic quarrel.

Sarsfield was a Catholic, so it was natural that after James II's landing in Ireland he rallied to the monarch's cause. William landed in November of 1689 and thus began in earnest the Jacobite War in Ireland. Although on the surface the war appeared to be a straightforward affair, there were three major interests involved. The first was that of the Irish who desired to make use of James for the sake of Ireland, and of course there were the Anglophiles and many of the British who wished to use Ireland as a stepping stone for the restoration of James. However, there was a further group — the tool of France — which was endeavouring to enhance the power of Louis XIV in Ireland by turning the country into a military base for operations against England, the English and any other part of the Continent, when opportunity presented itself.

The intricacies of the whole political situation involved Scottish settlers in the north and absentee Irish chiefs, particularly Tyrconnell, of whom a Frenchman wrote : 'If he were born a Frenchman, he could not be more zealous for the interests of France.'[4]

During the early days of the war Sarsfield's military responsibility appears to have had very little significance. However, in late 1689 he was made a Brigadier despite the fact that he was not liked by Tyrconnell. The French general Count D'Avaux wrote of him : 'I had all the trouble in the world to get him made a brigadier, although my Lord Tyrconnell strongly opposed this, saying he was a very brave man but that he had no head'.[5]

But despite this, at no time were his honour or his probity in question. In his new command he was sent to Connaught to hold that province for James II. Here he commanded five regiments and on his arrival found that in his command were many who did not favour James and considered him an enemy of the Irish.

Sarsfield's military record in Connaught was most praiseworthy. There is ample correspondence to prove that James II looked upon him with very great favour while at the same time Louis XIV was anxious to get him back to France and into the French Army. At the time of the exchange of troops with France, every effort was made to procure Sarsfield as one of the senior officers in the Irish group which left Cork. However, Sarsfield remained behind and took an active part in the Battle of the Boyne which was the beginning of the end of the Jacobite War in Ireland. During the retreat which followed the defeat of the Jacobites, Sarsfield was the personal bodyguard of the monarch.

There are some revealing stories about the behaviour of James II after the Battle of the Boyne. Apparently, James complained to Lady Tyrconnell that the Irish had betrayed him and had run before the Prince of Orange. Perhaps it is apocryphal but her Ladyship supposedly retorted to the King : 'But your Majesty won the race.'[6] The French historian Philippe Erlanger in his biography of Louis XIV says that during the battle 'he was the first to turn tail. . . .'[7] Subsequent events in Ireland showed all too clearly that instead of deserting James the Irish were to make a supreme sacrifice in his interests.

The defeat at the Boyne caused the Irish to retreat on Limerick and it was here that Sarsfield performed one of the most daring of his many feats. Limerick was heavily fortified with five bastions, a double wall, and some towers. The army within the city numbered some 20,000, poorly armed. William advanced on the city with some 40,000 men. He was aware that the capture of Limerick would require a very heavy train of armour and artillery. Consequently, he sent for six 24-pounders, two 18-pounders, five mortars, 153 wagons of ammunition for the artillery, boats, pontoons, and 400 draught horses to come to the city under the command of a Captain Pulteney. The night before they were to reach Limerick they settled down to rest at Ballyneety. Sarsfield knew that the train was on the way from Cashel and realized that its arrival would mark the end of Limerick. (This intended siege must not be confused with the siege of 1691 which resulted in the treaty. The siege under discussion took place in August of the previous year.) Sarsfield volunteered to destroy the train and took with him as his guide an Irish hero — half outlaw, half bandit, 'one gallopping Hogan' who knew every boreen and road and bridle path over the mountains. He collected around him a special group of picked horsemen and set out to destroy the train before it reached its destination. Fate was on his side because as he approached the Williamite camp one of his troopers whose horse was lame had met with the wife of one of the Williamite soldiers. She too had lost her way and in her endeavour to reach the convoy camp disclosed that the password for the night was 'Sarsfield'. Basking in the false security of their position, the siege convoy slept soundly until the middle of the night. A sentry challenged an intruder and the last words he is supposed to have heard were : 'Sarsfield is the word and Sarsfield is the man.' The slaughter of that siege train has been the subject of many tales, legendary and otherwise. But there is little doubt that the whole train was totally wrecked; only a few soldiers escaped the massacre.

Gerald O'Connor, who was with Sarsfield on that particular night, describes it in his memoirs. Apparently Sarsfield called him aside and said :

'The enemy has made an enormous mistake. He has challenged and warned us with guns that are of no use; but I have learned that his heavy artillery is on the way; I will make him pay dearly for his false over-confidence.

'The peasantry joyfully became our guides; we surprised
and suddenly fell on the enemy encamped in complete security in a valley of a hilly tract which had been worked for
mines, and some miles distant from the main army. Our
swords soon drank deeply in Saxon blood; only one fugitive
escaped to tell the tale of slaughter; in a few moments the
whole artillery park, with its trains and munitions had fallen
into our hands. We buried the weighty guns which were
being brought up for a siege mouth foremost, and filled with
powder, in the ground; we made a pile of the trains and set
the whole on fire; our backs had only been turned for some
hundred of yards when a tremendous explosion rent the
troubled air; the sound must have reached the usurper's
leaguer.'[8]

Because of the loss of the train, William's assault on Limerick failed and, indeed, as a result of it, leaving General Ginkel
in charge, the future king returned to England.

After his brilliant exploit at Ballyneety and his further dash
and gallantry at the Battles of Aughrim in 1691 and at Galway,
Sarsfield was one of the signatories on the Irish side of the
Treaty of Limerick. For those who questioned his integrity and
suggested that he had betrayed the Irish in doing so, one incident is of great significance. More French aid was expected to
help in the defeat of William's forces in Ireland but, unhappily,
fate stepped in again to write a page of Irish history : the
French fleet arrived two days after the treaty had been signed.
Many Irishmen made every effort to persuade Sarsfield to
scrap the treaty, to help the French to land and to take on William's forces again. But Sarsfield was adamant. He had given
his pledge and as far as he was concerned that was the end.

He marched with many of his soldiers to Cork and embarked
there for France. Gerald O'Connor who was with him wrote :
'Our transports dropped slowly down the stream of the Lee,
its shores stretching in desolate plains for miles.'[9]

On arrival in France, the Cork and Limerick contingents
met at Brest where Sarsfield took over one of two troops of
guards which were the Household Soldiery of James II. The
Irish troops were kept at Brest for a considerable period of
time, impatient, inactive and hoping for a further chance to

attack the Williamites. Many of them were hoping that a further invasion of Ireland would be mounted but they were bitterly disappointed for in the spring of 1692 Sarsfield at the head of his troops marched into Normandy. Later he joined the army of Marshal Luxemburg in 1693 and fought in many of the engagements against the Williamite forces in the Low Countries. The army of William numbered something in the region of 80,000. On 29 July of that year Luxemburg's troops stormed Neerwinden in Holland but were met with fierce resistance. Luxemburg was using the Irish troops in the hope that their daring and tenacity would make a breach in the defences. In O'Connor's words : 'I was with Sarsfield in the line with these brave horsemen; they remained under the fire of the breastwork for at least two hours but steadily closing up their shattered ranks. William, I have heard, broke out in an exclamation of praise.'[10]

This was not the first time that the Dutch monarch praised the courage of the Irish. Ginkel had told him of Sarsfield's courage and daring, and one of William's greater disappointments was that Sarsfield refused to accept a commission from him after the fall of Limerick. The final chapter at Neerwinden came when the Maison du Roi with Sarsfield in the lead, followed by a crush of exulting Irish horsemen, furiously cut through a small gap where they came face to face with English cavalry. The latter found themselves completely overrun and in a short time the victory was complete.

Immediately following this success the last hours of Sarsfield are best recounted by one who was there :

'As I was walking over the field a message from Sarsfield reached me, he had been wounded to death in one of our last charges; he sent an aide de camp to call me to his side. The noble form of the hero lay on a pallet in a hut; he feebly lifted up his nerveless hand and gave me a letter, which he had dictated in my behalf. It read : "I am dying the most glorious of deaths; we have seen the backs of the tyrants of our race. May you, Gerald, live to behold other such days; but let Ireland be always uppermost in your thoughts." '[11]

And so, with his close friend and constant companion, Gerald O'Connor, kneeling beside him in the hut at Neerwinden, the great Irish patriot died.

Sarsfield left behind him an Irish tradition which through the centuries that followed his brave example became a creed — the belief that Irish warriors are second to none.

One further reference to Sarsfield may help to throw some light on the character of this man :

Patrick Sarsfield may be quoted as a type of loyalty and patriotic devotion. In his public actions, firm and consistent; in his private character, amiable and unblemished; attached, by religious conviction and hereditary reverence for the right divine of kings, to the falling House of Stuart, he drew a sharp sword in the cause of the monarch he had been brought up to believe his lawful sovereign, and voluntarily followed him into exile when he could wield it no longer.[12]

Sarsfield was buried with full military honours on the Landen battlefield in Flanders where centuries later many of his fellow countrymen were to lie beside him. He had one son; his widow married in 1695 the Duke of Berwick. Of his son James we will read more later for he afterwards joined the army of Spain and was decorated by Philip V for his gallantry during the Battle of Barcelona.

1. Quoted by John Todhunter in *The Life of Patrick Sarsfield*, p. 2.
2. *Ibid.*, p. 8.
3. *Ibid.*
4. D'Avaux, quoted by Todhunter, *Ibid.*, p. 30.
5. D'Avaux, quoted by Todhunter, *Ibid.*, p. 42.
6. *Ibid.*, p. 73.
7. Philippe Erlanger, *Louis XIV*, p. 236. (Erlanger won the Grand Prix d'Histoire de L'Académie Française in 1969.)
8. William O'Connor Morris, *Memoirs of Gerald O'Connor*, p. 83.
9. *Ibid.*
10. *Ibid.*, p. 100.
11. *Ibid.*, p. 102.
12. Elliot O'Donnell, *The Irish Abroad*, p. 241.

CHAPTER IV

The Ancient Race

What shall befall the ancient race
The poor, unfriended, faithful race?
Where ploughman's song made the hamlet ring,
The hawk and the owlet flap their wing;
The village homes, oh, who can trace —
God of our persecuted race?

—Rev. M. Tormey, quoted in
Gill's Irish Reciter

Irishmen who have experienced the pangs of exile will find it easy to sympathize with the loneliness, misery and frustration of the Wild Geese who idled away the days in Brest after their arrival from Limerick and Cork. Not only had they to suffer the anguish of questionable defeat at home, but even their own leaders had, to some extent, deceived them about their families. Had they been accompanied by their wives and children life would have had some purpose, but the long days of waiting without domestic companionship and the suspense about their future were conditions they did not expect.

Although they were the Irishmen who established a great tradition that will endure for all time, the irrefutable but frequently forgotten fact remains: they started to tread the path of glory while they were still the minions of a dethroned British sovereign King James II. It was he who offered them the only word of welcome when they arrived in France. His letter read:

James *Rex.*
Having been informed of the Capitulation and Surrender of Limerick, and of the other places which remained to us in our Kingdom of Ireland, and of the necessities which forced the Lords Justices and the General Officers of our Forces thereunto; we will not defer to let you know, and the rest of the officers that came along with you, that we are ex-

treamly [sic] satisfied with your and their conduct, and of the valour of the souldiers [sic] during the siege, but, most particularly, of your and their declaration and resolution, to come and serve where we are. And we assure you, and order you, to assure both officers and souldiers that are come along with you, that we shall never forget this act of loyalty, nor fail, when in a capacity, to give them, above others, particular marks of our favour. In the mean time, you are to inform them, that they are to serve under our command, and by our commissions; and, if we find, that a considerable number is come with the fleet, it will induce us to go personally to see them, and regiment them. Our brother, the King of France, hath already given orders to cloath them, and furnish them with all necessaries, and to give them quarters of refreshment. So we bid you heartily farewell. Given at our Court at St. Germaine, the 27th of November, 1691.[1]

Although 1691 is the arbitrary date given for the flight to Brest, the actual movement of the Irish army was not completed until January of 1692; by then some of the miseries of the troops had been alleviated by the arrival of a number of their families. John Cornelius O'Callaghan in his *History of the Irish Brigades in the Service of France* gives some vital statistics:

From the returns of the French 'Commissaires', obtained through the Lord Marshal of Thomond and Clare, the Irish officers and soldiers, who followed the King to France, are specified by Mac Geoghegan at 19,059; which number, added to the previously-arrived Brigade of Mountcashel of 5,371 military of every rank, would make 24,430 officers and soldiers; and these, with others, who came over at different times not specified, would, according to the English and Irish authority of King James's Memoirs, and a letter of the Chevalier Charles Wogan, nephew of the Duke of Tyrconnell, amount, in all, to about 30,000 men.[2]

Sarsfield was one of the last to arrive and when he did King James visited Brest to inspect the troops he had so cowardly left in the lurch when he fled from Ireland. He took this opportunity to reorganize the army in order to establish a force which was to act under his personal command as opposed to the forces that were later to become part of the French army. This change added considerably to the dissatisfaction of the troops: many senior officers were reduced in rank; the O'Neill clan which at one time had been the backbone of the Irish army was relegated to the unimportant, while pay and allowances were pared for most because French rates of pay were far below those of the Irish. Admittedly James 'by an instrument under his hand and seal . . . made a solemn promise he would pay them what their actual pay wanted, to make it full English, whenever God was pleas'd to restore him, and so made it his own and the Crown's debt.'[3]

Despite the monarch's pretty speech it would seem that he was a financial cheat. In a document from MS 12161 in the Fonds Français of the Bibliothèque Nationale, Paris, is a copy of a letter written by an Irish officer of the time to his son, stating: 'No sooner had we arrived in France than King James made an arrangement with Louis XIV by which he had put us on a French footing; reserving for himself the difference in our pay for his own upkeep and that of his house.'

What was even more disturbing about the royal behaviour was that James gave much more favourable financial terms to British and Scottish mercenaries who had come to France to help him. The anger of the Irish was quite justifiable; their loyalty was not just that of the mere mercenary. Many of the Irish clans were denuded of their chiefs when they followed James, leaving their people at home leaderless. The motives of the chiefs were both religious and political because they harboured the erroneous idea that the restoration of a Stuart to the English throne would bring them religious as well as national freedom.

King James formed the Irish into four regiments. The first was called the Prince of Wales' Regiment; the King's nominee for command was probably Henry Jermyn, Lord Dover. The second and third were commanded by the Duke of Berwick and his brother Henry Fitzjames. The fourth was led by Lord Lucan.

To clarify the picture of the Irish military set-up in France at this time two important points need reaffirmation. Although the Second Flight of the Wild Geese did not occur until 1691, three regiments under Lord Mountcashel, the Honourable Colonel Daniel O'Brien and the Honourable Colonel Arthur Dillon had been formed in France as a result of the 1690 exchange for the French force which had arrived in Ireland under the command of the Count de Lauzun. These three Irish regiments became known as the Mountcashel Brigade which was, in fact, the nucleus of what was to become later the famed Irish Brigade of France.

The second important point is that the 1691 contingent were initially formed into the four regiments reorganized by James. Later many of them amalgamated; others went on independent missions. One of the more disturbing elements of this shuffle was that Patrick Sarsfield was separated from his own troops on the grounds that he was a cause of dissatisfaction and was stirring up trouble amongst the Limerick contingent. Narcissus Luttrell's diary refers to his commander Sarsfield and contains the following notation when referring to the discontent amongst the Wild Geese: '. . . so that Sarsfield was posted away to appease the said discord.'

Mountcashel's own regiment had an interesting history. It had been formed in 1683 'out of several Independent Companies of Irish, which King Charles II withdrew from Tangier, in Africa, when he caused it to be demolished. The corps was composed of two battalions in sixteen companies, variously stated, or, as it would appear, at different times, consisting of eighty or one hundred men a company. Its 1st Colonel was James Butler, afterwards 2nd Duke of Ormonde, who, being made Colonel of a Regiment of Horse in the Irish army, resigned his previous post to the Honourable Justin MacCarthy, subsequently Lord Mountcashel. After the destruction of this regiment at the unlucky affair of Newtown-Butler, in August, 1689, it was renewed with fresh recruits, and brought to France, in May, 1690, by his Lordship.'[4]

O'Brien's regiment had been formed in 1689 by Daniel O'Brien, Viscount Clare, to serve under James II. Armed and clothed and paid at the Viscount's own expense, it illustrated the kind of loyalty which was given to James but which he so ill-deserved. The regiment was handed over to a Colonel Lee who proved himself so distinguished an officer that later the Marshal de Luxemburg appointed him Inspector-General of

Irish Troops. This regiment became known as Clare's Regiment when the son of the founder became 4th Viscount Clare.

Dillon's Regiment was levied in 1690 also to serve James II. The Honourable Arthur Dillon, only twenty years of age, was appointed its first colonel. Later the regiment fought in Spain and Italy.

As soon as the 1691 troops had been organized into their various units at Brest, naturally the first thought of most of the Irish leaders was the preparation for a successful landing in Ireland and another attack on William of Orange. The two monarchs, James II and Louis XIV, were in frequent conference on this issue. The latter's chief interest was that a favourable Britain, created by a Stuart restoration, would enable him to destroy the League of Augsburg.

An invasion plan was agreed upon but the Irish expeditionary force was to exclude Mountcashel's Brigade. Typical of Louis XIV, he had other plans for this splendid fighting force. The remainder of the Irish force, totalling some 14,000, was to be a part of an army of 30,000 men which was nominally led by James II himself. The real military commander was Maréchal de Bellefonds who had as second-in-command Sarsfield with the rank of Major-General. Hope for the success of this mission was based on the belief that Jacobites both in England and Ireland would rally to James's colours as soon as the expeditionary force landed.

Early in April of 1692 the Irish and French invasion force assembled in Normandy between Cherbourg and La Hogue; King James and the Duke of Berwick (who was the natural son of James) were with the troops. Like so many of James's efforts the whole plan was a disaster. It is summed up succinctly by John Todhunter in his *Life of Patrick Sarsfield*:

A great fleet was assembled at Brest, eighty ships of the line and some 300 transports. Bellefonds was commander-in-chief, and De Tourville, admiral. James himself, with the Duke of Berwick, was to embark with the expedition. He counted on the English admiral, Russell, and other captains, and hoped that the fleet would declare for him. Russell, disgusted by a stupid proclamation of James, frankly told his agent that he would fight the French if he met them, even if the King himself were on board; and fight them he did, defeating and destroying the French fleet off La Hogue, after several days' engagement, on May 24th, 1692.

This was a severe blow to James, who proposed to retire to a monastery; and to Sarsfield it must have been among the great disappointments of his life. In June, Luttrell says, it was rumoured he had been 'clapt up in the Bastille for holding correspondence with the king's enemyes', having been but badly used. This seems to have been a false rumour, for in July he was in high command at Steenkirk.[5]

A more accurate description of the catastrophe was that the troops were hindered from embarking on the French fleet assembled for the purpose because of adverse winds described by the British as 'Protestant winds'. Also, a combined force of British and Dutch ships under Admirals Russell and Van Allemonde gave the French fleet a thorough trouncing.

This disaster was a turning point in the fate of the 13,000 Irish troops awaiting embarkation; as soon as it was realized that there was little further hope of an assault on the English at home, they were scattered through Europe. They were ordered to join the French armies in Flanders, Germany, Spain and Italy. There has always been confusion in the minds of many students of the Wild Geese as to the dissemination of so many of the Irish units while the French Irish Brigade as a specific force seemed to remain intact. The abortive invasion explains it. Some of the scattered Irish units did fight beside the French Irish Brigade later but this was due to the fortunes of war rather than to deliberate planning.

The Irish troops who were sent to Flanders did have an opportunity in 1692 to vent their spleen on William of Orange by helping the French in the capture of Namur. On this occasion they fought under the direct command of Louis XIV; later they came under the orders of the Marshal Duke de Luxemburg, whom the French King appointed as commander after Namur. Both Patrick Sarsfield and the Duke of Berwick were with Luxemburg, who gained a further victory over the Williamites at Steenkirk. A senior French officer, the Marquis de Quincy, writing of the engagement said that among the officers who 'gave proofs of a great valour and a rare capacity'[6] were the Duke of Berwick and the Earl of Lucan. Luxemburg himself, writing to Louis XIV, said 'Monsieur, the Duke of Berwick, was present from the commencement, when we proceeded to reconnoitre the enemy; and behaved, during the entire combat, as bravely as I have rendered an account to your Majesty, that he had done the last campaign. The Earl of Lucan was with him; in whom we have particularly noticed the valour, and the intrepidity, of which he had given proofs in Ireland. I can assure your Majesty that he is a very good and able officer.'[7]

Unhappily, as has already been recounted, Sarsfield's career ended the following year in what was the most important engagement of the 1693 Flanders campaign — the Battle of Landen — fought between Luxemburg and William III of Orange.

The Irish troops who went to Germany were the most fortunate for there they met many of their old comrades under the command of Mountcashel. The German campaign was an easy one for the Germans had no stomach for a fight and the capture of Heidelberg was the only significant event. The French army was commanded by the Marshal Duke de Lorges. A note in O'Callaghan's book sums it up : 'Henceforth, to the end of this war, *no* mention is made of the Irish corps serving in Germany, since nothing has been found related to *distinguish* them from their French fellow-soldiers there.'[8]

The troops sent to Italy, however, had a different story to tell for their service was an active and interesting one. William's allies in Italy were very strong and consisted of Italian, English, Spanish and Huguenot troops; their commanders were formidable soldiers of the calibre of Prince Eugene of Savoy and the Duke of Schonberg. Marshal de Catinat was the French commander who, because of the strength of the enemy, was most of the time on the defensive until the Battle of Marsaglia in 1693.

Catinat had amongst his men some outstanding Irish troops. Chief amongst them was Clare's Regiment which had been especially seconded to face Savoy. To reinforce them were many of the men who had fought at Limerick and whose dash and daring turned the tide of battle afer an initial success by Savoy. The one Irish contingent killed over a thousand of the enemy with swords and clubbed muskets. It was in this battle that the Irish used a dramatic artifice reminiscent of Benburb. A regiment commanded by General Arthur Dillon found itself outflanked by the enemy so, turning their muskets upside down with the butt ends facing upwards, they continued their forward advance. The enemy, thinking they intended to surrender, allowed them to approach, whereupon the demeanour of the Irish soldiers changed suddenly to a terrifying force, put the enemy to flight and helped secure the victory.

(This kind of onslaught seems to be peculiar to the Irish. During the Second World War at the Battle of Bou Arada in North Africa, a company of the London Irish were attacking a German stronghold at the top of a bare hill. The late Major John Lofting, realizing that he was to be the victim of a fierce German air attack by Stuka bombers, ordered his men to remove their helmets and wave wildly at the attacking planes. The pilots, thinking the advancing troops were their own, flew away leaving Lofting to take the position and inflict heavy casualties on the Germans. Little wonder that he was one of the few officers of the war to win the Military Cross and two bars.)

A feature of the Battle of Marsaglia was that the Irish were so eager to come to grips with the Orange troops that they overran their orders, 'and Catinat, seeing there was no recalling of them, commanded the whole army to follow. Great was the slaughter of the Confederates. The Irish pursued so swiftly, that their foot overtook some of the hostile cavalry. The Duke of Savoy narrowly escaped with 10 horsemen, into his capital citty of Turin.'[9] Of the Jacobite officers who were killed, having fought with great valour at the head of the Irish regiments, were the Major-General and Brigadier Thomas Maxwell, Colonel of the King of England's Dismounted Dragoons, Brigadier John Wauchop, also Colonel of Dragoons, both Scots; Brigadier Francis O'Carroll, Colonel of the Queen of England's Dismounted Dragoons, and others, worthy of lasting memory. Daniel O'Brien, 4th Viscount Clare, was acting as Colonel of his family regiment and was so severely wounded that he subsequently died at Pignerol. James de Lacy, of the family of Ballingarry-Lacy, County of Limerick, Brigadier, Quarter-Master-General, Colonel and Commandant of the

Prince of Wales' Regiment of Infantry in Ireland, was like-wise mortally wounded. His young nephew, Peter de Lacy, who had been an ensign under him in Ireland when only 13, and whom, after the Treaty of Limerick, he brought into France, was in this battle as a Lieutenant in the Regiment of Athlone. Ultimately he became Field-Marshal de Lacy in the service of Russia and father of the celebrated Field-Marshal in the service of Austria. The Duke of Schonberg whose father had been killed at the Battle of the Boyne was slain in the battle.

The Irish soldiers sent from Cherbourg to fight in Spain were in a special category. In the first place there were thousands of Irishmen on the Spanish side who had fled from Ireland with the Earls in 1607 so that, in effect, in many of the actions in the Spanish campaign Irishmen were fighting Irishmen. And not only was the quarrel a physical one but also a diplomatic struggle to lure Irish soldiers to opposite sides.

One of the principal participants was Brigadier Don Hugh O'Donnell, known on the Continent as Earl of Tyrconnell, who was making a strong appeal to the Jacobite Irish in Catinat's army to desert. According to himself, he had 'a design for forming Irish Regiments in Spain for the service of that state, in order to draw off the malcontents against the government of King William III.'[10] As a method of achieving his objective he had 'officers, on all the passes in the neighbourhood of their encampments, to receive 'em and invite 'em.'[11]

Both the French and the Spanish realized that the Irish soldiers were far from home, had few friends outside their comrades-in-arms, and were almost totally dependent on their military pay.

Tragedy seemed to haunt these exiles in that, far from the land of the original conflict between two rival monarchs, the Royal feud caused Irishman to fight Irishman deep in the heart of Europe. Probably the first time the soldiers of Sarsfield found themselves in this position was at the Battle of Ter in Catalonia, called after the river of that name. No doubt when the French and Spanish armies faced each other across the river, there were Irish spies on both sides of the river encouraging desertion. The Spanish army in Catalonia was under the command of the Duke of Escalona and while there is no specific record of any Irish regiments being at Ter, there is abundant proof that many exiled Irish leaders and their followers were, in fact, in Catalonia. This is confirmed by the fact that the registers of Irish regiments and officers in the service of Spain in the Low Countries received no mention after 1688. Obviously, most of them had been transferred to the homeland where the pressure from Louis XIV was greatest, especially during the years 1694 and 1695.

There is considerable data on the Wild Geese fighting for France. When the Spaniards were defeated at Ter and suffered the loss of some 4,000 men killed, O'Callaghan states that on the French side, among the 'officers praised by the Marshal, for having been "several times distinguished" during the day, was Charles O'Brien, 5th Viscount Clare.'[12] One of the puzzles arising from this reference is the fact that on the Spanish side and serving in Catalonia at the time was an Earl Clare. It would be interesting to know how closely they were related and if, in fact, a son was fighting his father.

The Spanish campaign in which the Irish were so deeply involved reached its climax in 1697 at the siege of Barcelona, which was defended by Prince George of Hesse-Darmstadt who had 11,000 regular infantry, 1,500 cavalry and about 4,000 civic militia. The defences of the town were formidable; to add to the strength of the walls and buttresses the Viceroy of Barcelona, Count de Velasco, was encamped about six miles away with 3,000 cavalry and sundry other troops amounting to 20,000 men. Also adjacent to the town was the Fort of Mont-juich. In effect, this meant that the town could not be surrounded and that there was also an open approach to bring supplies to the town.

With the French forces were Simon Luttrell's two Dublin-raised battalions, a battalion of the Clancarthy Infantry Regiment and an Irish unit under the command of Roger Mac-Elligot. The Honourable Arthur Dillon was there also with a battalion of his regiment as was Colonel Oliver O'Gara commanding a force of Irish Dismounted Dragoons. The performance of the Irish troops on that important battlefield has been recounted by the French in words of glory but they were prejudiced since they succeeded in reducing the city. But the unbiased report of a Whig writer, Forman, is without embellishments : ' "That, in the siege of Barcelona, in the year 1697, the great Vendosme was so charmed with their courage, and so amazed at the intrepidity of their behaviour, that the particular esteem and notice with which he distinguish'd them, even to the day of his death, is yet very well remembered in France. If what I say here is not literally true, there are Frenchmen enough, still living, to contradict me." '[13]

O'Callaghan continues : 'And this assertion, concerning the high opinion of the Irish as soldiers by Vendome, is corroborated by the testimony of the Chevalier de Bellerive, who afterwards fought under that great commander with the Irish in Spain, and who, noticing their gallantry there, under him, in 1710, says :

"M. de Vendosme, who had a particular esteem for this warlike nation, at whose head he had delivered so many combats, and gained so many victories, confessed that he was surprised at the terrible enterprises which those *butchers of the army* (it is thus that he named them) achieved in his presence."

— Among the garrison of 10,000 men, placed in Barcelona by Vendosme, was the Regiment of Dillon; in connexion with which, the veteran Peter Drake of Drakerath, in the County of Meath, observes — "And here I cannot omit the mention of a very extraordinary event. The centinels placed on the breach confidently affirmed that they saw, in the night, numbers of dreadful apparitions, who were wont to engage one another as in an attack; furiously crying, *kill, advance,* and such like expressions, commonly used on those occasions; and what added the greater authority to these assertions was that several centinels on that post were found dead without any visible marks of violence, and so supposed to have died of their fears. This occasioned orders for doubling the centinels, and, being sometimes of the number, imagined I both heard and saw the like." '[14]

However, the hero of Barcelona was Dillon; but for his daring in dislodging the Spaniards from the neighbouring hills, victory would not have been achieved.

Their defeat at Barcelona brought an end to the Treaty of Augsburg which was replaced by the Treaty of Ryswick in 1697. It was signed by Holland, Spain, England and the German emperor and marked the end of that particular war against Louis XIV.

1. John Cornelius O'Callaghan, *History of the Irish Brigades in the Service of France*, pp. 29-30.
2. *Ibid.*, p. 29.
3. *Ibid.*, p. 31.
4. *Ibid.*, p. 32.
5. Pages 198-199.
6. Quoted by O'Callaghan, *History of the Irish Brigades*, p. 168.
7. *Ibid.*
8. *Ibid.*, p. 176.
9. *Ibid.*, pp. 177-178.
10. Quoted from a letter written by O'Donnell and abstracted in Thorpe's Catalogue for 1834 of the Southwell Mss.
11. *Ibid.*
12. O'Callaghan, *History of the Irish Brigades*, p. 180.
13. Quoted by O'Callaghan, *History of the Irish Brigades*, p. 187.
14. *Ibid.*, pp. 187-188.

CHAPTER V

Cremona

'Are ye mad, or in a trance?
Waken, gentlemen of France!'
(Shout, boys, Erin's the renown!)
'See your lilied flags are flapping,
And your Marshal is caught napping
In Cremona town.'

Again and yet again,
Though the third of us are slain,
(Shout, boys, Erin's the renown!)
Though Sieur Villeroy is taken,
And the lilied flags are shaken,
Till our tardy comrades waken
We keep the town.

—Emily Lawless, *With the Wild Geese*

The Treaty of Ryswick marked the onset of a new phase in the lives of the Irish who had left their homeland in 1691. For many, particularly the more honourable, it was the beginning of a dark interlude which was to bring much soul-searching.

Following the Treaty of Ryswick in 1697, Louis XIV was compelled to reduce his military strength in order to lessen the vast expenditure that the Augsburg war had necessitated. Since he had made peace with William of Orange and acknowledged him as the lawful monarch of England, it was natural that he should look upon the followers of James II as the force least likely for retention. The official Irish Brigade was too solidly entrenched as part of the French army to be tampered with; also, its incomparable achievements made it too valuable to disband. Consequently, Louis's military advisers looked to the various Irish units which were scattered throughout his armies for excision. And, with ruthless disregard for the sacrifices they had made and his own exploitation of their service, he disbanded them leaving the soldiers penniless and forsaken in a strange land.

The consequences of this action were, indeed, severe, especially for the non-commissioned fighting men who knew no trade and did not speak the language of the country. In desperation they turned to the only means of survival they knew — the gun. A good many became highwaymen and robbers with the result that, as a chronicler of the period, Dr Doran, wrote : 'The route between St Germains and Paris was not safe, because of them; and they added murder to robbery when they met with resistance.'[1] Naturally, many of them formed themselves into gangs and roamed the roads and farmlands in search of prey. When they were caught, their punishments were extremely severe. The usual fate for being apprehended was to be 'broken alive' upon the wheel, a form of torture that was as savage a one as ever conceived. There are numerous incidents on record of the capture of Irishmen, sometimes individually and at other times in roving bands.

The Irish officers outside the official Irish Brigade had a particularly hard time, for even after the Treaty of Ryswick they were forbidden on pain of death to return to Ireland. As members of the leading Irish families there was little hope of their returning without recognition. Besides, their lands had been seized and, for the most part, were in the hands of English settlers. To add to the anguish of their being outlawed from Ireland, the promised Jacobite patronage never materialized. This was a tragic consequence for those who had forfeited their own lands in Ireland to join James II. They appealed to Louis in 1698 :

They presented to him, that they have remained silent until now, in expectation of what it might be his Majesty's pleasure to order respecting them; but that the extreme necessity, to which they have been reduced, has constrained them to break that silence, in order to lay before his Majesty the pitiable condition of their affairs. That they had fought, during 10 years, in defence of their religion, and of their legitimate Sovereign, with all the zeal, and all the fidelity, that could be required of them, and with a devotion, unparalleled, except among those of their unhappy nation.

That, for this cause, they had made a sacrifice of those who were the authors of their birth, of their relatives, their property, their country, and their lives. That they had the happiness of rendering some important service to his Majesty, by a diversion of three years, during which they had sustained, in Ireland, the brunt of the choicest troops of his enemies. That they had subsequently served in France, with a zeal scarcely differing from that of the King's natural subjects; as his Generals, under whose commands they were placed, had borne testimony to his Majesty. That, by the Peace, they not only found themselves deprived of the properties to which they had legitimate claims, but were likewise prohibited returning to their country under pain of death.[2]

The petition of the Irish officers was partially successful; Louis XIV probably anticipated the War of the Spanish Succession which broke out in 1701. They were formed into a special corps of officers to be used as and when Louis needed them. Later, due to their heroism, they were referred to as 'an invincible phalanx, that, if owing much to the munificence of the French Monarch, was, upon all occasions, deserving of the honourable treatment experienced from him.'[3]

The larger proportion of these officers fought in Spain with Louis's grandson, Philip V. Others joined the Duke of Berwick and were attached to the expeditionary force under Prince James Francis Edward Stuart in 1708 who, as the son of James II, claimed to be James III of England. James II had died in September 1701; his legitimate son, although entitled 'The Pretender' was a genuine Stuart because some forty-two persons of rank were present at his delivery. Of these, eighteen were of the Privy Council, while twenty were women who actually witnessed the birth of the child.

It will be remembered that when James II left Ireland, his intention was to return in triumph. In fact, as far back as 1696, James II's illegitimate son, the Duke of Berwick, had gone to England in disguise to organize a concerted rising which would put the Stuarts back in power. He had even raised an army containing a cavalry regiment fully equipped and ready to take the field at a moment's notice. However, the English plotters were very wary and were adamant in their refusal to make any move until French troops arrived. Louis had promised these, but his promises meant little to the English; they wanted to see the men on the ground. The Duke of Berwick, quoted by O'Callaghan, describes the situation:

The Most Christian King [Louis XIV] had readily consented to supply these; but he insisted that, before they should be embarked, the English should take up arms; as he was not willing to risk his troops, without being sure of finding there a party to receive them. Neither side being desirous of relaxing from what it had resolved upon, such fair dispositions could not lead to any thing; which determined the King of England to send me over, as his envoy on the spot, to endeavour to convince the English of the sincerity of the intentions of the Court of France, and to engage them to take up arms, without waiting for the descent; promising, that, as soon as they should do so, the Marquis d'Harcourt, who was nominated General of this expedition, would cause the troops to embark. I then passed over in disguise to England. I proceeded to London, where I had several conversations with some of the principal Lords. But, it was to no purpose, that I said to them whatever I could most strongly conceive, and represented to them the necessity of not allowing so fine an opportunity to escape. They continued firm in their desire, that, previous to their rising, the King of England should land with an army. To tell the truth, their reasons were good; for it was certain, that, as soon as the Prince of Orange would have witnessed the revolt, or would have had information of the project, which could not long remain concealed, on account of the preparations which it was necessary to make for the landing, he would have immediately ordered a fleet to sea, and would have blockaded the ports of France; by which means, those who might revolt, finding themselves driven, with their hastily-raised troops, to fight against a good army, composed of veteran and disciplined soldiers, it was certain, that they would have been very soon crushed.[4]

The ink on the Treaty of Ryswick was scarcely dry before

a fresh need arose for Irish troops and officers. Louis XIV must have cursed himself for treating the Irish troops so churlishly, for in 1701 the War of the Spanish Succession plunged Europe into another contest of arms.

Charles II of Spain died in 1700; he was the last Spanish monarch of the Austrian line and nominated in his will as his successor, Philip, Duke of Anjou, grandson of Louis XIV. The Emperor of Austria and the Elector of Bavaria would have none of this arrangement and together with their allies, the Dutch and the English, formed another alliance against Louis XIV. Prince Eugene of Savoy was appointed to command the army of the allies while his kinsman, the Duke of Savoy, with Catinat commanded the French armies. Of the two Savoys, the one on the British side was the better soldier; the duke turned out to be a traitorous and useless leader who ultimately joined the enemy. The battlefield was northern Italy and the French army included the Irish Brigade under Dillon, Burke, Galmoy and Berwick. The latter's peregrinations in Britain had led to nothing so he was happy to be back as a fighting soldier — a job he preferred to the endless intrigue in which his father, James II, and stepbrother, the aspiring James III, specialized.

The first major clash between the two armies took place at Chiari where Prince Eugene, anticipating an attack by the French troops, set the scene for his own advantage. By this time the French army was under the command of Marshal Duke de Villeroy who was sent to replace the treacherous Savoy. The engagement turned into a massacre instead of a battle, with the French losing nearly 2,000 men amongst whom were two unnamed Irish colonels. Prince Eugene's losses totalled only 117 men. In his official report of the battle, de Villeroy wrote to Louis: 'The Irish and Médoc who attacked upon the right, performed *all* that could be expected from the bravest troops.'[5]

In his *Military History of the Irish Nation,* Matthew O'Conor describes how, unhappily, the highest losses of the day were sustained by the Irish. 'The loss of the Irish surpassed that of any of the other regiments: two of their colonels, and several other officers killed and many more wounded, attested their matchless bravery in this most sanguinary conflict.'[6]

After the defeat at Chiari, which was partially the result of Savoy's treachery, the French commander planned a more careful campaign. With his headquarters established at Cremona, he enticed Prince Eugene to do battle there. The latter obliged him. But for a small band of Irish troops the French would have suffered a much worse fate than at Chiari.

In the beginning Prince Eugene showed little or no enthusiasm for a contest, but later, having bribed a priest, Gianantonio Cozzoli, Rector of the Parish of Santa Maria Nueva, to help in a rather precarious plan, he determined to seize Cremona. The Rector's house and church stood within the walls of the city. A grating in the Rectory wine cellar led to a nearby sewer which connected with a trench surrounding the walls. A promise of ecclesiastical advancement added to a sizable lump sum payment persuaded the priest of his enthusiastic Imperialism following which plans were made to take over the city.

The lethargy of the military which had prevailed in Cremona, due to inactivity, fostered particularly amongst the French officers debauchery and drunkenness of which Prince Eugene was very much aware. Consequently, he decided on surprise as the most important element in his attack. He divided his army into two parts to approach the town from either bank of the River Po. The first body, which was to come from Ostiano, was to have about 400 troops inside the town ready to open the gates of Cremona; the second body was to approach the town through the Parmesan territory and overwhelm the surprised and disorganized garrison.

On the night of 1 February 1702, the operation began; by daylight the following day Prince Eugene himself was in the town at the Hôtel de Ville. The consternation which prevailed is described by an Italian historian :

Confusion, terror, violence, rage flight and slaughter were everywhere! Dreadful for all was the awakening! Still more dreadful what they saw when awake! The citizens believed, that their last hour was come! The French, between fury and surprise, arming themselves hastily and irregularly, seized their muskets, sabres, and bayonets, and sallied out from their lodgings or posts, naked and bare-footed, or covered only with a shirt, ignorant of where they were rushing, what enemy they were going to engage, or what had reduced ill-fated Cremona to such extremities, during that horrible night. The Austrians believed that victory was already within their grasp.[7]

The most dramatic incident in the proceedings was the fate that befell the French commander, Marshal de Villeroy. During the surprise attack he was awakened from his sleep by the excitement. He rushed from his quarters, mounted his already-saddled horse, and galloped towards the sound of musketry. He had not gone far before he was wounded slightly and probably would have been killed but for the intervention of an Irish officer named Francis MacDonnell who was in the Austrian army. (This same officer presented a fascinating sidelight on the drifting of the Wild Geese which obviously had already started through Europe. MacDonnell was the nephew of James Mac-Donnell of Mayo, who had become a Count, a General, Imperial Chamberlain and Inspector-General in Austria. When he died in 1766, he was succeeded to the title by de Villeroy's captor.)

At first de Villeroy kept his name and rank secret from Mac-Donnell, but when the latter found himself being offered handsome rewards and even the command of a cavalry regiment in the French army he became highly suspicious and sent for his superior officer, General Stahremberg, who recognized the French marshal and made him prisoner. This incident is confirmed, although with some slight difference, in the military memoirs of O'Conor :

Villeroy, roused by the firing, jumped out of bed, burned his papers, proceeded to the square, and arriving just as D'Entragues received his death wound, was himself borne down by the cuirassiers, trampled under foot, and in danger of being killed, when rescued by Francis MacDonnell, an Irish officer of the regiment of Bagni. Villeroy whispered : 'I am the Marshal Villeroy; I will make your fortune, bring me to the citadel; you shall have a pension of 2,000 crowns annually, and a regiment.' MacDonnell replied, he had hitherto served with fidelity; he would never be disgraced by perfidy; he preferred honour to fortune, and hoped to attain, by honourable services in the Imperial army, the rank offered to him in the French, as the reward of treachery. He conducted the Marshal to the most distant *corps de garde,* and was again tempted by a bribe of 10,000 pistoles; but MacDonnell's honour was beyond the reach of corruption, and he gave up his prisoner to General Stahremberg.[8]

From all appearances the seizure of most of the town and the French commander spelled the end of Cremona. But, in fact, the drama was only beginning. Two battalions of the Irish Brigade, who could neither afford the debauchery of the French nor had the opportunity by virtue of their strict discipline, were strongly entrenched near the Po gate. The battalion from the Dillon regiment was commanded by Major Daniel O'Mahony, who led a fierce assault on the Imperial troops when he learned that they were in the city; he succeeded in foiling the efforts of the Germans to open the gate at the last moment. This was the first unexpected setback to Prince Eugene's plan.

The other battalion of the Irish, attacked by Austrian Grenadiers, allowed the enemy to come as close as possible, then with 'a line of bayonets, and of musket-mouths vomiting fire and death'[9] repulsed the Imperial troops.

Prince Eugene, realizing that the quick subjugation of the Irish troops was tantamount to success, now turned to bribery. He chose as his emissary the same MacDonnell who had captured de Villeroy. MacDonnell approached with a flag of truce and addressed the soldiers of the Brigade :

'Countrymen, Prince Eugene sends me to say to you, that if you will change, you shall have higher pay in the Imperial than you have had in the French service. My regard for my countrymen in general, and especially for brave men like you, induces me to exhort you to accept these offers. If you should reject them, I do not see how you can escape certain destruction. We are in possession of the whole town except your part. His Highness waits my return only to attack you with his whole force, and cut you to pieces, if you do not accept his offers.'

'Sir, [replied one of the Irish officers] if your general waits only for your return to cut us to pieces, he shall wait long enough; we will take care you shall not return. You are my prisoner. You come not as the deputy of a great captain, but as a suborner. We wish to gain the esteem of the Prince by doing our duty, not by cowardice or treachery, unworthy of men of honour.'[10]

One of the real tragedies of this incident was that it highlighted the inevitable consequences of Irish versus Irish. MacDonnell himself was stalwart in resisting the bribery of de Villeroy; one wonders whether he believed honestly that he could move his fellow countrymen. Why should he expect less honour from them than from himself? Perhaps there was some clannish pride involved; nevertheless, his temerity was equalled only by that of clerical interference in a war in which the Pope seemed to be fighting on both sides. This aspect of the war is shrouded in mystery although there is some evidence that the Pope had secret treaties with both sides.

The negotiations with the Irish gave the French forces time to recuperate from the dissipation of the night before and, to quote O'Conor: 'Thus ended the surprise of Cremona, one of the most remarkable events in modern warfare. A garrison of 7,000 men, in a town strongly fortified, surprised in their beds, obliged to march in their shirts, in the obscurity of night, through streets filled with cavalry, meeting death at every step; scattered in small bodies, without officers to lead them, fighting for ten hours without food or clothes, in the depth of winter, yet recovering gradually every post, and ultimately forcing the enemy to a precipitate retreat.'[11]

Mahoney, the commander of Dillon's battalions, was the hero of the battle; of his 600 men, 223 were killed. He was selected to bring the despatches of the battle to Paris. He gave the news personally to Louis XIV who said to him: ' "You have said nothing of my brave Irish." Mahoney replied, "They fought . . . with the other troops of your Majesty." '[12] It is hard to determine whether Mahoney was being loyal to his captured commander or was naturally of a modest disposition. O'Conor, who tends to be biased, suggests that it was 'a memorable instance of the modesty of merit, or of pride, conscious of merit and disdainful of vainglory.'[13] At any rate, as a result of the battle Mahoney was raised to the rank of Colonel as were two officers from Burke's regiment. All the officers and men of the Irish units received increases in pay.

De Villeroy, now a prisoner, was succeeded by Marshal Vendôme who was a grandson of Henry IV and something of a fire-eater. His army was strengthened by the addition of a further part of the Irish Brigade under Clare and three other independent Irish units. There followed French successes at Caneto and Mantua; then came the Battle of Luzara in which Prince Eugene, whose military genius had been compared with that of Hannibal and Napoleon, faced Vendôme, revered by his troops for his personal courage and audacity. 'On a field of battle [he] shone like a meteor in a clouded sky.'[14] The battle for Luzara was one of frightful carnage with the Irish troops sustaining a terrible onslaught which lasted nearly twelve hours. Prince Eugene was determined to defeat them at all costs; it is significant that he had his own Irish troops (Taffe's regiment) but kept them in reserve.

The outcome of the battle was something of a stalemate; although military students award the honours to Prince Eugene's Imperial army, '*Te Deums* sung at Vienna and Paris claimed the victory for each and affronted the Supreme Being with conflicting thanks, for the inhuman immolation of his creatures to the ambition of kings.'[15]

The futility of the slaughter was magnified by the appalling loss of Irishmen on the French side; more than 10,000 Irishmen, nearly a third of those taking part in the battle, were killed. After this sickening butchery considerable changes took place in the Irish units. Some of them were augmented with recruits from Ireland; the pool of officers formed by Louis was much in use so that Irish troops were on many fronts. Dillon himself had command of his own regiment and since the conflict was moving to the Tyrol, he joined his regiment there. One of the more peculiar facets of the campaign as it advanced was the clash between the Irish and the Germans. Maybe Martin Luther had something to do with it but often the crack German troops found themselves face to face with the crack Irish ones. In fact, as a result of the defeat of the Germans by the Irish at Cremona, a Munster piper became famous for his tune, 'The day we beat the Germans as Cremona.'

> *By honour bound in woe or weal,*
> *Whate'er she bids, he dares to do;*
> *Tempt him with bribes, he will not fail,*
> *Try him in fire, you'll find him true.*
> *He seeks not safety; let his post*
> *Be where it ought, in danger's van,*
> *And, if the field of fame be lost,*
> *'Twill not be by any Irishman.*—Orr[16]

The War of the Spanish Succession was increasing in intensity. By 1704 the Duke of Marlborough had joined the Imperialist Army under Prince Eugene; the Elector of Bavaria had crossed sides and was now with the French and Spaniards, their armies being known as the Gallo-Bavarians. The French commanders were de Marcin and de Talland. Of the important clashes affecting the Irish, the Battle of Blenheim fought on 13 August 1704 was one of the fiercest. The French were defeated. In the Spanish peninsula, however, the Duke of Berwick leading Irish troops brought great credit on his forces due to the particularly daring exploits of Brigadier Daniel O Mahoney of Cremona fame. It was not, however, so much for winning a battle as for covering a successful retreat from the Portuguese. There was little accomplishment by the Irish during 1705 except that Irish troops fighting for Marlborough deserted in great numbers to join the French, most of them coming from the Flemish and German regiments.

This desertion was testimony to the sad disillusionment of so many of the Wild Geese. The idealism which generated their departure from their homeland must have been a very hazy memory by this time as it became increasingly obvious to them that they were the merest of ciphers in the European cockpit. Their bitterness must have been even more painful as they observed the two nations, in which they placed their hope for a free Ireland, at each other's throats. At this stage the Irish were being treated by both sides simply as mercenaries; their numbers were strengthened regularly by recruits from Ireland who had been deceived into believing that to fight on the

Spanish Imperialist side was to fight for Ireland. This deception was aggravated by their strong religious belief. Amongst the officer class the idealism still remained although they were also aware that they were men without a country and that their hope of survival lay in outstanding military achievement — an ambition that was fully realized and culminated in the Battle of Fontenoy.

Wherever Irishmen fought they brought nothing but credit on their bravery and fighting skill. Their losses were inestimable; their blood drenched the earth in countless faraway places where the Treaty of Limerick cast its bitter and poignant shadow. It was always their desire to engage the English in battle but this prize was reserved for Fontenoy where for the first time they were able to challenge those who had forced them into exile.

1. Quoted by John Cornelius O'Callaghan in *History of the Irish Brigades in the Service of France,* p. 189.
2. *Ibid.,* pp. 189-190.
3. *Ibid.,* p. 191.
4. *Ibid.,* pp. 183-184.
5. *Ibid.,* p. 196.
6. P. 238.
7. Quoted by O'Callaghan, *History of the Irish Brigades,* pp. 199-200.
8. Matthew O'Conor, *Military History of the Irish Nation,* p. 248.
9. O'Callaghan, p. 204.
10. O'Conor, pp. 249-250.
11. *Ibid.,* p. 253.
12. *Ibid.,* p. 254.
13. *Ibid.*
14. *Ibid.,* p. 258.
15. *Ibid.,* p. 268.
16. O'Callaghan, p. 217.

CHAPTER VI

Fontenoy, 1745

Before the Battle; night

Oh bad the march, the weary march, beneath these alien
    skies,
But good the night, the friendly night, that soothes
    our tired eyes.
And bad the war, the tedious war, that keeps us
    sweltering here,
But good the hour, the friendly hour, that brings the
    battle near.
That brings us on the battle, that summons to their
    share
The homeless troops, the banished men, the exiled
    sons of Clare.
Oh little Corca Bascinn, the wild, the bleak, the
    fair!
Oh little stony pastures, whose flowers are sweet,
    if rare!
Oh rough and rude Atlantic, the thunderous, the
    wide,
Whose kiss is like a soldier's kiss which will not
    be denied!
The whole night long we dream of you, and waking
    think we're there, —
Vain dream, and foolish waking, we never shall see
    Clare.

The wind is wild to-night, there's battle in the
    air;
The wind is from the west, and it seems to blow
    from Clare.
Have you nothing, nothing for us, loud brawler of
    the night?
No news to warm our heart-strings, to speed us
    through the fight?

*In this hollow, star-pricked darkness, as in the
    sun's hot glare,
In sun-tide, moon-tide, star-tide, we thirst, we
    starve for Clare!
Hark! yonder through the darkness one distant
    rat-tat-tat!
The old foe stirs out there, God bless his soul
    for that!
The old foe musters strongly, he's coming on at
    last,
And Clare's Brigade may claim its own wherever
    blows fall fast.
Send us, ye western breezes, our full, our rightful
    share,
For Faith, and Fame, and Honour, and the ruined
    hearths of Clare.*

— Emily Lawless, *With the Wild Geese*

Poetry has flowed from many an Irish pen about the Battle of Fontenoy which was a fulfillment of a hope for the Wild Geese, a climax of Irish military genius, and a glorious expression of pent-up patriotism. Pages of documentation of all kinds have been written about a battle which, under ordinary circumstances, would be classed as just another event in the long-drawn-out struggle for European royal supremacy. But the circumstances were not ordinary. Military strategists have made it the subject of considerable controversy while politicians have endeavoured to underrate the importance of the Irish contribution to the French victory. For the Irish nation a bitter memory was now assuaged by pride that on a far-off field some little retribution had been made for the infamous Treaty of Limerick.

There remains one strange truth about the battle which still gives many people food for thought : Irish people at home commemorate defeats they have suffered in history, such as 1691 and 1798, yet there has been no national effort to recognize Fontenoy which must always stand as a great landmark in Irish history.

In April 1745 the Allied forces assembled in Brussels under the command of the Duke of Cumberland, son of George II, to campaign in Flanders. This struggle was a continuation of a war which began over the Spanish Succession and which later was followed by the Wars of the Polish Succession and the Austrian Succession. These confrontations all amounted to the same thing; a clash of the British, Austrians and Dutch united against Louis XIV (and his few allies, chief of which was Prussia) and later continued against Louis XV. In retrospect one wonders about the point of the Treaty of Ryswick, for the Augsburg alliance still appeared to be going strong.

Some idea of the Irish part in these struggles can be gleaned from the following figures of Irish losses in Europe given in *The Irish Sword* :

'War of the League of Augsburg, 1688-1697, 21,000 killed and wounded;

'War of the Spanish Succession, 1701-1714, 20,000 killed and wounded;

'War of the Polish Succession, 1733-1735, 2,000 killed and wounded;

'War of the Austrian Succession, 1740-1748, 5,000 killed and wounded."[1]

In his *History of Ireland*, published over two hundred years ago, the Abbé MacGeoghegan estimates (allowing these figures for the years 1691-1745 only) that they constitute only about ten per cent of the total Irish casualties in France. From this statistical analysis it may be deduced that 480,000 Irishmen gave their lives for France. The thought that during these years the blood of half a million Irishmen was lost in Europe makes one wonder why the Irish 'Curse of Cromwell' was not replaced long ago by the 'Curse of the Stuarts' who started the whole sad story of the Wild Geese.

Louis XV himself was present at the Battle of Fontenoy but the real commander-in-chief was Maréchal Maurice de Saxe. In fact, King Louis is reputed to have said to him, 'In confiding to you the command of the army I intend that everyone shall obey you, and I will be the first to set an example of obedience.'[2]

The Irish Brigade by this time had been expanded to six

regiments which was an indication of the number of recruits from Ireland. One of the main reasons for the influx of new blood was the belief that James II's grandson could be restored to the Scottish and English throne. An attempt, this time by Bonnie Prince Charlie, to land a force in England in 1744 proved abortive due to adverse winds. The effort is described by O'Callaghan :

Early in March, when the Prince, and the Count de Saxe, having shipped 7,000 men at Dunkirk, were actually at sea with a fair breeze, for the English coast, and protected by their men-of-war, the wind shifted to an adverse point in the evening, and a violent tempest of several days' duration commenced, which dispersed the fleets of both nations that had been in sight of each other about Dungeness, and sank, drove back, or shattered the French transports in such a manner that the proposed invasion had to be abandoned. A contemporary French historian has observed that Louis XV might have exclaimed, on this occasion, like Philip II formerly, with reference to his Armada — 'I did not send my fleet to war with the elements!'[3]

Despite this failure, Irish recruits came to the Brigade. A letter addressed to Monsieur de Ceteret from the Court of Versailles dated 29 February 1744 states :

Sir, — The King having been informed that several Irishmen present themselves on the frontier, with the intention of serving in the regiments of their nation actually in his service, and that most of these regiments being complete, the supernumeries could only find their means of subsistence at the expense of the captains, if it were not otherwise provided for; His Majesty, in consideration of the useful services which he has received in the preceding wars, and of those which his Irish troops continue to render him daily, commands me to acquaint you, that the Commissioners of War appointed to the direction of the five Irish regiments which are in his service, are to comprise, in their returns, all the supernumeraries capable of serving, who may present themselves, taking care to hold a separate register of those who shall exceed the full number of each regiment, in whatever number they may come, and shall see that their pay be remitted to them, at the rate of six sols six decimes per day each, until His Majesty shall come to a determination of raising the regiments of this nation which he maintains by one or more battalions. I request you to make known this resolution to M. Deseichelles, Prefect of Flanders, in order that he may act conformably, and, on his part, look to its exact performance. I have the honour, & c., (signed) D'Argenson (foreign minister).[4]

Apparently the supernumeraries were many for on the eve of the battle there were the six Irish regiments of Clare, Dillon, Bulkeley, Roth, Berwick and Lally. There was also a separate Irish cavalry regiment under the command of Fitzjames. The latter was detached from the main Irish force — a fact that was responsible for conflicting accounts later on about Irish behaviour during the battle. [There is considerable confusion about Fitzjames who took over the regiment in 1733, became a count and was afterwards Marshal of France. His regiment was disbanded in 1762 and in 1777 he entered the Austrian service where he became a count, Field-Marshal, Imperial Chamberlain, Councillor of State, and Knight of the Golden Fleece.] The overall commander of the Irish troops was Charles O'Brien, 6th Viscount Clare and 9th Earl of Thomond, then a Lieutenant-General.

Both the Allies and the French realized that Fontenoy was to be a major event in the war. Sir Charles Petrie describes it as 'among the most murderous conflicts of the eighteenth century.'[5] The actual location for the battle was chosen by Maréchal de Saxe who, knowing that the Allies were approaching to raise the siege of Tournai, had decided that this was the most advantageous ground.

The armies were evenly matched comprising about 60,000 troops each. On the French side there were nearly 4,000 Irish soldiers. In the vicinity of Tournai itself there were about 20,000 troops; the remainder of the French army with de Saxe and the King took up their position on a cultivated plateau five miles to the south and west of Tournai. The village of Fontenoy, heavily fortified, was in the centre of their line;

their left flank was Barri wood, the right the fortified village of Antoing and the Scheldt. The French reserves were on the left flank, covered by Barri wood, and in the first line of these were the six regiments of the Irish Brigade; they were supported by the Normandie regiment, one of the six senior infantry regiments in the French army, and other picked units.

One of the most graphic descriptions of the position comes from John Manchip White, one of the biographers of Maurice Comte de Saxe :

When Maurice took up his final position, he rested his left on the village of Ramecroix, protected by a wood and by swampy ground. On the extreme left he posted the little regiment of five hundred Corsicans which had been with him at Dunkirk. Next to them he placed his large Irish contingent, six battalions strong, behind wood breastworks and equipped with eight cannon. The Irishmen would prevent the British from debouching from the woods in the early stages of the battle — if, in fact, they ever managed to make their way through the wood at all. At the worst, the Irish would form a reserve for the hard-pressed battalions in the exposed centre, for Maurice recalled that Villars had owed his defeat primarily to the fact that he had weakened his centre in order to reinforce his left wing. In the present battle that danger would at least be minimized : on what finer reserve could a general call in a moment of crisis than six battalions of the Wild Geese?[6]

Reconnaissance began on the night of 10 May; one strong British patrol drove one of de Saxe's outposts back with the result that he was forced to burn a small hamlet near Fontenoy. Squadrons of Dutch cavalry skirmished on the verge of the enemy strong points but it was not until six o'clock on the morning of the 11th that the battle really began. Before the action started both the King and the Dauphin rode up and down amongst their troops and received loud applause.

The British, amongst whom was the Brigade of Guards, launched an early assault on Barri wood, but their effort to capture it failed, as did two attacks on Fontenoy and Antoing. After about three hours' fighting, the Allies had made little progress, whereupon Cumberland decided to launch a frontal attack on the main body of the French troops. Sir Charles Petrie gives a vivid description :

> Cumberland then gave the order to advance, and to do him justice he took his place at the head of the first line, though as commander-in-chief it would have been more convenient had he been in a position to observe the progress of the battle as a whole. Sixteen thousand men, the flower of the British army, began to move forward up the slope to Fontenoy, raked by a murderous fire from the French redoubts. Whole ranks were swept away, but still the dense mass continued to press forward over the heaps of dead and dying, while the sergeants dressed the ranks with their long halberds as if they were on parade. It was without question one of the most memorable feats of valour in military history, for in spite of the terrible flanking fire from the redoubts, and of the efforts of one French regiment after another, the British moved steadily on, until they stood proudly in the centre of the French position, apparently masters of the battlefield.[7]

Up to this point the Irish Brigade as a whole had taken no part in the battle. Dillon's regiment, however, had been taken from the Brigade and was part of the force which took a bad beating during Cumberland's main attack. De Saxe, realizing his critical situation, consulted both the King and Dauphin; all recognized the need for a quick change in tactics. The aide-de-camp to the King, the Duke de Richelieu, was present at the conference; he had made a complete survey of the situation and while doing so had met Lally, who complained that 'the devotion of the Irish Brigade was not turned to account.'[8] He had noted also that four pieces of cannon on the Irish flank had not been used. In all reports of the battle much has been made of these four guns; probably in no battle in history have four pieces of artillery been discussed more.

Louis took Richelieu's advice; the Irish Brigade, supported by the four cannon, was literally hurled at the British. Five of the regiments were fresh, but despite the mauling he had received already Dillon with two French units was ordered to join them. This was to be the effort that would dislodge Cumberland or lose the battle.

To the tune 'The White Cockade' the Irish advanced with fixed bayonets into what O'Callaghan describes as

> a great oblong square (made up of Cumberland's men), keeping up in front, and from both flanks, a terrible fire of musketry, as well as of cannon loaded with cartridge-shot, but, by this time, so unluckily curcumstanced, that it could not make use of its cannon without injury to itself, was now within due range of the four pieces of French artillery, pointed in the best manner to make an opening for cavalry through the van of that as yet impervious and invincible mass, while the infantry should assault it on each side. The well-served discharges of the four cannon having raked rapid chasms through the opposing 'wall of men,' Richelieu . . . gave the word to charge.[9]

The particular job of the Irish was to smash through Cumberland's right flank. Led by Lord Clare, their effort is best described in Thomas Davis's immortal poem 'Fontenoy' of which the following verse presents the drama of the occasion :

> *How fierce the look these exiles wear, who're*
> *wont to be so gay,*
> *The treasur'd wrongs of 50 years are in their*
> *hearts to-day!*
> *The treaty broken, ere the ink wherewith 'twas*
> *writ could dry,*
> *Their plunder'd homes, their ruin'd shrines,*
> *their women's parting cry,*
> *Their priesthood hunted down like wolves, their*
> *country overthrown, —*
> *Each looks, as if revenge for ALL were stak'd*
> *on him alone.*
> *On Fontenoy, on Fontenoy, nor ever yet*
> *elsewhere,*
> *Rush'd on to fight a nobler band, than these*
> *proud exiles were!*

Facing the Irish was the English Brigade of Guards. The emotional pitch of the situation was heightened by the impatience of one young Guards officer who rushed out in front of his men to meet in single combat Anthony MacDonough from County Clare. The encounter caused both sides to halt hostilities momentarily. MacDonough smashed the sword arm of the Guardsman and sent him to the rear as a prisoner.

MacDonough's daring onslaught aroused the Irish to fever pitch with shouts of *'Remember Limerick, and Saxon perfidy!'* They were met with a formidable tempest of bullets from the British square, but despite appalling casualties they strode on to smash through the enemy and to win the battle. The leading English authority on the battle, Francis Henry Skrine, in his book *Fontenoy and the War of the Austrian Succession,* writes : 'Among French infantry regiments those of the Irish Brigade stood first. Their desperate valour was a factor of great importance in our disaster.'

The biographer of Maurice de Saxe may be relied upon for an accurate and informed summary : 'As the French regiments ran down the slope, one regiment was ahead of the others. It yelled its ferocious battle cry : REMEMBER LIMERICK! REMEMBER LIMERICK! The words echoed grimly in the ears of the English and Dutch. The Wild Geese of Ireland had many scores to settle, not least of them a failure at Malplaquet in face of Schulenburg, and a failure earlier that day at Fontenoy when Lord Clare had had to rally them after the first broadside of the English infantry. Now the Papishes were determined to be revenged on the Proddies. They advanced shoulder to shoulder, running with muskets levelled towards the bayonets of the English. A minute later the rival regiments had coalesced. The fighting was hand to hand. After a confused mêlée, it was seen that the Irish had achieved their ambition. They had sent the English reeling back. But the cost had been terrible. Thirteen of their officers, including the Chevalier Dillon, colonel of the *Regiment de Dillon,* and two hundred and sixty-one men were killed; fifty-nine officers and three hundred and twenty-four men were wounded. The Irish losses were higher in proportion than those of any other unit on the French side at Fontenoy. *Normandie* too, coming up with Lowendahl's brigade from Rumignies, charged heavily in the

universal onslaught, and they also suffered heavily, although
their casualties were mercifully lighter than those of the Irish
Brigade. The Wild Geese had sacrificed themselves to compel
an English retreat."[10]

That the Irish suffered the heaviest casualties is undeniable.
Out of a total of 3,870 they suffered 656 casualties in all,
among whom was Clare himself who received two bullet
wounds. Two colours of the Coldstream Guards fell into the
hands of the Irish as well as fifteen of the twenty cannon
taken from the enemy. The Irish leader responsible for their
capture was the brother-in-law of the late Duke of Berwick,
Lieutenant-General Count Francis Bulkeley. 'The learned Dr
Maty, Principal Librarian of the British Museum, and Secretary to the Royal Society, in his contemporary *Memoirs of the
Life of Lord Chesterfield,* referring to the very creditable behaviour of the British at Fontenoy, speaks of them, as owing
their defeat there to the Irish Brigade, or as "retiring with this
consolation, if it could be one, that they yielded the palm to
their own countrymen." To which assertion the Doctor ap-
pends this note : "The great share which the Irish Brigade had
in the success of the day was fully ascertained by one of their
most respectable countrymen, Colonel Dromgold. He published
two letters in French, on purpose to expose the fallacious account, given by Voltaire, in his poem on the battle of Fontenoy; a poem which Lord Chesterfield, notwithstanding his
partiality to the author, very wittily ridiculed in one of his
French letters." And there could not have been a more respectable authority, in opposition to Voltaire, than this Irish officer,
named by Dr Maty."[11]

The French account of the battle sustains the Irish claim.
It reads :

'The six Irish regiments sustained by those of Normandy
and Vaisseaux being thus drawn up, they marched to the
enemy without firing, and broke them with their bayonets
fixed to their pieces, while the Carbineers charged them in
flank.

'In fine, the Artillery charged with cartridge shot, playing
then upon that English Infantry, began to stagger them, and
the Household Troops charged at the same time so vigorously
and so opportunely, that all the valour of the English column

could not bear up against it. They were repulsed with considerable loss — a great way beyond the field of battle even to the Rivulet of Vezon.

'During this attack the enemies that came back towards Antoin to form themselves in two lines of infantry and cavalry, between the redoubts occupied by the Brigade of Bettens and that of Grillon, a battalion of which lay before the redoubt on the right hand, were to terribly galled, only by the cannon in those redoubts, that they retreated with precipitation, abandoning their artillery, which was taken by the brigade of Grillon.

'The Second Regiment of English Foot Guards, who had Bulkeley's Irish regiment to deal with, must be almost destroyed. The latter took from them a pair of colours, and two pieces of cannon with the horses belonging to them, which were before the battalions!

'As the great fatigue the troops had gone through in the day of battle did not permit us to follow the enemy immediately through an uneven country, full of hedges, besides woods where the cavalry could not have acted to advantage, the army of the Allies, who returned to their camp in great disorder, quitted it the same day (May 11th) at eleven o'clock at night, and marched directly to Aeth without stopping.

'We had about 520 officers and 4,000 private men killed and wounded.

'As for the Allies, their loss amounts to 15,000 men killed, wounded and deserted; which together with the loss of almost all their field pieces, whereof we took nearly 50, must disable them from undertaking anything of consequence for this campaign.

'The 15th we sang *Te Deum* in the camp under a triple discharge of 160 pieces of cannon and 40 mortars against the citadel of Tournay, as likewise three discharges from the small arms of the whole army.'[12]

Why all the controversy about the performance of the Irish? Political denigration by the English was one obvious reason especially as they did not wish to encourage any further hope of Stuart reinstatement. There was also a more acceptable explanation for the clash of opinion : the first assault of Dillon's Regiment against the allies did result in a definite repulse;

also, Fitzjames's cavalry was unsuccessful and was one of the units forced back by the Blues, the Scots Greys, and the Royals.

One further aspect of the battle must be considered : King Louis was so impressed by the behaviour of the Irish that he lavished awards on them and promoted many of the officers — MacElligot, Kennedy, Creagh, Hennessy, O'Neill, O'Connell and many others. One officer from County Cork, Captain James Creagh, had his Cross of St Louis smashed through his body. He recovered, became a Maréchal de Camp and was alive in 1789.

The gallant Anthony MacDonough who had participated in the single combat was also promoted and singled out for special assignment and sent to Ireland to recruit more men for the Brigade in County Clare. This he did very successfully but while on his mission he met a young girl from his native county, married her and did not return to France. He lived to be eighty and passed on to one of his grandchildren, one Anthony Hogan, from Kildare Street, Dublin, stirring details of the battle.

In England when George II heard of the battle he is reputed to have said of the Irish troops, 'cursed be the laws which deprive me of such subjects',[13] a sentiment that was driven home by Henry Grattan when arguing for Catholic Emancipation : 'We met our own laws at Fontenoy. The victorious troops of England were stopped, in their career of triumph, by the Irish Brigade which the Penal Laws had shut out from the ranks of the British Army.' (Hansard).

But hanging over the battlefield was that ever-present Irish ghost — Irish fighting Irish — for on the British side were many thousands of Irishmen. Immediately following the combat the Irish troops on the French side rested while their officers walked amongst them. One officer, finding many of the men in tears, asked : 'What is the reason for this when you have so ably done your duty?' Their reply was that although they would fight all over again, 'it was hard they should have to fight against their own countrymen, and, perhaps, some of them even relatives.'[14]

Note: A Celtic cross now marks the battlefield of Fontenoy; it was erected in August 1907 by the Irish Government of the period but not before an outraged Irish American visitor to Fontenoy named O'Sullivan, in a fit of anger at seeing no memorial to the Irish, erected in 1903 his own plaque. It stated that it was the Irish who had won the battle.

In 1965 Sir Charles Petrie unveiled a bronze plaque on the battlefield; it was provided by the Irish Historical Society.

FONTENOY, 1745
After the Battle; early dawn, Clare coast

'*Mary Mother, shield us! Say, what men are ye,*
Sweeping past so swiftly on this morning sea?'
'*Without sails or rowlocks merrily we glide*
Home to Corca Bascinn on the brimming tide.'

'*Jesus save you, gentry! why are ye so white,*
Sitting all so straight and still in this misty light?'
Nothing ails us, brother; joyous souls are we
Sailing home together, on the morning sea.

'*Cousins, friends and kinsfolk, children of the land,*
Here we come together, a merry, rousing band;
Sailing home together from the last great fight,
Home to Clare from Fontenoy, in the morning light.

'*Men of Corca Bascinn, men of Clare's Brigade,*
Harken, stony hills of Clare, hear the charge we made;
See us come together, singing from the fight,
Home to Corca Bascinn, in the morning light.'

— Emily Lawless, *With the Wild Geese*

1. Richard Hayes in *The Irish Sword*, vol. I, pp. 198-201.
2. Quoted by Sir Charles Petrie in *The Irish Sword*, vol. I, p. 167.
3. John Cornelius O'Callaghan, *History of the Irish Brigades in the Service of France*, p. 343.
4. Matthew O'Conor, *Military History of the Irish Nation*, appendix pp. 387-388.
5. *The Irish Sword*, vol. I, p. 171.
6. Jon Manchip White, *The Life and Times of Maurice Comte de Saxe (1696-1750)*, p. 154.
7. *The Irish Sword*, vol. I, pp. 168-169.
8. Quoted by O'Callaghan, *History of the Irish Brigades*, p. 353.
9. *Ibid.*, pp. 356-357.
10. Jon Manchip White, *Maurice Comte de Saxe*, p. 163.
11. Quoted by O'Callaghan, *History of the Irish Brigades*, p. 360.
12. *The Celt* (Dublin, John O'Daly), nos. 19, 20 (5 December, 12 December 1857), pp. 317-318.
13. Quoted by Francis Plowden in *An Historical Review of the State of Ireland*, vol. I, p. 291.
14. Quoted by O'Callaghan, *History of the Irish Brigades*, p. 366.

CHAPTER VII

Gerald O'Connor and Peter Drake

'When we read of the Flight of the Wild Geese, after Limerick, we seldom dwell upon its consequences in after years, on the constant traffic that went on between the Continent and quiet places in Munster, where today the mention of Spain or France or Austria is as infrequent as reference to Alaska or Japan.'

— Pierce Fitzgerald, quoted by Daniel Corkery in *The Hidden Ireland*

Two very different short biographies of Gerald O'Connor and Peter Drake, provide interesting speculation on the kind of lives the Wild Geese led. They may constitute the extremes, for undoubtedly a routine military life was the lot of the vast majority. But throughout the course of history it is the throwoffs from the roving Irish regiments that have made their mark and have provided the most colourful, adventurous and famous stories.

I shall never see the dear land again, nor yet the few remaining kinsmen of our race. I have reached my 78th year and bring to a close these records of a life of many and strange vicissitudes. There is much in the state of my adopted country I regard with misgivings. France is no longer the France of the great king; but I have hopes for the future of the noble land which has caught to its heart the Irish exiles and has placed them high on the roll of her renowned armies. I look at the sword I wore at Blenheim and Dénain; my aged hands will never wield it again but my descendants, I trust, will draw it, should the occasion arise in the service of the nation which has given us the Brigade, and, whether in good or in evil fortune, will prove themselves worthy of their people and their name. To France I owe all that makes life most prized — a wife, who has been the best of helpmeets, sons, daughters, friends, companions, home; I love her as if she were a second mother. Yet my thoughts often turn to our fallen Offaly, to the scenes of my boyhood and first youth, to the castle by the lake, to our broken clansmen, to the parents of two generations who nursed me on their knees.[1]

These thoughts expressed in his memoirs by Gerald O'Connor, one of the ancient Offaly families, might well have been those of thousands of other Wild Geese who left the shores of Limerick and Cork. We are fortunate in having the story of his life for it traces a pattern of the lives of so many of his colleagues.

O'Connor was a descendant of the great Earl of Kildare; his grandfather Gerald had fought with Hugh O'Neill at the memorable and victorious Battle of the Yellow Ford. Few conflicts in Irish history have presented so exciting a drama as the defeat of the famous English General Bagenal when his forces were led into a trap by O'Neill. The ground had been dug up and lightly covered over with sods of turf. Bagenal's cavalry plunged headlong into it and were slaughtered like sheep.

After the death of Sarsfield, in command of a detachment of Luxemburg's army O'Connor was sent to the Rhine. He has left behind a vivid description of the devastation which war left in its wake in the Palatinate; although he was not present at the sack of Heidelberg he has nonetheless recorded terrible tales of its destruction. The French army on the Rhine, the cavalry of which was under the command of the renowned General Villars, was itself led by the Dauphin although a General Lorges was the real leader. Villars had known Sarsfield and because of the letter given by the latter to O'Connor he was put on the staff of the cavalry commander. The main army did practically nothing during the campaign but O'Connor was sent to take part in hostilities on the Italian frontier, which he described as follows:

'I beheld, for the first time, the giant heights of the Alps; the precipitous cliffs, the narrow valleys and defiles, the torrents rolling down the masses of rocks, made a profound impression on eyes that had only gazed on the low hills of Ireland.'[2]

O'Connor remained two years with Villars, either soldiering on the Rhine or on special military missions. He recalls some interesting events of those two years. Apparently, Luxemburg died in 1694 and was succeeded by a playmate of the king who was considered to be 'utterly unfit for high command.'[3] He records that the defeat of the French at Ramillies need never have occurred, that it was due entirely to the incompetence of the new commander.

On his return from the Rhine, O'Connor lived in Paris where, as he says, 'I devoted my hours of leisure to exploring the vast and stirring world of Paris . . . Accustomed as I had been to the sight of the poor towns in Ireland I used to gaze with astonishment at these scenes of wonder.'[4]

The most fascinating and romantic incident of O'Connor's life began at the Battle of the Boyne and had its aftermath in France. O'Connor had captured a French officer in the Williamite army known as Monsieur de Bacquancourt and had accepted from him his word of honour not to try to escape. Prior to O'Connor's leaving Limerick, prisoner and captor had to part company. When he was handed back to the Williamite Army, Bacquancourt said to O'Connor: 'Strange is our lot. Would that I could return to France, and you are mourning because you will behold her shores; but we shall remain friends whatever fate has in store for us. I have a brother in Normandy who holds the ancient faith, and several kinsmen in the Low Countries; they will be kind to you if it were only for my sake.'[5]

Later in France, O'Connor had a letter from Bacquancourt's brother inviting him to visit the family home in Normandy. Apparently, it was a large château near the little town of Caudebec which was mid-way between Rouen and Havre de Grace. During this visit O'Connor developed a true feeling and understanding of the politics and aspirations of the French monarch. But in less serious moments he had discussions of another kind. These were with Estelle who was the daughter of Bacquancourt. His own words best describe how this discussion developed :

Our hearts had soon joined in close and tender sympathy; we became deeply attached to each other; her mother did much to prevent our union; and the authority of a mother in France is immense in these matters. Love, nevertheless, overcame all obstacles; and Monsieur de Bacquancourt, who had treated me as one of the family, at last consented that I should become his son-in-law; he was good enough to say that, though a poor exile, I was a soldier who had a future before him. I was married when in my 29th year; half a century has passed over our heads, bringing with it the manifold changes of life; yet from the hour that my Estelle placed her hand in mine and vowed before the priest to be my true wife, to the present time, when we are both drawing near the grave, our union has been one of unmixed happiness.[6]

After the rout of the French Army under the command of Talland at Blenheim, O'Connor joined it and described how fewer than 6,000 men escaped and how scarcely a gun or any ammunition were left. After this defeat Villars sent O'Connor to make a study of some of the regiments of French troops. Admitting that the spectacle which the French troops made was grand, O'Connor still stated that 'it was not equal to that of our race in 1689 and '91.'[7]

Apparently, during all this time the Maison du Roi still remained in a French army which by 1705 was somewhere in the region of 80,000 men. In the meantime the great Marlborough had landed in France and at the head of 100,000 men was determined to destroy the power of Louis XIV. The intricacies of European politics at this time were so involved that they must tax the ingenuity of any historian, especially since propaganda was quite rife in those days just as it is today. Coxe, in his *Life of Marlborough,* disagrees entirely with the figure of 100,000 men and states that is was only 42,000.[8]

Beyond the Pyrenees at this time Philip V of Spain was heading a monarchy which was deteriorating as rapidly as that of Louis XIV. At the same time Archduke Charles was hoping for the destruction of France and Spain so that he could take over the Spanish throne.

O'Connor took part in the Battle of Ramillies and gives a vivid account of not only his own part in it but of his own personal effort to capture Marlborough. His regiment was placed in the second line of the cavalry, the old Maison du Roi; the flower of the heavy cavalry of France together with the Gray and Black Musketeers — the renowned Gendarmes especially chosen — and veteran soldiers were in the front lines. A few hundred yards to the left of O'Connor were the three Irish regiments under Lord Clare who, according to O'Connor, had been 'more than true to the standards of their adopted country.'[9]

The battle began at noon and apparently the shock of the hostile squadrons as they charged at each other was terrific. O'Connor's own line received the overflow of the first shock, and this description, in his own words, is probably the most realistic :

> Our horsemen had now the better of the fight; but soon we beheld fresh bodies of horsemen, hastening to the relief of the half-defeated squadrons. Marlborough was at the head of this reserve of cavalry, no doubt, as I had feared, detached from his right, which really was in no kind of danger. I can still see him as, undauted and serene, he rode forward amidst the cheers of his troops, shouting 'Corporal John' the name they had given their hero; he was surrounded by his staff, evidently receiving his commands. I fell on his men with my whole regiment; he narrowly escaped being made prisoner — oh! that heaven was so unpropitious to France — but he was extricated, and my troopers were compelled to retreat.[10]

After the final defeat at Ramillies, O'Connor escaped with only thirty men; with these he made his way back to Brussels where he took refuge with some kinsfolk of his wife. Unfortunately, he had to leave this city in a hurry because, had he been taken prisoner by the British, he would unquestionably have been hanged as an Irish rebel. He escaped by disguising himself as a peasant and made his way toward the borders of France and then to Hainault.

In 1708 O'Connor also fought at the Battle of Oudenarde, having previously served in the Italian campaign at Turin. His active life as a soldier ended with the Peace of Utrecht in 1713, which was confirmed by a further peace at Baden in 1714.

By this time O'Connor was over forty; he was the father of five children, two of whom were being prepared for the army. As he wrote : 'I passed several months in this quiet retreat — it is unnecessary to say what my feelings were at enjoying a season of fresh happiness which seemed to me like a new union.'[11]

The next important event in his life was the death of Louis XIV of France. Apparently, Louis had contracted gangrene in one leg and, according to O'Connor, although the monarch was over seventy-seven and not very popular his demise caused something of a shock. His description of the funeral certainly gives food for thought : 'The spectacle was a sorry, nay a most painful sight. The funeral procession to St. Denis was ill-attended and mean; the people along the roads showed at best indifference, ribald jests and murmurs were occasionally heard. Such was the end of a reign of unparalleled grandeur; it proved how utter is the vanity of earthly things but it was discreditable to the character of the French nation.'[12]

After the king's death and with the formation of a collective array known as the Irish Brigade (which will be dealt with in other pages), O'Connor lost his own troop of guards but was made a major in one of Lord Clare's regiments. According to him, the actual brigade consisted of 10,000 men. By this time one of O'Connor's sons was actually serving in Clare's regiment. O'Connor himself remained on the staff of Villars and was regularly sent on tours of inspection throughout France to report on the state of the cavalry; he remained in this honourable position until he left the army when he was some sixty years of age. He did not fight at Fontenoy which to him was a very serious disappointment although he took great pride in the fact that the Irishmen turned the tide of battle.

When O'Connor left the army in 1731, his eldest son, John, had a company in one of Lord Clare's regiments near the city of Rouen. John invited his father to a special banquet to celebrate his retirement, but for the old soldier it was one of the more disappointing episodes of his life : *not one single officer present had remembered Sarsfield or knew very much about him.* On that occasion also he was invited to visit his old commander Villars who gave him a cogent description of the English soldier : 'He is slow and heavy and must have his belly full but he fights like a bull dog, and never gives in. I saw the red coats to my cost at Malplaquet; they were the best of the enemy's troops in the field. I prefer 20,000 Englishmen to 30,000 Germans.'[13]

In many ways O'Connor was one of the luckiest of the Wild Geese for in 1725 he was able to return to the land of his birth without restriction. In those days the place to land, apparently, was 'Ring's End', which he described as 'a collection of poor dwellings on a dreary marsh beside the Liffey — it had scarcely a sail on its waters.'[14]

Although O'Connor had not seen Dublin since the Battle of the Boyne, he remained there only a very short time and then began the two-day journey to Offaly. His description of Dublin is by no means complimentary for he wrote that the public buildings were few and mean, the churches were unsightly, and the whole place had an inanimate and squalid aspect. He described the main part of the city as an assemblage of narrow alleys and lanes and typical of the home of a conquered race.

O'Connor remained altogether six months in his homeland and his most vivid and bitter reflections found expression in his caustic feeling towards the conquerors. One of his references is : 'The Treaty of Limerick had been shamefully broken . . . the Colonial Parliament with the full consent of the men in power in England made a series of laws which placed the Irish Catholic in a position of permanent and degrading bondage, in some respects worse than when he was under the iron rule of Cromwell.'[15]

During his stay in the country his own kinsfolk had become deeply involved with the authorities, so with a strange mixture of despair and melancholy he returned to France. Writing afterwards of that first journey home, the only good word he had to say about any place was Portarlington where his prisoner, the famous Monsieur de Bacquancourt, had changed his name to Desvoeux. The latter was dead but O'Connor and his wife were very hospitably received by a Huguenot colony which had been developed in Portarlington and he was able to discuss at considerable length old swords and pistols that had done service at the Boyne. He also had occasion to discuss the strategy of the Boyne and the battle that succeeded it.

While he was in Dublin he met Dean Swift. To quote him : 'We met him in a street, followed by a thronging mob shouting out "The Drapier" and "Wood's Halfpence"; even the best citizens took their hats off to him.'[16] O'Connor's brother was a close personal friend of Swift.

Fifteen years later Gerald O'Connor wanted once more to see the land of his birth. His brother was an old man, both his sisters had died in a religious house in Kerry, and his family name was fast dying out in that country. On this occasion he records considerable improvement in his homeland since his first visit, but he still found it under the shadow 'of a most dire calamity.'[17] The previous winter — 1739 — was one of intense frost. It was the year that the potato crop failed all over the country and the price of corn and bread rose far beyond the means of the poor. Consequently, O'Connor, who witnessed the frightful effects of the famine, returned to France for the last time bearing in mind the words of the English poet Spenser : 'Out of every corner of the woods and glens, they came creeping forth upon their hands, for their legs could not bear them; they looked like anatomies of death; they spoke like ghosts crying out of their graves; they did eat the dead carrions, happy when they could find them.'[18]

O'Connor's last visit to Ireland was quite short; the misery that prevailed all around him was so appalling that he was glad to return to France where he died some eight years later. One wonders whether in truth he would have believed the words of the poet Thomas Davis who wrote in later years :

> *I would almost venture another flight*
> *There's so much joy in returning.*

While O'Connor's life followed a fairly regular military pattern there were many others who led much more dramatic and less orthodox careers. A Captain Peter Drake has also left us his memoirs which provide glimpses of a life in fascinating contrast to that of Sarsfield's aide. It is equally deserving of study because it outlines an entirely different kind of exile. It is of particular importance because it is filled with the spirit of adventure that sent so many of the Wild Geese wandering, not only through Europe but all over the known world.

Peter Drake, like O'Connor, went away after the Treaty of Limerick but on arrival in Brest was considered too young for military service. His patron, Lord Trimlestown, sent him to the Marchioness of Catulan 'with directions that I should be instructed in the French tongue.'[19]

In 1694 Drake left the custody of the Marchioness, probably because of some rakish incident. According to himself, the parting occurred in Paris — very conveniently. Drake glosses over his life in Paris. His next admission was that he sought aid from Sarsfield's mother who with her two daughters was living in comparative poverty about thirteen miles northwest of Paris at Saint-Germain-en-Laye. Apparently, the exiled Stuarts held court here; in fact, James II died and was interred there in 1701.

This kind of life was not for Drake so he next went to the Earl of Limerick whom he described as his best friend, but to whom he was also related. His association with the Earl proved to be a stormy one, so much so that he had to leave the patronage of his friend and join Colonel Arthur Dillon's regiment of foot. The latter proved to be one of the most famous units in the French army; later, in 1706, Dillon was promoted to Lieutenant-General and was undoubtedly one of the most successful of all the Irish officers who won French commissions. He was surpassed only by the Duke of Berwick who founded the Regiment of Berwick. The latter whose name was James Fitz James and who later became the Duke of Berwick was the illegitimate son of James II and Arabella Churchill. She was the sister of the Duke of Marlborough, under whom Drake fought during the Duke's last campaign in Flanders. He had changed his allegiance from the French to the British.

Drake had fought with the French at Ramillies and was wounded at Malplaquet. He tired of the French with whom he was dissatisfied because he was not given a commission; so he decided to return to Ireland. He landed in Cork in 1699 but was recognized as a former member of Sarsfield's army and was promptly clapped in jail. He spent six months in prison but managed to escape — this through the aid of an attractive young woman. Evidently he was particularly appealing to the fair sex and throughout most of his life was able to make full use of them in pursuit of his objectives, legitimate and otherwise. The fact that he was well-connected, socially, always proved a boon in his various adventures. Although he was condemned to death he still managed to avoid the hangman's noose. For example, he describes the last few days of his prison life : 'I had the pleasure of seeing my benefactress at least twice a week and sometimes oftener.'[20] The fact that these meetings took place was due to the financial assistance which his lady friend was providing for him. Her name was one Elizabeth Toomy. After his escape Drake made his way to Dublin where he appeared to have had little difficulty in finding considerable sums of money and living a luxurious life.

This was not the only time he saw the inside of a prison. In 1707 he joined a French privateering group which set out from Dunkirk to attack English ships at Dover. It was a harebrained escapade; it ended disastrously and put Drake in Marshalsea Prison. He was sentenced to death for treason but by the middle of 1708 his sentence was commuted to life imprisonment. By the following year he was completely free having been granted Royal pardon by Queen Anne. All this was effected because of the influence of his friends at court, many of whom were women. Even while under sentence of death (and, indeed, during most of the time he was in prison) he was permitted to leave the jail. Most of the time he spent carousing and womanizing in London.

By 1710 Drake was in the British Army under Marlborough, but this time with the rank of sergeant; he was attached to Lieutenant-Colonel Sir Robert Montgomery who was the Acting Military Governor of Ghent. In this position he exploited his job to the full; it is hard to determine which one was the bigger rascal, Drake or his Colonel. One thing is certain : both of them made considerable money, so much so that the Irishman was able to return to London once more to wallow in the fleshpots. Here he became acquainted with the Marquess of Harwich in whose regiment of horse he enlisted. This did not prevent him from having an abundance of leave.

In London he met one Mrs Viers who later became Mrs Jolly. The latter title seemed most appropriate for she had a rip-roaring affair with Drake which lasted for many years and which enabled the Irish rogue to make a great deal of money out of an old Dutch woman whom he pretended to marry. He called her his 'Old Woman'. Her wealth was apparently considerable; it even enabled Drake to set up in London one of the finest of inns which later passed into the hands of Mrs Jolly who later made a whore house of it.

Drake's own description of some of these events makes fascinating reading. Whenever he sought lodgings in London his practice was to refuse to accept any unless they were run by a widow. By this means he always tried to assure not only the comforts of the house but the pleasures of the bed. Referring to the Dutch woman he writes:

> I gave a thundering knock and the maidservant came to the door; I asked what rooms they had to let. She desired me to walk in and shewed me into a handsome parlour, saying she would call her mistress. The widow came in; she was a little plump woman about 5 or 6 and 50, was well-dressed, and had the remains of a good face . . . I fixed my resolution and waited for the first favourable opportunity to make a general attack, which soon happened; the storm was made in the dead of night and after some faint resistance I entered.[21]

The sham wedding which followed later is described in the most fascinating style. Apparently, in London, Catholic clergy could not perform public marriages. Naturally the Dutch woman's three sons and friends wanted to be present at the nuptials. Drake, with well-thought-out rascality, used the marriage law to full effect, and 'told the company that . . . no priest would perform the ceremony in the presence of so many people, it being against the law.'[22] Drake simply took another woman friend of his, Mrs Holland, who was supposedly the witness; in fact, she was a partner in the whole scheme and it can be deduced that she was Drake's mistress as well. In all fairness it must be made clear that the Dutch woman was as ill-inclined to wedlock as Drake.

The 'bridegroom' lived peacefully and quietly 'at home with my old woman, often going to the play and partaking of the other diversions of the town for the remainder of this year 1712.'[23]

The diversions which Drake refers to are undoubtedly visits to brothels because he gives an intriguing description of one in his memoirs:

It may not be amiss to give my reader a short detail of the ways, customs, and manners of those houses. They are within a few doors of each other; numbers of people resort to them, where those who are so disposed may dance; the first room you go into is spacious, and fitted for that purpose; they have a band of musick, begins to play at a fix'd hour; and there immediately appears six or eight (sometimes more, never less) well-dressed, merry, undone, pretty girls, who take their places at one corner of the room, to separate them from those modest fair ones, who may go thither to see diversion. Those ladies are hired by the people of the house to oblige their customers; they have no clothes of their own, for on entering here, they are stripped of their rigging, whether good or bad, which is kept for them in case of ill behaviour, or some other misfortune, that may render them incapable of service, and if they are dismissed, or sent to an hospital, their clothes are returned. The company pays no money coming in, as is usual in such places in other countries. Here you are no sooner seated, than a man with a white apron, his hat on, and smoking his pipe, presents you with a glass, containing about a gill of bad wine, for which he demands a skilling, (about sixpence English). The company then begin to dance minuets, the men taking partners of the house ladies. My women begged that I would take one, and dance a minuet; I went and took a tall, clever, fair woman, dressed in crimson velvet, and a black velvet cap, then in fashion . . . When the waiter was gone, I resumed my discourse, and told her, I was sorry she was so confined; I had a great liking to her, and should be glad to pass a few hours with her, if she could contrive how. She was pleased to say I did her a great deal of honour, but if I was so inclined, it was in my own power, for I might now, or at any other time I should please to come, go upstairs, and, might be by ourselves with freedom.[24]

Once his inn was established as a respite Drake returned again to the British Army in pursuit of further adventure. The opportunities were few, so he left the army and ultimately made his way to Ireland where he lived with the gentry, moving from house to house as, strangely enough, a welcome guest. He died in Ireland when he was nearly eighty years of age.

Despite Drake's coming and goings as a soldier and his life of genteel debauchery he was undoubtedly a very brave man and would never hear a word said against the Irish. This is exemplified by one incident which is worth recording in his own words :

There was then in London one Captain Hardyman of whom I had heard a great deal but never had the honour to see him though I had often wished it. This gentleman was reputed brave but quarrelsome which are rarely to be met with in one and the same person. These two talents he chiefly put in practice against the Irish, publickly professing a mortal hatred to that nation, having or pretending to have so good a nose that he could smell an Irishman from the rest of the human specie. I had not been long in the house but I saw 6 or 7 gentlemen drinking their pints; whom I knew. I called for a pint, but before I had finished it, in came a portly gentleman and called for a pint of Derby; some of the gentlemen got up wishing him a good morning by the title and name of Captain Hardyman. I was glad to see him though I neither intended or expected any dispute with him, but soon found to the contrary. He was not 10 minutes in the room, before he began to suck his breath through his nostrils, as if taking snuff, swearing, damn him, he smelt an Irishman. I heard one of these who sat at the next table say, 'Now the game begins.' In a very little time, the Captain repeated his words again; I looked very earnestly at all the company, and was sure there was no Irishman in the room but myself . . . I called for a fresh pint of ale, got up and walked very gravely towards him, and addressing him in this manner : 'Sir, as I am the only Irishman in this room, whose rank smell could be so offensive to you' — Without hearing anymore, he asked me in a lofty manner, 'What then, Sir?' 'Why, Sir, I think I am obliged in honour to prevent (as much as in me lies) its having a worse effect on you, by washing it way, which I shall do in this manner,' flinging the pint of ale in his face, which blinded him for a while.[25]

Hardyman did nothing to accept the challenge offered by Drake; the most interesting part of the story is that later they both met in the same British regiment and became fast friends.

1. William O'Connor Morris, *Memoirs of Gerald O'Connor,* p. 310.
2. *Ibid.,* p. 103.
3. *Ibid.,* p. 105.
4. *Ibid.,* p. 111.
5. *Ibid.,* p. 82.
6. *Ibid.,* p. 123.
7. *Ibid.,* p. 165.
8. Coxe, *Life of Marlborough,* vol. I, p. 278.
9. William O'Connor Morris, *Memoirs of Gerald O'Connor,* p. 180.
10. *Ibid.,* p. 181.
11. *Ibid.,* pp. 265-266.
12. *Ibid.,* p. 268.
13. *Ibid.,* p. 280.
14. *Ibid.,* p. 289.
15. *Ibid.,* pp. 293-294.
16. *Ibid.,* p. 304.
17. *Ibid.,* p. 308.
18. *Ibid.,* p. 309.
19. *Amiable Renegade. The Memoirs of Captain Peter Drake, 1671-1753,* p. 12.
20. *Ibid.,* p. 25.
21. *Ibid.,* pp. 309-311.
22. *Ibid.,* p. 312.
23. *Ibid.,* p. 313.
24. *Ibid.,* pp. 344-345.
25. *Ibid.,* pp. 330-331.

CHAPTER VIII

The Fate of Lally

'*My God!*' *Lally exclaimed while imprisoned, 'oh, my*
God! is this the reward of forty years faithful service
as a soldier?'
— Quoted by James Grant, *The Cavaliers of*
Fortune

The Irish Brigade in France reached the pinnacle of its success
at Fontenoy and, although it survived as a special unit of the
French Army until 1791, it was important more because of
the men it produced than for any further distinctive military
achievement.

The immediate sequel to the battle was the birth of new
hope in the heart of Bonnie Prince Charlie that the way to
the Scottish throne was now open. Consequently, the Prince,
accompanied by seven companions known as 'the seven men
of Moidart', landed in Scotland. Of the seven four were Irish.
Three were the Marquis of Tullibardine (by right the Duke
of Athol), Mr Aeneas MacDonald, and Francis Strickland, a
man of very questionable integrity. The Irishmen were Sir
Thomas Sheridan, Colonel John O'Sullivan, Sir John Mac-
Donnell and Mr George Kelly.

George Kelly was a Protestant clergyman who had worked
incessantly to put James III on the throne. He was far more
concerned with issues of politics than with those of his church;
it is little wonder that he ended up in the Tower of London
charged with treason. His health deteriorated during his in-
carceration and, despite the fact that while he was imprisoned
he had managed by trickery to dispose of the relevant documents which formed the evidence against him, he was allowed
to take the country air up to a distance of ten miles outside the
city. Although he was always accompanied by a warden, he
made contact with a relative, the Rev Myles MacDonnell.
The latter was a Catholic priest who helped Kelly escape.

From St Germains (the Stuart stronghold in France) he wrote
to James III in 1747 and described Kelly as 'not only my very
near kinsman, but a person for whom I exposed my life, to
release him out of the Tower of London, and for whose sake
I am actually in exile.'[1] Later Kelly became secretary to Prince
Charles — an appointment which brought many onslaughts
on his probity and honesty.

Sir Thomas Sheridan, whose recorded Irish ancestors dated
back to 1087, was the son of the Secretary of State, Privy
Counsellor, and Commissioner of Customs in Ireland under
King James II. Sheridan had followed the king after Limerick
and remained at court under James II and James III. There
is some evidence that he was tutor to Bonnie Prince Charlie
but this has never been proven. Sir Thomas had a son in the
Irish Brigade; he served in Dillon's Regiment and was also
one of the men who sailed to Scotland with Bonnie Prince
Charlie.

Colonel John O'Sullivan, the third of the Irishmen of
Moidart, was a descendant of the Sullivans of Kerry. He was
one of the more dramatic and colourful figures of the Irish
in Europe. One of his earliest assignments was that of tutor
to the son of Marshal Maillebois. The latter, however, discovered that he was 'better adapted to the sword than the
gown.'[2] Later he went to Corsica as secretary to the Marshal
where, due to the constant over-indulgence of the Frenchman
in most things, O'Sullivan ran the war and earned an outstanding reputation as a 'guerilla'; in those days guerilla activities were referred to as *irregular* warfare. In a letter to a M.
de Argenson an unknown French general wrote : '. . . he (Mr
Sullivan) understood the *irregular* art of war better than any
man in Europe; nor was his knowledge in the *regular* much
inferior to that of the best General then living.'[3]

Apparently, of all the Prince's companions, O'Sullivan
was by far the most popular, so much so that the Prince rarely
went anywhere without the Irishman's company. Because of
his service to the Prince, James III made him a knight; there
are numerous records of him in the French and Italian court
documents of the period. He married a Miss Fitzgerald from
Kerry by whom he had a son who fought afterwards in the
American War of Independence. This young man had a

strange career; he was quarrelsome and undisciplined in his youth, fought in the American, British and Dutch armies and died a major in the Dutch service in 1824. In the meantime he had established his respectability and was the progenitor of brilliant and world-famed diplomats. His family served in the Canary Islands, Portugal and Morocco.

Of Sir John MacDonnell little is known except that he was a member of the Irish Brigade and was later taken prisoner at Culloden. There is some doubt about his ancestry but in an unpublished history of Kerry forming a portion of the Chevalier O'Gorman's mss. in the library of the Royal Irish Academy, we learn that he served in Corsica and also on the Rhine.

Despite the fact that Prince Charles had taken Irishmen with him to Scotland, his campaign received little support from the Irish at home. And, of course, the success and hopes of the Irish regiments were based on Irish recruitment. Although it had taken them a long time to realize it, the Irish acknowledged the fact that they were the victims of Stuart failures. If they had to serve an English monarch, why not throw in their lot with the successful one? Consequently, the sequel to Fontenoy was paradoxical; the gallant victory produced results contrary to those expected. Irish recruiting for the French Army decreased while for the British Army it increased. There was another interesting effect of that battle: the men who were to leave a permanent mark in world history began to become prominent in regiments and politics, with outstanding and varied achievements to their credit.

One of the more noteworthy was Thomas Arthur Lally who was born at Romans in Dauphiné in January 1702. His father was Sir Gerard Lally, from Tullaghnadaly, County Galway. Probably because of the difficulty of pronouncing the name of the village the elder Lally became known as Lally-Tollendal, and left Ireland in 1691 with the Second Flight of the Wild Geese. He married a Frenchwoman, Marie Anne de Bressac; Thomas Arthur was their son.

Thomas was commissioned into Dillon's Regiment in 1709, while only seven years old, and fought at Barcelona and Fontenoy. His service at the latter battle was such that, having been wounded, he was promoted Brigadier on the Field by Louis XV. He remained with his regiment until war between France and

England terminated with the Peace of Aix la Chapelle in 1748.

By this date India had become the focal point for exploitation by both England and France. Each of the nations had set up its own company but the British East India Company after 1748 was very much the stronger, financially and politically. The reason was simple : the British loved the sea and braved all elements to go to India while the French preferred to wait for clement weather. Finesse in diplomacy was required to tread warily down the Indian political pathway, for at every turn ruler was fighting ruler, and the whole scene was a permanent flaring, fighting brawl.

It was into this mess that Lally was sent by the French Government in 1756. Comte d'Argenson, the French Minister in charge of the French project, objected to his appointment for, while he admired Lally's brilliant military qualities, he considered that he was far too impatient to cope with the complicated intrigues of India. But his objection was unavailing and Lally was promoted Lieutenant-General and appointed Commander-in-Chief of all the French establishments in the East Indies. He was to take with him a force of 3,000 men, three warships, and a war chest of 3,000,000 livres.

Whatever Lally's enthusiasm at his appointment, it was sadly dampened before his departure. At first, he was subjected to inexplicable delays and then, just as he was about to leave, both his military force and money were reduced by one-third. He refused to depart but was persuaded to do so, ultimately, with a most solemn undertaking that the remaining promised resources would be forthcoming.

Like so many honest soldiers in history, Lally fell a victim to the chicanery of politicians; in May 1757 he sailed for India with instructions, according to the Directory of the Company at that period, 'to reform the abuses without number, the extravagant prodigality, and the vast disorder, which swallowed up all its revenues.'[4] In consideration of the fact that the French East India Company were just as rotten as the English and just as full of rogues, the task needed a giant in diplomacy. The headquarters of the French organization were at Pondicherry and, indeed, part of the directive to Lally read : 'As the troubles in India have been the source of fortunes, rapid and vast, to a great number of individuals, the same system always reigns at Pondicherry; where those who have not yet made their fortune hope to make it by the same means, and those who have already dissipated it hope to make it a second time.'[5]

Due to a variety of problems at sea, Lally did not arrive in India until April 1758. Much had happened in a year : Clive had established himself as leader of European interests in India, he had won the Battle of Plessy, and French influence was sadly on the wane.

No preparations had been made for Lally's arrival; in fact, as he entered the harbour his ship was fired upon. Voltaire in *Fragments sur L'Inde, sur le Général Lalli etc.* (Paris 1773) suggests that under the pretence of firing welcoming salutes, the garrison had been ordered to sink his ship. Certainly five cannon balls were on target : three pierced the ship while two others hit the riggings. Apparently, the fame of his personal integrity and his love of discipline had preceded him, and those afraid of any forthcoming reforms were determined to stop him.

Sometime after Lally's arrival in India to fight for the French East India Company, Theobald Wolfe Tone's brother, William, born in 1764, arrived in the country as well; he had run away from Ireland at the age of 14, had made his way to India and joined the British East India Company. He returned to Europe after a few years but went back to India a second time to serve as a soldier with the Nizam of Hyderabad. George Thomas, the 'Rajah from Tipperary',[6] was serving in the same army; it would be interesting to know if the two Irishmen ever met, but that is probably one of the secrets history will never reveal. William Tone was a poet and a littérateur but, according to his brother Theobald, 'He was as brave as Caesar and loved the army.'[7]

Although William died fighting for the Indian leader, Holkar, in 1802, he left behind him a definitive work on the Mahrattas entitled *Some Institutions of the Mahratta People*. Lewis Ferdinand Smith, who has so ably recorded details of the Tipperary Rajah's life, described Tone, '. . . as a man of undaunted valour and persevering enterprize (sic); an unfortunate gentleman whose abilities and integrity were as great as his misfortunes had been undeservingly severe.'[8]

Upon his arrival in India it took Lally little time to discover that he was in the midst of a financial and military rot equal only to that of the British company. Ever the man of action, he was not to be deterred by a mountain of debts, enormous financial losses and an ill-equipped army, for although he arrived only on 27 April, by the following evening he was investing the British company's fort at Cuddalore. Within a week he had seized and occupied it, at the same time picking up whatever supplies and ammunition he could. Then came his decision to march on Fort St David — a formidable undertaking considering that he had been little more than a week in India. He was fortunate in that the politicians on the British side were as untrustworthy as the French. Although the Fort, one of the strongest in India, had nearly two hundred cannon, it was short of troops and ammunition. The garrison consisted of over 2,000 men, of whom about 500 were Europeans and the remainder Sepoys.

Although he had practically no supplies and only forty guns, Lally had the great advantage of his own veteran regiment from the Irish Brigade. The defenders were no match for these experienced troops who were anxious to get at the British throats. He led his own Irish troops in the assault on the fort where, according to a French report, 'Without a moment's interruption, even throughout the burning day in the hottest season of the year, he was everywhere present, shrinking from no exposure to the tropical sun, and restricting himself to the smallest portion of rest during the calm sultry night, when the works were carried on by the light of torches and lamps.'[9]

After open trench warfare lasting seventeen days, the fort surrendered; on 13 June the garrison also gave themselves up as prisoners, Lally destroyed the fort, seized the serviceable guns, as well as a large sum of money and a considerable quantity of supplies.

Buoyed up from the success at Fort St David, Lally decided now to attack Madras, the most powerful and important of the British companies in India. He arranged for a French naval squadron to engage the British at sea. The result of this action was in the nature of a draw so Lally prudently abandoned his Madras objective and turned his attention to the collection of debts for the French company. One of the largest debts was that of the King of Tanjore; he became the chief target for the General's army.

Lally knew little or nothing of the Indian mind, especially its attitudes towards money. With the advantage of this knowledge he would have reconsidered the use of force to collect debts. Tanjore's immediate reaction, on learning Lally's plans, was, naturally, to appeal to the British at Madras who were only too anxious to give their aid. If the British knew all there was to know about 'divide and rule', the Indian rajahs had a monopoly on 'let others fight it out while we hold onto the cash.'

Tanjore's action forced Lally to turn again to the conquest of Madras — a task that had become more dangerous since he was running short of supplies. The French Government failed to send the promised money and equipment, so the unfortunate General had to make do with what he could grab en route.

His attack on Madras marked the beginning of a series of disasters: he had no money to pay his troops even though, initially, he drew on his own private resources; many of the Sepoys deserted to the enemy; his health broke and his enemies in the French company exerted every endeavour to malign and destroy him. Despite all these troubles he met with some early success and actually captured Madras itself while the British withdrew to Fort St George which was the East India Company stronghold in Madras; in fact, it was the more important part of the town and Lally failed to capture it.

An interesting incident occurred during the struggle for Madras which illustrates the somewhat strange gentlemanly code governing battles at the time, notwithstanding the ferocity and bloodshed that were inherent in them. It appears that, contrary to the 'courtesies of war', Lally's headquarters had been fired upon, whereupon he complained bitterly to the British. Pigott, the British Governor, sent a letter in reply, under a flag of truce, which read:

To M. Lally. In war mutual civilities and mutual severities can be expected. If the first has been wanting, it has not been on my part. Upon your entrance into the Black Town, I gave orders to the Commandant of Artillery that no fire

should be directed at the Church of the Capuchin Friars,
where I heard you intended to reside, although it is nearly
within Point Blank shot of the Cannon of the Fort, a distance
very unusual for a General's Headquarters. These orders
were not revoked until I received information that you had
removed from there, and that your Guards often paraded
there. If you will inform me at what Pagoda you fix your
headquarters, all due respect shall be paid to them.[10]

Lally fought a series of battles after his failure to capture
Fort St George, but disaster followed disaster. The French
Squadron at sea accomplished little; no supplies were forthcoming and the Admiral Comte D'Aché embarked on a smear
campaign against Lally, one which has few equals even in
these days of rotten politics.

Ireland's ever-present paradox was to the fore again. Lt Col
Eyre Coote, an Irishman from County Limerick and a brilliant
soldier, opposed Lally at the Battle of Wandiwash. Coote had
come to India in 1754 where he had for a time served under
Clive and ultimately had become Commander-in-Chief of the
East India Company's forces. Apart from the fact that Lally
was short of every kind of supplies, the British commander was
the better strategist, and at the end of the battle in January
1760, the French were totally defeated and forced to retreat
to the company's stronghold at Pondicherry. Events there
proved no more fortunate; the town was forced to surrender
in 1761, thereby ending the French holdings in the Indian
Empire.

The last weeks in Pondicherry were humiliating ones for
Lally, mostly because of his fellow countryman Coote. Lally,
who was so sick that he had to be carried everywhere on a litter,
was all for holding out against the enemy. The French company officials, already with well-lined pockets, acted to the
contrary; it was they who arranged the terms of surrender
with Coote. It was customary in those days for opposing
generals to dine together; Coote refused to dine with Lally
and had dinner instead with Duval de Leyrit, Governor of
the French East India Company. Coote's attitude is inexplicable when one considers that he wrote one of Lally's greatest
tributes: 'There certainly is not a second man in all India,

who could have managed to keep on foot, for so long a period, an army without pay and without any kind of assistance.'[11]

There is, however, an unconfirmed story that on the evening of the battle Lally and Coote drank in many toasts : 'Damnation to the Saxon!'

To add to his humiliation Lally was sent to England as a prisoner; the captain of the merchantman *Onslow* in which he sailed treated him with the utmost discourtesy. On his arrival in England, he was detained but treated with kindness and respect. There he heard of the many charges levelled against him by the officials of the French company and, relying on his own innocence, asked for parole to return to France to face his accusers. He wrote to the Prime Minister, Pitt :

London, September 29th, 1761. Sir,—Since my departure, now almost 5 years, from Europe, for the Asiatic climates, I am historically acquainted but with 2 men in this world, the King of Prussia and Mr. Pitt; the one by a series of distress, the other of success; the former snatching at fortune, the latter directing her. But, when I shall have seen and heard here of Mr. Pitt all I have already read of him, I shall always remember I am his prisoner, and liberty to me, though a Frenchman, is of an inestimable value; therefore I earnestly beg your interest, with his Majesty, to grant me leave to repair to my native soil, either upon parole, or upon the terms of the cartel, in accepting my ransom. Nothing, but my sense of gratitude for this favour, can add to the high regard, with which I am, Sir, your Excellency's most humble and most obedient servant, Lally.[12]

Pitt agreed to the request 'on his parole of honour' so on 5 October 1761, Lally set out for France where, immediately on his arrival, he was arrested and sent to the Bastille. He could have saved himself that indignity had he been prepared to withdraw his charges against Admiral D'Aché and the charlatans involved in the East India Company swindle. This he refused to do, believing at the time that the worst that could happen was that he would be cashiered from the army. However, he had been warned that the consequences might be worse, for en route to Paris he stayed with an old friend, Robert

MacCarthy, Earl of Cloncarthy, who lived at Boulogne. Mac-Carthy had his finger on the political pulse of the country and he knew that the reaction to the loss of the French colonies was a bad omen for Lally. He was quite right; the Irishman remained, untried, in the Bastille for fifteen months.

Lally did everything possible to get a fair hearing and addressed a letter to the Duke of Choiseul:

> My Lord,—The rumours, which prevail in Paris, have brought me here. My enemies will never be able to terrify me, since I depend on my own innocence, and am sensible of your equity. The King is master of my liberty, but my honour is under the safeguard of the laws, of which he is the protector. I do not ask you, my Lord, who are my slanderers; I know them; but what their slanders are, that I may obviate them; and repel them with such proofs, as will cover the authors of them with shame. I have brought here my head and my innocence, and shall continue here to wait your orders.[13]

He selected the wrong man, for de Choiseul, apart from being related to Admiral D'Aché, was also one of the most powerful of King Louis XV's advisors and friends. Finally, he was brought to trial; his request to be tried by court martial was evaded deliberately, so he faced a civil court. During his trial, according to the official testimony, even his accusers admitted that his conduct 'did display the greatest ardour in the service, the greatest disinterestedness, fidelity, and perseverance, with no common share of military talent, and of mental resources.'[14] Nevertheless, after nearly four years in the Bastille, in May 1766 he was sentenced to be decapitated having been found guilty of betraying the interests of the King, the State, and the Company of the Indies. The 'guilt' of betraying his King was his severest insult and despite many pleas for a fairer trial on his own part and thousands of requests by his friends for a pardon, by a process of legal chicanery he was executed on 9 May 1766. He tried to commit suicide before his execution and when he was led to his place of execution in Paris, he was subjected to humiliation reserved only for the lowest criminals. Lest he make a speech at the execution block, he

1   William of Orange's departure from Helvoetsburgo and his arrival in England at
Torbay, 5 November 1688

2   James II landing at Kinsale, holding a parliament of French and Irish

3   The defeat of James II and the Earl d'Avaux at the Battle of Enniskillen, 1689

4   Battle of the Boyne, 1 July 1690, by Romeyn de Hooghe

5   The flight of James II, by Romeyn de Hooghe

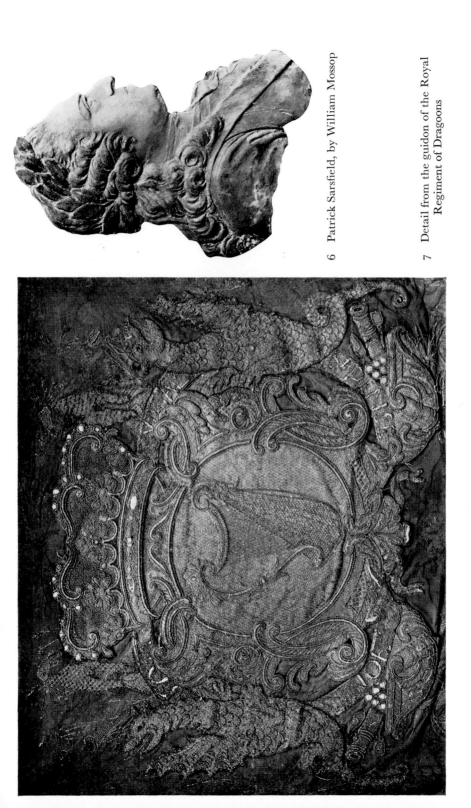

6 Patrick Sarsfield, by William Mossop

7 Detail from the guidon of the Royal Regiment of Dragoons

8 England's defeat at Fontenoy, 11 May 1745

9   Detail from a military document of the Irish Brigade in France

10   Peter de Lacy

11 The regimental badge of the San Patricio Battalion which was formed from the deserters from the American Army in Mexico

12 Captain Myles Keogh at the Battle of Spoleto

13　John Forbes, founder of the Austrian navy

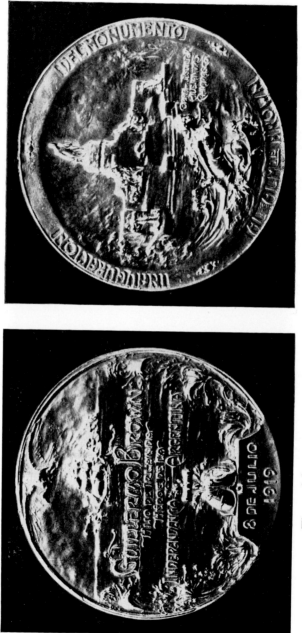

14 The medal struck to commemorate William Brown, founder of the Argentinian navy

15   General Meagher at the Battle of Fair Oaks, 1 June 1862

16 The Celtic cross which commemorates the Wild Geese who fell at Fontenoy

19 Colonel John Franklin
Blake in the Boer War

18 Keogh's medal found
round Sitting Bull's
neck after the Battle of
Little Big Horn,
25 June 1876

17 Bernardo O'Higgins,
the liberator of Chile

20 Michael Davitt

ARTHUR O'CONNOR ESQ.

(a State Prisoner in the Castle of Dublin.)

22 Irish soldiers in the American Civil War

was gagged, and even the executioner muffed the job. Fisher sums it up admirably :

> The unfortunate Lally lost India for the French on the hard-fought field of Wandiwash. There is no aspersion on his courage or loyalty; but in Eyre Coote he met a soldier hardly surpassed by Clive himself. Magnanimity in face of disaster is not one of the special French virtues. Six years after the fall of Pondicherry (1761) a barbarous crowd gathered in the Place de la Gréve to enjoy the last agonies of this son of Erin as, under the clumsy axe of the Paris executioner, he expiated a proconsul's failure. To Clive a grateful but not uncensorious country awarded a medal, a statue and an Irish Peerage.[15]

Voltaire, Madame de Pompadour and all of the few honest men in the French Colonial service were outraged at the sixty-five-year-old count's execution. The injustice exercised in the trial by the *Parlement,* which even denied counsel to the accused, was the harbinger of the Revolution which followed so shortly after.

The Irish Brigade was incensed and dangerously near revolt upon hearing of Lally's death. One Irish officer, a Colonel Butler, was 'so much affected at the injustice to his gallant countryman, that, appearing at the head of his regiment, he took the cockade from his hat, and spurned it upon the earth; and solemnly swore, he never more would serve a king and people, who with such ingratitude, so ungenerously sacrificed his friend and countryman the brave Count Lally. Although, at that time, the family estate was enjoyed by his elder brother, yet, with a noble and disinterested generosity of soul, he maintained his word, and withdrew from the service of France.'[16]

But the injustice was not to be forgotten. Before his death, Lally wrote to his son, then at school, and charged him with the task of exonerating his father. And this he did with the aid of Voltaire and members of the Irish Brigade. In May 1778 King Louis XVI in Council 'by unanimous opinions of its members, advised by a panel of magistrates pronounced that the court and sentence of twelve years previously acted without authority. As soon as this royal decree was promulgated,

D

Voltaire described it as an official murder carried out with a sword of justice. In his onslaughts on the Establishment he made the Lally case one of ceaseless reference and a poinard of official injustice. On hearing the King's verdict he wrote, although near death himself: "The dying man revives on learning this great news. He embraces very tenderly M. de Lally. He sees that the King is the defender of Justice. He will die contented." [17]

A century and half later the French Army, probably due to a belated conscience of the Irish Brigade, remembered with pride one of its former great officers. In 1929, with a full ceremonial parade, it publicly exonerated General Lally. In retrospect one wonders whether the parade was to expiate the same kind of events that were to shame it again so disgracefully eleven years later when it deserted the British Expeditionary Force on the sands of Dunkirk.

1. Quoted by John Cornelius O'Callaghan in *History of the Irish Brigades in the Service of France,* p. 370.
2. *Ibid.,* p. 376.
3. *Ibid.*
4. *Ibid.,* p. 508.
5. *Ibid.*
6. Maurice Hennessy, *The Rajah from Tipperary.*
7. *The Autobiography of Theobald Wolfe Tone, 1763-1798,* Edited by R. Barrie O'Brien, p. 2.
8. *Ibid* p. 4.
9. Marquis de Lally-Tollendal, *Plaidoyer du Comté de Lally-Tollendal.*
10. J. A. Maccauley, M.A., *The Irish Sword,* vol. 5, p. 83.
11. Quoted by O'Callaghan p. 567.
12. *Ibid.,* pp. 568-569.
13. *Ibid.,* p. 570.
14. *Ibid.,* p. 572.
15. H. A. L. Fisher, *A History of Europe,* pp. 764-765.
16. Quoted by O'Callaghan, p. 578.
17. *Fragments Sur L'Inde sur le Général Lalli,* etc.

CHAPTER IX

Disbandment

*'Throughout their history Irishmen have always wrought
better for others than for themselves, and when they unite
in Ireland to work for each other, they will direct into
the right channel all that national capacity for devotion
to causes for which they are famed.'*

— A. E. Russell in *The National Being*

The cruel injustice of the death of Lally, the demoralization
of the officers and men caused by the behaviour of the French
politicians, and the realization that the Stuarts were for all
time doomed to failure started a decay in the Irish Brigade.
Although in the Seven Years War between France and England, from 1756 to 1763, the Irish regiments still fought in
Europe, they did so as attachments to French units rather
than as a separate brigade. The Irish at home were so disillusioned by Lally's death that recruiting dropped off drastic-
ally.

Meanwhile, many of the Irish officers sought opportunities
to enlist in the other continental armies. Aware of the nepotism
and dishonesty prevalent in the French Army, they sought
more promising careers. The Austrian Army, in particular,
had special appeal; already it had many Irish officers who
were well-respected and treated with courtesy. When Francis
I of Germany died, the following paper was found : 'The more
Irish officers in the Austrian service the better; our troops will
always be disciplined; an Irish coward is an uncommon
character; and what the natives of Ireland even dislike from
principle, they generally perform through a desire of glory.'

The Spanish service, both because of its Catholic tradition
and its past association with the Earls O'Neill and O'Donnell,
was also popular. In the Austrian Annual Register of March
1766, the following appears :

On the 17th of this month, his Excellency, Count Mahony,

Ambassador from Spain to the Court of Vienna, gave a grand entertainment in honour of St. Patrick, to which were invited all persons of condition, that were of Irish descent; being himself a descendant of an illustrious family of that kingdom. Among many others, were present Count Lacey, President of the Council of War, the Generals O'Donnel, McGuire, O'Kelly, Browne, Plunket and McEligot, 4 Chiefs of the Grand Cross, 2 Governors, several Knights Military, 6 Staff Officers, 4 Privy-Counsellors, with the principal Officers of State; who, to shew their respect to the Irish nation, wore crosses in honour of the day, as did the whole court.

Other nations in Europe held out a welcome for Irish soldiers and, indeed, with little wonder. The Italian military archives contain the story of an Irish officer named Carew who was in the service of the Neapolitan Army at the siege of Tortona. Carew was ordered to take a detachment to a particular post. Having given him his orders, his commanding officer called him aside and whispered to him : 'Sir, I know you to be a gallant man. I have therefore put you upon this duty. I tell you, in confidence, it is certain death for you all. I place you there, to make the enemy spring a mine below you.' Apparently, Carew merely bowed to the General and turned to lead his men to their designated and dreadful post. On arrival there he called for a bottle of wine, opened it, and in the presence of his men drank a toast to those who fall bravely in battle. The story had a happy sequel because Tortona capitulated before the mine exploded.

There were other factors which affected the Irish Brigade as such. Although with considerable reluctance the British politicians recognized that the Penal Laws were appallingly unjust; they advocated a more mitigated policy for Ireland. Fontenoy had taught them the value of Irish troops and they were most anxious to enlist as many as possible. The great Wellington, in his address in 1829 to the House of Lords in favour of Catholic Emancipation, included in his speech the following :

'My Lords, if on the eve of any of those hard-fought days, on which I had the honour to command them, I had thus

addressed my Roman Catholic troops : "You well know that
your country either so suspects your loyalty, or so dislikes
your religion, that she has not thought proper to admit you
amongst the ranks of her citizens; if on that account you
deem it an act of injustice on her part to require you to shed
your blood in her defence, you are at liberty to withdraw"
— I am quite sure, my Lords, that, however bitter the recollections which it awakened, they would have spurned the
alternative with indignation; for the hour of danger and
glory is the hour in which the gallant, the generous-hearted
Irishman best knows his duty, and is most determined to
perform it. But if, my Lords, it had been otherwise; if they
had chosen to desert the cause in which they were embarked,
though the remainder of the troops would undoubtedly have
maintained the honour of the British arms, yet, as I have
just said, no efforts of theirs could ever have crowned us
with victory. Yes, my Lords, it is mainly to the Irish Catholics that we all owe our proud pre-eminence in our military
career; and that I, personally, am indebted for the laurels
with which you have been pleased to decorate my brow —
for the honours which you have so bountifully lavished on
me, and for the fair fame (I prize it above all other rewards)
which my country, in its generous kindness, has bestowed
upon me. I cannot but feel, my Lords, that you yourselves
have been chiefly instrumental in placing this heavy debt
of gratitude upon me — greater, perhaps, than has ever
fallen to the lot of any individual; and, however flattering
the circumstance, it often places me in a very painful position. Whenever I meet (and it is almost an every-day occur-
rence) with any of those brave men, who, in common with
others, are the object of this bill, and who have so often
borne me on the tide of victory; when I see them still branded
with the imputation of a divided allegiance, still degraded
beneath the lowest menial, and still proclaimed unfit to
enter within the pale of the constitution, I feel almost
ashamed of the honours which have been lavished upon me.
I feel that, though the merit was theirs, what was so freely
given to me was unjustly denied to them; that I had reaped,
though they had sown; that they had borne the heat and
burden of the day, but that the wages and repose were mine

alone. My Lords, it is a great additional gratification to me
to advocate these principles in conjunction with a distinguished member of my family, so lately at the head of the
Government of his native country — a country ever dear
to me from the recollections of my infancy, the memory
of her wrongs, and the bravery of her people. I glory, my
Lords, in the name of Ireland; and it is the highest pleasure
I can ambition, to be thus united with the rest of my kindred,
in the grateful task of closing the wounds which seven centuries of misgovernment have inflicted upon that unfortunate land.'

Napoleon also valued the Irish troops for when the possibility of Catholic Emancipation was mentioned to him by a
Dr O'Meara at St Helena, he said : 'When the Catholic question was first seriously agitated, I would have given 50,000,000
to be assured, that it would *not* be granted; for it would have
entirely *ruined my projects upon Ireland.*'[1] Later, Napoleon
bemoaned the fact that he did not go to Ireland instead of
to Egypt in 1798. In view of the many Irishmen he had to fight
later on, his sentiments are not surprising.

One further European event seemed to affect the Irish Brigade : the fate of the Corsicans at the hands of the French
and Genoese was very similar to that meted out to the Irish
by the British.

The final official dissolution of the Irish Brigade in France
came in July of 1791 when a decree of the National Assembly
embodied all troops into the French Army, with one exception — the Swiss. The latter was still clad and fed as a foreign
regiment. It was a decision that France would come to regret
later; however, in all probability if events had been allowed
to take their own course, the Brigade would have disintegrated
on its own. Already Clare's regiment had been sent to India
because of trouble in the Falkland Islands; Dillon's and Walsh's
regiments were in the West Indies. Walsh was a descendant
of the Fitzjames family and his cavalry had become part of
the Brigade.

The last Colonel of the Brigade at the time of its disband-
ment was General O'Connell, uncle of Daniel O'Connell, the
Emancipator. The O'Connells had fought in France since
Maurice O'Connell was commissioned in the French Marine

Corps in 1692. The General was devoted to the Bourbon cause and when he could no longer serve it in France, he left the army and returned to his home in Kerry. Prime Minister Pitt in England was also interested in the restoration of the Bourbons and interviewed a number of French officers in London to discuss a plan.

General O'Connell was one of the officers consulted and he so impressed Pitt that the Prime Minister asked him to form an English Brigade which was to consist of six regiments. 'This determination was carried into effect, and one of those regiments was placed under the command of General O'Connell. It was stipulated that Colonels should not be raised to the rank of Generals in the British service, but should receive full pay for life.'[2]

Later, when O'Connell returned to wind up his estates in France, he was seized and imprisoned until the restoration of the Bourbons following the downfall of Napoleon. He was then too old to soldier on, so with the permission of both the British and French governments he remained in France drawing simultaneously full General's pay from the French and full Colonel's pay from the British. These were his halcyon days and not destined to last; he refused to take the oath of allegiance to Louis Philippe after the 1830 revolution and as a result lived in considerable poverty. However, he remained in France where he died at the age of 90 in 1833.

After the final dispersal of the Irish Brigade and with the restoration of the Bourbons a further attempt was made to form a new one in France. This failed but Louis XVIII (Monsieur) did, on behalf of his family, pay tribute to the services of the Irishmen and had a banner prepared which was accompanied by these words:

Gentlemen, — We acknowledge the inappreciable services that France has received from the Irish Brigade, in the course of the last 100 years; services that we shall never forget, though under an impossibility of requiting them. Receive this standard, as a pledge of our remembrance, a monument of our admiration, and of our respect; and, in future, generous Irishmen, this shall be the motto of your spotless flag —

'1692-1792,'
'Semper et Ubique Fidelis.'[3]

This banner was given to the remnants of the regiments of Dillon, Walsh and Berwick.

Before the final disbandment of the Brigade one historical event occurred which was to be of vital importance and of special concern to the Irish. It was the American War of Independence in 1775. While the British recruited large numbers of troops in Ireland to help fight their war in America, the French sent some of their Irish troops to oppose them. And so, on a fresh battlefield that stark tragedy that dogged the Irish throughout their history began again : kinsmen were to fight kinsmen once more on far-off fields. They had already done so in Europe and Asia, and now it was to happen all over again, across another ocean, not just once but twice, for in less than a hundred years after the Revolutionary War Irish troops were to oppose each other in the American Civil War.

Let us take a look at a facet of the Irish soldier's character that is rarely discussed. In every single army in which Irishmen have served they have become totally integrated within the warmth and great companionship that play such a part in regimental life. And, strangely enough, officers and men from south of the Boyne who have served with troops from the north of that river can recall no rifts or quarrels arising out of politics and religion. The historic Connaught Ranger 'mutiny' in 1921 in India, on the other hand, does show that where there was a *totally southern* regiment, a nationalistic spirit was strongly entrenched. Apparently, although Irish regiments in the British service, such as the London Irish Rifles, the Faugh O'Ballaghs (the Enniskillen) and the Royal Irish Rifles, consisted of a large proportion of Southern Irishmen, they were amongst the most closely-knit and harmonious units in the army.

1. Dr Barry O'Meara, *Letters from St Helena* (1837).
2. John Cornelius O'Callaghan, *History of the Irish Brigades in the Service of France*, p. 637.
3. From the French MSS given by the late John O'Connell to John Cornelius O'Callaghan.

CHAPTER X

The Irish in Eastern Europe

In the Austrian Empire 'lack of numbers precluded the existence of Irish regiments to compare with the units of the great Brigades of France or, Spain, and we can find little trace of the Celtic ranker who in the first half of the eighteenth century was to play such a significant part in the making of Irish military history elsewhere : to all intents and purposes the Irishman who appears in these pages is the Irish officer and general.'

> — Christopher Duffy in *The Wild Goose and the Eagle*

Most of the saga of the Wild Geese thus far has been confined to their exploits in Western Europe; it is time to take a look at them against the backdrop of Eastern Europe where their story is just as colourful and their accomplishments certainly much more appreciated.

One of the more oustanding figures acquired fame in a land whose stark bleakness was in sharp contrast to the soft green hills of Erin. He was a young ensign who, at the age of thirteen, left Ireland with the army after the Treaty of Limerick and grew up to be the famous Field-Marshal Peter de Lacy serving in far-off Russia.

The Lacys were a County Limerick family, having come to Ireland during the reign of Henry II, and were descended on the distaff side from Roderic O'Conor, King of Connaught. The 'Russian Peter' was born in 1678 and sailed with James II; his father was a member of the King's bodyguard (and in later years became a Field-Marshal in the Austrian Army) while Peter's uncle was also a Colonel in one of the emigrant regiments. The latter was killed at Marsaglia in 1693 while Peter's two brothers were also both killed in the service of France. Peter fought with Catinat's army in Italy but when the Treaty of Ryswick was signed he found himself without a commission. He entered service in Hungary but this was short-lived; subsequently he fought against the Turks but after the Peace of Carlowitz in 1699 he was once more within an appointment.

About this time Tsar Peter of Russia, concerned about the slack discipline in his army, commissioned the appointment of 100 European officers to strengthen the fibre of his troops. Among those selected was Peter de Lacy. He was made a company commander with the rank of captain; his commanding officer was a Colonel Bruce who was in charge of an infantry regiment. In 1700 he was sent to fight in the campaign against Charles XII of Sweden. He distinguished himself to such a degree in the conflict that he was appointed to a company called the 'Grand Musketeers' which was composed of Russian nobles who were responsible for arming and providing themselves with mounts. His service must have merited high commendation to win this honour, especially since he was changed from infantry to cavalry, the latter being considered the élite of the Russian army. In 1705 he served with the Tsar in Poland where again his courage and skill in strategy marked him out for special reward; this time he was promoted to Major and returned to the infantry where he was given command of the Russian Marshal Scheremetoff's personal infantry unit. The following year he covered himself with laurels again in the same campaign and was promoted Lieutenant-Colonel on the personal instructions of the Tsar and given the task of training three newly-raised Russian regiments. At this point in his career his fame was spreading rapidly through Europe; in 1708 he was given complete command of the Siberian Regiment of Infantry. By this time, also, he had become the bête noire of the Swedish army. One of his major triumphs was the capture of Rumna which was defended by King Charles himself. Despite the fact that the greater part of the Swedish army was in the environs of the town, Lacy with only three battalions, a company of grenadiers, a regiment of dragoons, and 500 Cossacks achieved his objective.

Success followed success, and by 1720 Lacy was a Marshal in the Russian army and was largely responsible for the defeat of the sturdy Swedes. In 1723 he was summoned by the Tsar to Petersburg to become a member of the Imperial College of

War, and when the Empress Catherine I was crowned he was one of a small group of officers selected to follow her carriage.

Honours were showered on Lacy by the Empress Catherine and it was rumoured that he was one of the many young men to whom she extended intimate favours. The probability is that he did, in fact, serve her 'at home' as well as abroad. In view of her nymphomaniacal tendencies the real wonder would have been had he *not* been looked on with preference by her, especially since he was a most personable individual.

In 1733 Lacy was given one of his more important assignments : he was ordered to put Augustus of Saxony on the Polish throne in place of Stanislas. Once more, as in the case of Sarsfield, an Irishman was in the rôle of kingmaker. The following year, with a force considerably inferior in numbers to his enemy's, he succeeded in capturing Danzig, thereby forcing Stanislas to escape from the country in disguise. The siege of the town lasted 135 days and some idea of the severity of the struggle can be judged from the fact that 8,000 men and 200 officers were killed.

Augustus's gratitude to Lacy took the form of a gift — a portrait of himself set in diamonds worth 25,000 crowns — and the bestowal on him of the Knighthood of the Order of the White Eagle of Poland.

The establishment of Augustus on the throne did not mean that the war was over; the followers of Stanislas were still determined to return their leader to the monarchy. Their endeavours resulted in one of the most remarkable battles in history. It was that of Busawitza, where Lacy with only 1,500 dragoons, 80 hussars and 500 Cossacks defeated over 20,000 Poles.

On the Eastern European scene at this time Austria was again in conflict with France on the issue of the Polish Succession. Lacy was sent with some 10,000 troops to the aid of the Austrians. He came under the command of that veteran warrior, Prince Eugene of Savoy. There were many favourable comments on the discipline and bearing of Lacy's troops, although they saw little action in the campaign. In 1736 Lacy went to Vienna for a personal interview with the Emperor and Empress. Giving away portraits as a token of esteem was something of a royal vogue in Eastern Europe at this time and

Lacy came away with one of the Emperor of Austria richly set in diamonds. It was accompanied by a gift of 5,000 ducats.

As the Polish Succession was now settled, Lacy was needed to fight the Turks. On his way back to St Petersburg he was met by a courier bringing him the glad tidings that he had been made Field-Marshal but also bearing his orders to begin another campaign; he was to seize the Fortress of Azoph. This was very nearly his last journey for on the way he was attacked by about 2,000 Tartar bandits; his only defence was his bodyguard which consisted of thirty-six dragoons. However, he managed to escape on horseback, only because the Tartars, having seized his coach, became too engrossed in pillaging it even to notice Lacy slipping way; he was joined later by about fifteen of his dragoons.

The initial campaign against the Turks was successful. Lacy, forcing Azoph to surrender, freed some 300 Christians and captured a large supply of artillery and ammunition. His next move was to the Crimea and the Ukraine where he set up headquarters. His particular enemies were the Tartars who at every opportunity plundered villages, drove away cattle, and carried off peasantry into Mohammedan bondage. Lacy surprised one such onslaught which was under the personal command of the Khan of the Crimea and destroyed 300 of his force, captured 400 horses, and released as many as 3,000 Christian prisoners. Between 1736 and 1739 the Irishman was pre-occupied with the Tartars and Turks, a task which he undertook with particular enthusiasm. He was born into an atmosphere of religious intolerance; his Catholic upbringing made his attitude to the Mohammedan 'infidels' one of fierce bigotry enthusiastically harnessed to oppose Islam.

Lacy's subsequent campaigns included the following: he fought in Finland, he returned to Sweden for further hostilities, he quelled a revolution in the Russian army, and he engaged the Turks. Finally, he retired to Livonia where as Governor he passed the remaining years from 1743 until his death in 1751 at the age of seventy-three.

He was in person tall, and well made, [writes O'Callaghan] in mind distinguished by enlarged views, clearness of perception, and soundness of judgment; or a due combination of vivacity and vigour, with coolness, secrecy, and the power of varying his conduct, according to the enemies with whom he had to deal — Swedes, Poles, Turks and Tartars. He was admired and beloved, among his 'companions in arms', for the example he gave of intrepidity, endurance of fatigue, and the maintenance of discipline; accompanied by a concientious solicitude to acquaint himself with the wants of his troops, and an uncommon attention to their health and preservation. The zeal and ability he had uniformly displayed in subordinate posts elevated him to the chief command of the Russian forces; and, at their head, his successes proved how worthy he was of that command. Hence, it was noted at the time of his decease, that, if his death was in Russia a subject of regret to the nation at large, it was still more so among all such, as were qualified to be judges of real merit.[1]

While Lacy was in Vienna he met a fellow countryman who was making a name for himself in a career not unlike his own; he was the famed Marshal Maximilian Ulysses von Browne. His father, Ulysses, went to France as a captain of infantry, probably in 1690 with Mountcashel as one of the group of exchange officers. At that time the 'von' had no place in the family name but was added later. In 1699 Maximilian's father had married a clanswoman, Annabella Fitzgerald; Maximilian was born in 1705 and was sent to a Protestant school in Limerick, which was owned by the Rev R. Cashin. Attendance at a Protestant school in Ireland at that time was no indication of religious belief. The Penal Laws had closed the Catholic schools so many of the Protestant ones had the care of the sons of the Catholic gentry.

An example of the paradox so prevalent in Irish history was that Maximilian's uncle George was a close friend of the Duke of Marlborough who, although an adversary of the Irish, was really responsible for establishing the Brownes in the Austrian Imperial Service. At the age of ten, Maximilian was taken from his Limerick school and sent to Hungary to join his uncle's regiment. By this time his father was commandant of Landshut in Bavaria. George von Browne had attracted the attention of the Austrian military authorities particularly because of his service in the Italian and Spanish campaigns of the War of the Spanish Succession. In 1715 when young Maximilian joined him he was commanding his own regiment, with the rank of Colonel.

The specification 'own' was most important in those days for there existed then nothing comparable to current army regulations. Most owners of regiments wrote their own disciplinary rules and instructions; it is in this area that George Browne made a major contribution to the Austrian army. Some of his admonitions would not find overwhelming sympathy in a modern army: 'In as much as we can hope for success and victory from Almightly God alone, we must promote His fear and worship above all other things.'² This 'noble' sentiment was mouthed in many armies; the impertinence of it is as ludicrous today as it was yesterday, in the suggestion that the Almighty was a monster blessing the horrors of war.

George Browne's idea of what a colonel should be is, however, valuable to all military leaders. He should be 'an intelligent, earnest and brave man, from whom may be sought and obtained enlightenment concerning the welfare of the service; he must show a good example to all, so that everyone can follow in his steps. His own interests must not count for anything, nor can he allow a single drop of bitter blood, whether of officer or common soldier, to lie upon his soul and conscience. On the contrary, he must give every man his due, and content himself with what is his own by right. Through this he will always be able to fight with assurance, and after death carry no bad name with him into the grave, thereby not only winning the love of his subordinates, but being able to hold each one of them up to his duty with all the more authority.'³

So it was in an atmosphere of religious and regimental discipline that young Maximilian was brought up. The father, the uncle and the boy certainly carved out careers for themselves in their service to the Austrian Empire, so much so that on 13 March 1716 the Emperor Charles VI issued a patent of nobility for Ulysses and George which, of course, meant that his father's title would automatically pass on to Maximilian in time. The Brownes were, indeed, an ambitious family for they also persuaded the 'Young Pretender' James III to bestow upon them the titles Baron, Viscount and Earl of Browne with the titles to be handed down to the heirs of Ulysses. The Brownes' ambition resulted in much soul-searching and jealousy amongst the many senior Irish officers in Europe; most of them were descended from families far more ancient and better-known than the Brownes'. So Maximilian's young days were not altogether free of troubles. His uncle, who had surrounded himself with many Irishmen, appears to have been the complete nepotist. He gave ample leave to his friends, overcharged the Austrian troops, and spared the Irish when he could. His financial dealings were somewhat notorious for he made the soldiers pay for the soles on their boots. All this resulted in a bitter split within the regiment in which, apparently, Maximilian was involved. One thing was evident: George Browne did not practise what he wrote about leadership.

So Maximilian at an early age was exposed to the devious ways of intrigue, dishonesty and conflict; yet, he seemed to be little affected by it. At the age of nineteen he married in 1725 the Countess Maria von Martinitz whose family was one of the most distinguished in the country. According to Duffy: 'Maximilian was fortunate in beginning his family life in the only decade of comparative peace enjoyed by Austria in the eighteenth century, and though now holding the rank of Lieutenant-Colonel, he could have found little of importance to disturb the easy routine of life in his North Italian stations. On 2 June 1727, Maximilian's first child Philip George was born at Novara, followed on 17 October of the next year by a younger son whom he named Joseph Ulysses Maria.'[4]

The involvement of the Austrian Empire in war in 1731 marked the real beginning of Maximilian's active service which was to last almost until his death. The extensiveness of the Hapsburg dominions not only excited the jealousy of most of Europe but made them the objective of every power-drunk monarch and politician. By this time Browne was commanding a battalion of the O'Neillan regiment; the O'Neillans were close clansmen with whom the Brownes had intermarried. Although there is considerable controversy on the subject, the O'Neillans were not descendants of the O'Neills, as one would imagine, but were O'Nolans. Their descendants, now rejoicing in the name Neulau, are still to be found in Austria.

Maximilian's first battle was in Parma where his courage

and soldierly qualities marked him out from his companions. Although Parma was lost to the Empire, Browne was made a Major-General and earmarked for special duty. Apparently, the early military training sustained under his uncle's command, as well as the little practical experience, made him a brilliant tactician. He studied the strategy of the armies of France and Spain in particular and was convinced that these two forces were most susceptible to the immediate exploitation of initial success. Throughout his military career he proved it. Certainly he had ample opportunity.

Like his kinsman, Lacy, in Russia, Browne fought in Poland and Sweden and against the Turks; he played a major part in the Thirty Years War. He rose to the rank of General and was made Commanding General in Bohemia in 1751, a responsibility that carried with it the appointment of Town Commandant of Prague. In 1754 he was made a Field-Marshal by the Empress Queen Maria Theresa, the highest rank in her army. Like Lacy he also received the Order of the White Eagle for his part in the War of the Polish Succession. So brilliant had been his success against the Prussians under Frederick II in 1757 that he was awarded the Chain of the Order of the Golden Fleece.

Much has been written about Browne. Cognazzo, an Austrian strategist, claims that he was the 'greatest man to appear in the annals of Austria since the time of Eugene; with the method of a Khevenhüller and the shrewdness and foresight of a Traun, he combined Eugene's highest boldness and resolution. He would have become Austria's Turenne, had not the many enviers of his brilliant talents succeeded so often in laying obstacles in his path, and staid the glorious course of his career by their treacherous machinations.'[5]

It was natural that such greatness should arouse jealousy, especially since an Imperial envoy wrote: 'The military men, the statesmen, the courtiers and even the ladies can speak only of him. They admired his conduct, they fear that he may have exposed himself too dangerously, and everyone hopes to hear that he has returned safely to his camp.'[6]

In that same year, 1757, despite his success the Irishman

was superseded by the Prince Charles of Lorraine. Maria Theresa, knowing full well that an injustice had been done, sent him a very special gift : it was his new Order of the Golden Fleece set in diamonds. At the same time, she presented to his valet who had served him faithfully since he was a young officer, a golden snuff box and an annual pension of 500 florins. Despite the fact that he had been deliberately passed over, Browne repaid the Prince with complete loyalty. In one of his letters to the Commander he wrote : 'Flattering myself that Your Royal Highness will be so good as to agree with my arrangements, I make bold to beg you to rely upon my vigilance and attention : these I will never cease to employ, as my feeble talents direct, towards the good and the essential advantage of the service.'[7]

In the meantime, Frederick started the invasion of Bohemia, and Browne, with a force of 60,000 troops, found himself facing an enemy with 114,000. Browne was prepared to defend Prague but the Prince decided to abandon it. The Austrian officers were on Browne's side but Prague, nonetheless, was almost captured. During the battle for the city Browne was fatally wounded by a cannonball which shattered his left leg. With rest he might have survived, but a siege of the city called on all his resources and, though wounded, he was directing operations and was unable to receive proper medical treatment. He died on 26 June 1757.

Browne had left behind him a record rarely achieved by Austria's sons. Maria Theresa gave his regiment to his younger son, Colonel Joseph Browne. In 1758 at the Battle of Hochkirch another son, Philip, attacked Frederick's camp successfully, causing the Prussian to retreat. He became a Major-General and was awarded the Knight's Cross of the Military Order of Maria Theresa. Unhappily, in the same action Joseph was wounded in the foot as his father had been and died on 29 April 1759.

One biographer said of the old Marshal : 'Browne probably possessed the most comprehensive military talent of his day. When we think of a de Saxe, a Daun, of a Frederick, we think principally of one kind of warfare : none of these commanders excelled Browne in the justifiable confidence with which he could address himself to the exploitation of every technique and opportunity open to a general of the time. Here lies his chief claim to fame, and here also the danger of underestimation in the superficial judgment of posterity. However, in two respects at least, Browne was clearly in advance of his contemporaries: in the speed and boldness with which he could move his men, and still more in his enlightened notions of leadership and individual responsibility.'[8]

A relationship of considerable interest was that established between Lacy of Russia and Browne of Austria. They became fast friends, so much so that Lacy handed over his son Franz to the care of Browne. The relationship between the boy and the man was a lasting one; Franz attributed his later military skill to the teachings of his mentor.

Although Lacy and Browne were the two most brilliant stars in the military galaxy of Eastern Europe in the eighteenth century, there were many other Irishmen who are, indeed, worthy of mention. Thomas Baron von Brady was born in Cavan in 1752. He entered the service of Austria at the age of 17 and had a most successful military and diplomatic career. He was in turn on the military staff of the Imperial Army, became commander of the Tyrolese Sharpshooter Corps in 1793 and later became both Military and Civil Governor of Dalmatia and Albania. He married into one of the noble Austrian families but left no issue.

The Nugent family from County Dublin presented the Imperial service with no less than five very distinguished servants. Count James Robert, born in Castlenugent, entered the Austrian army at 15, took part in the Turkish War of 1737 and having become a Field-Marshal, was ambassador to Berlin in 1764. His son, Laval, who was born in Ireland where his father maintained a residence, became a privy councillor in Austria and later was appointed a Roman Prince by Pope Pius VII. He left the Austrian service for a while with permission from the Emperor and became Captain-General of Naples under Ferdinand V. He too became a Field-Marshal. The other members of the family had distinguished military careers also but one aspect of the family was that their children were born in Ireland. Count Laval's son was born in Dublin in 1796.

In the case of the O'Donnells, here again is that extraordinary arrangement about birth. Count John, Count Charles,

Count Magnus were all born in Dublin; other members of the family were born in Vienna. Most of them became Generals; Count Francis Joseph rose to great heights becoming Imperial and Royal Chamberlain and Minister of Finance. He died in 1810. Claudius became a privy councillor and Governor of Siebenburgen in 1768.

Two of three famous O'Flanagans were born in Ireland; in 1753 one of them, Count Colloredo, became assistant to the Austrian Minister Plenipotentiary to the English Court. To enumerate all the names is impossible but the Wallis family, the O'Connor-O'Connells from Kerry, the O'Gilvys, the von Plunketts, and Von Purcells are all worthy of mention. No less than nine of the Wallis family — later the Count von Wallises — are mentioned in the records of Austrian achievement. Unlike France, Britain was on a friendly footing with the Imperial powers; hence, permission was readily granted to the Irish soldiers serving in Austria to have their children born in Ireland. In France many Irish families did not have this opportunity because some of the more distinguished were classed as aristocrats; as a result a goodly number of Irish heads rolled into the guillotine baskets during the French Revolution.

Today, many descendants of Irish families remain in Austria but the names have been changed beyond recognition. Christopher Duffy has made a distinctive contribution in his works to trace many of the families but there is much research still to be done to elucidate more fully the many links that remain.

1. John Cornelius O'Callaghan in *History of the Irish Brigades in the Service of France,* p. 498.
2. Quoted by Christopher Duffy in *The Wild Goose and the Eagle,* p. 8.
3. *Ibid.,* p. 9.
4. *Ibid.,* p. 17.
5. Cognazzo in *Veterans in Hinsicht auf die Verhaltnisse zwischen Österreich und Preussen,* Breslau, 1788-1789, part II, pp. 196-197.
6. A. Ritter von Arneth, *Maria Theresias erste Regierungsjahre,* the first section of *Geschichte Maria Theresias,* Vienna, 1863-1879, vol. 5, p. 154.
7. From a letter from Browne to Prince Charles, Prague, 27 March (Feld-Acten) 1757, vol. III, p. 26.
8. Christopher Duffy, *The Wild Goose and the Eagle,* p. 261.

CHAPTER XI

Wives and Lovers

Must I bow when you speak!
Be silent and hear;
Inclining my cheek
And incredulous ear
To your voice, and command, and behest;
*   hold your lightest wish dear!*

I am separate still!
I am I and not you!
And my mind and my will,
As in secret they grew,
Still are secret; unreached, and untouched,
*   and not subject to you.*

— James Stephens, *Collected Poems*

The Irish women Wild Geese who left Ireland with their husbands have received little mention in history despite the fact that they were often as colourful and courageous as their men. They need a Women's Lib. Movement to find their right place in the narration of events. In recent years Micheline Walsh has carried out admirable research into their activities.

This chapter does confirm two arguments about them: whether they be Irish or otherwise, they nearly always meant money and trouble.

The first records of the Wild Geese womenfolk commence with the Flight of the Earls, and the stories available all show clearly that the Irishwomen brought with them the romance, sentiment and humanity — too warm at times — so characteristic of the Irish. They also illustrate that the peculiar strength, resolution and sensuousness of Irish womanhood revealed themselves in all their adventures.

Spain was very generous to the widows and orphans of the

Irish soldiers who fought for her in the seventeenth century. One group alone of Irish exiles in a small corner of north-western Spain was being paid £9,000 a month; in those days this was a sizable sum. A letter written by a Rose Geoghegan to the King of Spain in 1607 typifies the kind of communication which led to the tracing of these Irishwomen:

> Señor, I, Rosa Guegan, declare that Your Majesty granted me a pension of twelve crowns a month to be paid by the Governor of Galicia. But now my brothers and my sons have gone to serve Your Majesty in Flanders and without them here in Galicia I am sad and lonely. So I humbly beg Your Majesty to order that my pension be paid to me in Flanders so that I may go and receive it there as punctually and fully as I have received it in Galicia.[1]

The Spanish financial records for the year 1610 give a further indication of the type of transaction that went on:

> Doña Cathalina Geraldina. She is a sister of the Earl of Desmond who died in the Tower of London. She receives fifty-one crowns a month.
> Doña Cathalina Brenan. She comes from the land of the Lord of Biraven and she is a widow. Her husband died at the hands of the English in the wars of Ireland. She receives ten crowns a month.
> Doña Elena Sulivan. She is a daughter of Dermicio Sulivan who also receives an allowance in this kingdom. The English hanged her husband in Ireland. She receives thirteen crowns a month.
> Doña Eleysica Leyn. She is a widow and her husband was tutor to Don Daniel O Sulivan who was page to the King. She lives in Santiago with the Lord Biraven. She receives eleven crowns a month.
> Doña Joana Belona. She is a widow from the land of the Lord of Biraven. Her husband died at the hands of the English. She has one son with her and four in Ireland. She receives thirteen crowns a month.
> Doña Elena Geraldina. She lives at the Court where she receives her allowance. She receives twenty crowns a month.[2]

The Elena Garaldina was the widow of a brother of the Lord Kerry who had been killed in Flanders. Later she married an Irishman called Mateo Tulio whose real name was probably Tully. The latter had been secretary to Red Hugh O'Donnell and was with the earl when he died in Valladolid. Tully returned to Ireland but went back to Spain a second time.

Even in those days the path to matrimonial bliss had its obstacles for when Tully returned to Spain both he and Doña Elena ended up in prison charged with bigamy. A document dated July 1610 records the following :

I, Mateo Tulio, agent in this city for the Earl of Tyrone, declare that my wife and I were accused before the judges of being married twice, for which we were imprisoned and are now held in the city jail. This matter has already been before the Council of State when it was found that these accusations were false and an order was issued for our release. Despite this some people were dissatisfied and the case was tried a second time. On this occasion we were found not guilty of any offence. Neverthless, without an order from Your Majesty no one will set us free. I humbly beg Your Majesty to give this order without delay for I am ill and my wife is with child.

The King referred the matter to his secretary who, a week later, reported back to His Majesty : 'This noble and his wife,' he writes, 'have now been set free. I have dealt with the matter privately for if I followed the usual legal procedure we should never get to the end of it.'

The following year Mateo died in Madrid and Doña Elena, in accordance with the Spanish policy of grouping the Irish refugees in different parts of Spanish territory, was allotted Flanders and was to receive her pension there. Elena, however, had experience of low-lying Flanders and seems to have preferred the air of La Coruña; at any rate, on 20 September 1611, she appealed to the King :

I, Elena Geraldina, Irish widow, [she writes] state that Your Majesty granted me a monthly allowance of twenty crowns in La Coruña. On the death of my husband, Matheo Tulio, this allowance was increased to thirty crowns on condition that I go to Flanders. I am alone in the world, burdened with three small children and unable to undertake such a long journey. In consideration of this and of the services of my husband, I humbly beg Your Majesty to be allowed to remain in La Coruña.[3]

There was another Irish Ellen who had a somewhat different career. She was the Countess of Clancarthy who escaped to Flanders in 1612. She had married Florence MacCarthy Reagh, thereby uniting two of the most powerful families in the south of Ireland. Permission for the marriage should have been obtained from Queen Elizabeth who had her own matrimonial plans for the young woman. The young couple managed to escape the wrath of the Queen by hiding until the accession of the Stuarts when they were both pardoned.

The career of the Countess was open to question for there is every reason to believe that at one stage she did, in fact, spy on her husband for the English. The Spanish government took the matter sufficiently seriously to institute enquiries in London about her in 1612, through Don Alonso de Velasco, the Spanish ambassador in London. The following official report was sent to the Spanish monarch:

In fulfilment of the order sent to Don Alonso concerning the Countess of Clancarti, he writes that this is the information he has gathered: she was the heir to the house of MacCarthy Mor which is one of the richest and most noble of Ireland. She married Florencio Macarti Reagh who, in his province, waged war on the English at the instigation of the Earl of Tyrone. Florencio Macarti eventually made peace and came to terms with the English. Shortly afterwards on hearing of Don Juan del Aguila's journey to Ireland, Queen Elizabeth had Macarti arrested and brought to London, for she was suspicious of him. He is still in prison, without hope of liberty, and all his estates and those of his wife were confiscated. His wife, the Countess Clancarti, whose lands were ultimately confiscated and who had spent her wealth endeavouring to free her husband from unjust imprisonment, finding herself very poor, crossed to Flanders

with the intention of going to Madrid to seek help from
Your Majesty. She left London without saying anything to
Don Alonso or obtaining the permission of her husband
who had already found cause for anger in her indiscreet
conduct. Don Alonso advises that the wisest decision to take
would be to place the lady in some house of religion, as
this would be most becoming in the service of God and
most in keeping with the greatness of Your Majesty. It
would also be most pleasing to her husband.[4]

The sentence of the King's advisers was that she be forced
to enter a convent, a punishment that did not appeal to the
sensuous Ellen who, with the help of the Governor of Flanders,
made her way to Spain, where she conspired that her charms
might prove a valuable asset in the advancement of her cause.
Her hopes were realized for later she was to act as sponsor
to Donal O'Sullivan Beare, the famous chieftain of Dunboy,
when he made application to become a Knight of the Spanish
Military Order of Santiago. Donal's application was successful; some of the other sponsors were such distinguished per-
sonages as a former Rector of the Irish College of Santiago,
the Abbot of Boyle and the Archbishop of Tuam. One can
only wonder if somewhere along her very successful diplomatic
path Lady Ellen made spiritual restitution for her political
machinations engineered in and out of quite a number and
variety of beds.

Another countess who operated at this level was Catherine
Magennis, Countess of Tyrone, who was the fourth and last
wife of the great Hugh O'Neill. She, too, was accused of
spying on her husband and, apparently, was not too concerned
about the sheets she slept under when her own advancement
was at stake.

When Hugh O'Neill died in Rome in 1616 the Countess
appealed to the Spanish King for the same financial assistance
given to her late husband. On 10 September 1616 the King
wrote to Cardinal Borja, his ambassador in Rome: 'I have
resolved that the Countess should be given the same allowance
which her husband received. You shall inform her of this
and of the pleasure I take in giving it to her. You shall assure
her also that, as a mark of my esteem for her, I shall always

take the same pleasure in attending to anything that may concern her.'⁵

O'Neill's Irish dependents, furious at this decision, exercised all their powers to change it. The King, however, was very much on her side and in a further letter to Borja told him not to forward any further petitions on the matter as they would not even be considered. The O'Neills must have had some influence at Court because there is evidence that the good lady was kept waiting for her money on occasion. The following letter is proof :

Sacred Majesty, I am obliged to make known to Your Majesty that for the past seventeen months I have not been paid and suffer great want, for I have the responsibility of family and dependents. But I fear less to die of hunger than to become the ridicule of the English enemies for they say that my husband, the Earl of Tyrone, waged war on them at the instigation of King Philip II and of his son, Your Majesty, leaving his King and losing his estates in Your Majesty's service and that now Your Majesty is without concern for this afflicted and unprotected widow, who was his wife, but leaves her and his family to die of hunger.

I humbly beg Your Majesty to send an order to the Viceroy that I be paid what is owed to me and that, in future, I receive my allowance punctually. Your Majesty's most humble servant, The Countess of Tyrone.⁶

Thus far, these womenfolk Wild Geese seem to have spelled nothing but trouble; apparently, they did not confine it just to Spain. One Leonor Riano (Leonora Ryan in Ireland) became an absolute pest at the Royal Court in Madrid, although she lived in Portugal. So determined was she to get an increase in her allowance that she arrived in Madrid in August 1622 to present her petition to the King of Spain. The similarity to present-day bureaucracy made it hard for her to break through to the person of authority. Her uncle was Cornelius Ryan, Bishop of Killaloe; he helped with the final petition :

(my father) died in the army, leaving me an orphan without protection or means of livelihood, for which reason I came to Spain to seek the protection of the said Bishop, my uncle, and went with him to Lisbon where he died leaving me more orphaned and unprotected than ever. But my uncle, in his will, recommended me to Your Majesty as the heir to his services and, being a minor, I was granted an allowance of eight crowns a month paid to me in Portugal. This is such a small amount that it is not sufficient for my needs and I beg Your Majesty to increase the said allowance in view of my rank and my great losses.[7]

As a result, the Council of State sent the following recommendation to the King:

This Council has already seen several similar memorials from the petitioner. On the first two occasions she was answered that her request could not be considered. She was given the same answer on the third occasion for, on enquiry, it was found that (far from being an unprotected orphan) she had a husband, Don Andres Orleo, who also enjoys in Lisbon an allowance from Your Majesty of twenty crowns a month. Finally in March this year Your Majesty ordered that she be given travelling expenses of two hundred crowns (to enable her to return to her husband in Lisbon). For all these reasons the Council recommends that the petitioner be told to content herself with what she has already been granted and refrain from sending any more useless memorials.[8]

In 1622 another Irishwoman, who added a little more respectability to the scene, arrived from Ireland; she was Mariana MacCarthy from Cork who, according to Micheline Walsh, was remarkable 'only on account of the peculiar circumstances of her relations and those of her son with the Queen of Spain.'[9] Mariana and her husband landed in Portugal and having little or no money set out for Madrid on foot. Mariana was pregnant at the time and the result was that the child was born en route. There is a recorded story of the family's arrival; incidentally, the husband gave his name in Irish, which is the translation of O'Murphy:

Don Domingo O Mouroghu was born in Guarda in Portugal as his parents were on their way to Spain fleeing from the persecutions of the English in Ireland. They came to this court relying on the mercy and generosity of His Majesty. When they came to the Palace of El Pardo, Her Majesty the Queen chanced to see Don Domingo who was then a baby in his mother's arms. Her Majesty took a great fancy to him for he was a very beautiful child, and asked the mother to give him to her. The Queen took him with her and had him brought up in the Royal Palace in the care of the Condesa de Olivares. He was so well beloved by Their Majesties that he was allowed to enter their apartments as he pleased. Later he was given a tutor, a house close to the Church of San Juan and a pension of three hundred ducats a month, which he still receives today, and he was page to the King . . . His mother and his father were granted a maintenance allowance which they received until their death. They both died in Madrid, the father in the parish of San Nicholas and the mother in the Hospital de la Pasion . . . Don Domingo was married to a lady in waiting at the court and was sent to Naples with the Viceroy, the Duque de Medina de las Torres, when the latter married the Princess de Stigliano. In Naples he was majordomo of the Viceroy's household and was appointed to various posts in the army. He had also held several employments in the King's household.[10]

This young boy, born in such precarious circumstances, grew up to join the Spanish Army, served brilliantly and was knighted.

Teresa O'Berne, who was a descendant of the MacDonnells, came to Madrid at a later date, in 1725, and again the Spanish Court was ruffled by typical Irish romantic verve. Teresa's father was in the Spanish army, holding a commission in Crofton's Regiment of Dragoons. He was also something of a controversial character for, according to the Carte Papers in the Bodleian at Oxford, as a captain at the head of his troops and in the midst of a battle he shot at a Major Crane who disputed the command of the soldiers. The latter was seriously wounded, O'Berne was sent to prison but was later released and promoted to Major in the same regiment. One can assume that either he was in the right or that he had a greater influence in high places.

Teresa's life was as turbulent as her father's. She married the English Duke of Wharton who turned out to be a most thorough blackguard : he was a drunkard, a womanizer, and conniving liar. He was staying in Madrid with the Duke of Liria at the time he met Teresa. Wharton had been married previously and actually met Teresa the day following his first wife's death. At the time Teresa was one of the Spanish Queen's Maids of Honour, and a most respectable young woman; he fell in love with her immediately. Wharton informed his host of his intention of marrying her and said that he had become a Catholic, enhancing this statement with a tissue of lies. The Duke asked him to leave his house and did everything possible to prevent the wedding but failed. Wharton and his new wife ended up in Gibraltar where he died. Teresa with her grandmother, Doña Sarah O'Neill, later went to London to claim Wharton's estate only to discover that the rascal had forfeited them for disloyalty to the Crown.

Certainly, thus far, the women Wild Geese appear to have added little glory to their sex and few serious social contributions to their memory. Nor, indeed, did Doña María Jacinta Marco y Espejo. She did, however, throw some light on an interesting issue : 'breach of promise,' early nineteenth-century variety. Doña María was not born in Ireland but she did become entangled with one of the Wild Geese, José Butler, a Captain in the Spanish navy. Butler was a widower with two daughters; when she met him Doña María had been a widow for some six years. They fell in love, Butler proposed to her and was accepted and, according to custom, sought and obtained Royal permission to marry. After his fiancée had bought herself a very expensive trousseau, suddenly Butler changed his mind about marrying her.

Micheline Walsh, in her researches in the Archivo del Museo Naval, Madrid, found some of the blistering letters written by Doña María on pale blue paper and, for the most part, addressed to the King. An excerpt from one follows :

... the reputation of my late husband and especially my

own irreproachable conduct, not only as a married woman but also as a widow, are so well known to all who know me and to the greater part of the officers of this city that many have wished to marry me ... Among these Capitán de Navío Don José Butler distinguished himself by his extraordinary demonstrations and his persistence. He sent to me many persons of respectability who pleaded his cause that I might condescend to become his wife. I objected that there were many obstacles and inconveniences. Butler overcame these and succeeded, with no little trouble, in convincing me and all those who knew of his intentions, that his feelings were not only the most honourable but also the deepest and most noble that could be imagined ... so that I finally decided to condescend to this marriage which Butler desired with such eagerness.[11]

The law appears to have been on the side of Cupid for Butler was tried by court-martial and found guilty! His sentence : to be confined to quarters for six months and to pay for the trousseau. The latter was to be handed to him. But who ever heard of a woman handing over a carefully-prepared trousseau, no matter what the damage to her bruised heart? As a consequence, after the six months' confinement Butler appealed against the charges (despite the fact that he had paid for his 'crime'), adding strength to his case by stating that he had not received the trousseau which he had paid for. The lady had problems finding someone to represent her at the appeal; in all probability it was not heard. At any rate Butler was promoted Comandante de Pilotos in Cartagena just three years later in 1806, so the love storm seems to have done little harm to him professionally.

It is natural that, considering the puritanical attitude towards women of that period, only the more notorious were publicized. There was one, however, who has definite claim to fame — Lucy Fitzgerald, living in Gerona, which was garrisoned by the Spanish regiment of Ulster. It was commanded by Colonel Anthony O'Kelly who had with him such officers as Major Henry O'Donnell, Commandant John O'Donovan and Captains MacCarthy (spelled Makarti in Spanish), Sarsfield and Fitzgerald. The town revolted against

Napoleonic domination with the result that the French sent a force of over 6,000 men to quell the small garrison of just over 400 Irishmen. The defiance with which the little town held out for over eighteen months is in itself noteworthy, but more so were the events taking place within its walls.

Lucy Fitzgerald, impressed by the determination of her fellow countryman O'Kelly to defy the French, organized a women's unit which was named the twelfth Company of the Crusade, the Company of Santa Barbara; she became its first Commandant. Her duties were clearly defined : she was to be responsible for the movement of ammunition and food to the troops and to take over complete charge of transporting and caring for the wounded. Lucy's disciplined unit became an inspiration for the garrison while her personal courage in the face of that relentless siege was exemplary.

The 6,000 troops who came originally to take the town were sent scuttling, and this insult so enraged the French that the Marshal of France, General Augereau, with Lieutenant-General Saint-Cyr and more than 33,000 men were dispatched to reduce the town to ashes, as it was on the main supply road to France.

Colonel O'Kelly's personal intrepidity and determination in the face of such an onslaught were in themselves remarkable; when called upon to surrender, the dignity and valour displayed in his reply to the French General Duhesme give a good indication of the type of man he was : 'Señor, I have received Your Excellency's of today . . . In answer I have the honour of informing you that this town has taken its decision and we shall defend it in the knowledge that we have the means. May God keep Your Excellency many years. Gerona, 12th of August 1808. Antonio O'Kelly, Colonel.'[12]

A diarist who witnessed the siege wrote of Lucy's behaviour and final report; unhappily, the fort was ultimately forced to surrender but only after terrible slaughter. So fierce was the struggle that the Bishop of Gerona allowed the secular priests to take up arms and join a company of artisans. The diarist wrote :

In the Square of San Pedro were the women of the Company of Santa Barbara, noblest of their sex, who only moments

before were filing under a rain of shells, bombs and grenades
to administer to the needs of the defenders; with the silent
eloquence of example, more persuasive than any words,
they communicated their spirit and courage to the soldiers
of Montjuich; in their arms they carried the wounded to
the blood-covered floors of the hospital. Certainly Gerona
was that day the abode of heroines.

Fortunately Lucy Fitzgerald's official report to headquarters, written that night, is still extant; it reads :

Company of Santa Barbara.
The Commandant informs the High Command that, at
the sound of the alarm, at one o'clock in the afternoon, she
led her company to the Square of San Pedro. All ranks behaved with distinction. They administered untiringly to
the needs of the defenders at the various points of attack.
They brought much needed water and brandy to the fort of
Montjuich and carried back the wounded on litters and in
their arms. Despising the dangers of shells and bombs which
rained about them without stop, they displayed heroic zeal,
charity and supreme courage. Lucia de Fitzgerald, Commandant. Gerona, 10th of August 1809.[13]

Another woman of magnificent courage and more widely
travelled was the Marquise de La Tour du Pin, whose memoirs
were translated and edited by Felice Harcourt and published
in English in 1969. A lady of colourful background and history, Madame de La Tour du Pin lived through the
French Revolution and the subsequent terror, fled to America
where she farmed a remote region with constant contact
with the Indians, and ultimately returned to her native
France.

The Marquise was born Henrietta — Lucy Dillon — in
Paris in 1770. Her father was Arthur 11th Viscount Dillon,
second son of Henry. He was given command of the Dillon
Regiment, one of the original regiments of the French Irish
Brigade. He commanded it until the French Revolution when
he was executed by the Revolutionaries in 1794.

Arthur Dillon married twice; his first wife was Lucie de

Rothe who was descended from the Carys. She was Lady-in-waiting to Queen Marie-Antoinette but died at the age of thirty-one when her daughter Henrietta was only twelve. Of the Dillon family Henrietta wrote: 'My mother, married at seventeen to a boy only a year older than herself, who had been brought up with her and who owned nothing in the world but his Regiment.'[14] Henrietta's great uncle, after whom her father was named, was another Arthur Dillon who was Archbishop of Narbonne until 1806.

One of the more illuminating and significant remarks here is that of Lucy's having been brought up with de Rothe who was also a commander in the Irish Brigade; evidently the senior officers kept close together and probably created an intimate social life of their own.

The insight into pre-Revolutionary France which Henrietta presents is both revealing and shocking. Her intimate association with the Irish Brigade officers gave her an opportunity of studying the nepotism, chicanery and general corruptness of a fine regiment which was, obviously, deteriorating rapidly into some hybrid social military élite. She illustrates this by the story of one of her cousins who was a captain in Dillon's Regiment. When the island of Granada was captured the fort was taken by a Grenadier company of Dillon's Regiment and as a reward her cousin, Captain Sheldon, was sent back immediately to France to present the standards to the King. On arrival in France he went straight to the Minister of War at Versailles. Although he had dressed in his best uniform, Henrietta's own uncle forbade his seeing the King unless he changed into court dress. As she narrates in her memoirs: 'It was only when he had assumed a thoroughly civilian appearance that he was permitted to lay at the King's feet the colours he had risked his life to capture. Yet people are surprised that the Revolution should have destroyed a Court where such childishness prevailed.'[15]

Henrietta's father was anxious that his daughter should wed so after considerable intrigue she married in 1787 Frederic-Seraphim, Comte de Gouvernet, who succeeded to his father's title of Comte de La Tour du Pin de Gouvernet in 1794. Later he was created a Peer of France by Louis XVIII. The Marquis was a professional soldier, but during the Revolution he was

compelled to go into hiding during which period he escaped
to America.

Henrietta's description of her family's flight to America is
harrowing. She secured their passport by going to the passport
office just as it was closing, knowing that there was less chance
of their being recognized. After many difficulties they managed to sail in a small 150-ton ship which had only four sailors
and a cabin boy; apparently the captain was very young and
relied on an old Nantucket salt for advice. By this time she had
five children; their journey across the Atlantic on so small a
ship was an appalling experience. They were also captured
by a French frigate but when told to follow her they managed
to elude their captor in a fog.

The family arrived in Boston and found temporary accom-
modation in a small farmhouse outside the city. Later they
moved to Albany, then to Troy, New York.

In after years they were fortunate in being able to return
to France. From there they visited England and Spain and
Holland. The marquis later became one of the ambassadors
plenipotentiary of France at the Congress of Vienna. His last
appointment, which he held for ten years, was that of ambassador in Turin.

Henrietta wrote her memoirs when she was over fifty; as
an appendix to her work she has left a brief historical account
of the Dillon Regiment.

No account of remarkable Irishwomen would be complete
without some reference to Molly Pitcher ('Irish Molly') who
was described by the widow of General Hamilton, one of
George Washington's senior officers, as a 'pretty freckleface
Irish lass' who, at the Battle of Monmouth in the American
Revolutionary War, in which her husband was killed, took
his place at the cannon he was loading and rammed home the
charge herself. James Kelly, one of America's foremost sculp-
tors, included as part of the design for the 'Monmouth Battle
Monument' Irish Molly, her dead husband at her feet, ramming the charge into the cannon while a wounded soldier
thumbs the vent. The Irishman General Knox is shown in
the background directing the battle.

E

1. Quoted by Micheline Walsh in *The Irish Sword,* vol. 5, pp. 98-99.
2. *Ibid.,* pp. 99-100.
3. *Ibid.,* p. 101.
4. *Ibid.,* p. 103.
5. Quoted from *Archivo General, Simancas* Estado, legajo 1865.
6. Quoted from *Archivo General, Simancas* Estado legajo 1881.
7. Quoted from *Archivo General, Simancas* Estado, legajo 2751.
8. *Ibid.*
9. Micheline Walsh in *The Irish Sword,* vol. 5, p. 134.
10. Quoted from *Archivo Histórico Nacional (A.H.N.) Madrid,* Calatrava, expediente, 1830.
11. Micheline Walsh in *The Irish Sword,* vol. 5, p. 142.
12. Quoted from *Archivo del Regimiento Infantera Morteros 120 — Ultonia No. 59.*
13. Micheline Walsh in *The Irish Sword,* vol. 5, pp. 144-145.
14. *Memoirs of Madame de La Tour du Pin,* edited and translated by Felice Harcourt, p. 15.
15. *Ibid.,* p. 50.

CHAPTER XII

Famous Regiments

*The continuous history of the Spanish-Irish regiments
may be started on 1st November, 1709; but Irishmen
not only served under the Spanish colours, but had
formed whole units in the Spanish army for short periods
in the preceding century . . . Not only O'Donnell and
Tyrone, but thousands of other Irish rebels made their
way, some to Spain and some to the Spanish Netherlands . . . There was a similar development in the reign
of Charles I, when, from the moment of the sending of
Stafford to govern Ireland in 1633 down to the extinc-
tion of the Irish rebellion by Cromwell in 1652, there
was an enormous emigration of fighting men of the
Catholic party from the island. Those of them who
drifted to Spanish soil were welcomed, and embodied
in the ephemeral regiments of O'Reilly, O'Brien, Gage,
Murphy, Coghlan, Dugan and Dempsey . . . The first
Irish regiments taken into the Spanish service were those
of the Marquis of Castlebar and Dermot MacAuliffe,
both of which received their patent of creation from the
King of Spain at Saragossa on 1st November, 1709 . . .
When the Spanish War Office (long years before our
own made the same reform) resolved to give every unit
a permanent title, Castlebar received the name of Hibernia; MacAuliffe that of Ultonia (Ulster); Vendome that
of Limerick; Comerford that of Waterford; Waucope
that of Irlanda.*

— Sir Charles Oman (1918) in the *Journal
of Royal United Services Institute*

Any comprehensive account of the exploits of the Wild Geese
on the European scene must chronicle four regiments of particular renown: the Hibernia, Ultonia and Irlanda Regiment of the Spanish army and the Irish Battalion of St

Patrick which fought in the service of Pope Pius IX in the war against Sardinia. Of these the Hibernia was by far the most illustrious, for not only did it establish an Irish military élite which still exists in Spain, but it had a profound effect on the history of the Americas.

La Columna Hibernia originated in 1709 as part of the Royal Spanish Army; it was formed in Aragon by a Don Reynaldo MacDonald who was specially commissioned by the Spanish King to recruit Irish and other foreign nationals for the regiment. The Royal decree specified clearly that all officers in the regiment were to be Irish or of Irish origin, 'to give the young men of the Irish nobility the opportunity of following the honourable career of arms.'[1]

Initially, this regiment consisted of two battalions of thirteen companies; in 1792 this was altered to three b'ttalions, the first two of which consisted of four fusilier companies and a grenadier company, the third being restricted to four fusilier companies.

The first battles of record in which the Irish regiment took part were those of Zaragosa in 1710 and Brihuega and Villaviciosa; it also fought at the siege of Barcelona in 1714.

To their satisfaction the three Spanish Irish regiments faced the British again at the siege of Gibraltar but, unhappily for them, all their efforts were abortive; The Rock remained the unassailable stronghold it still is at the entrance to the Mediterranean. From Gibraltar the three regiments campaigned in Italy against the Austrians between 1742 and 1748 where their enemies were commanded by some of the most distinguished Irish generals in the history of the Austrian Army. It was Marshal Maximilian von Browne who inflicted on the Spanish Irish Brigade its most severe mauling. In August 1744 Browne, with a special force of 6,000 men including many Irish, led a night attack against the Spanish who were fighting with Charles, King of Naples. Charles had set up his headquarters at Velletri, situated about twenty-five miles southwest of Rome. Browne's main objective was the capture of King Charles himself.

The Irish on the Austrian side must have known that they were opposed by the three Irish regiments of Spain for an Irish grenadier from Browne's forces deserted and hastened to warn the Velletri garrison. Browne became aware of this treachery but was still determined to press the attack. He is reputed to have shrugged his shoulders, vowing at the same time : 'On with the advance. We'll try our luck!' It turned out that their luck was good that night. The missing grenadier had reached an outpost of the Irlanda Regiment. Lieutenant Burke in charge of the picket couldn't understand the man's words, but it was obvious that he was trying to say something of importance so they sent the deserter back to town for questioning. Meanwhile the relief guard arrived under the command of a Captain Slattery.

Just as Burke was about to march off his detachment there came the first alarm of the Austrian attack. The two Irish officers quickly formed up their men and managed to slam two volleys into the Austrian point before they were forced back. Lieutenant Burke was killed, but Captain Slattery managed to keep his tiny force together and make a fighting retreat. It is said he answered Browne's surrender demand by saying, 'by the breakfast I've just received I can judge what a fine lunch is being prepared for me.'

About a mile away the Irish regiments were encamped with a regiment of Walloons. Hearing the noise of musketry they roused themselves and managed to form a line of battle. These units took almost the whole weight of the enemy onslaught. The massed volleys of the Austrians cut them down by hundreds and after several minutes the attackers swept forward, overrunning the Spanish camp. However, the fight was not over. The surviving Irish and Walloons fell back on the Nettuno gate, Browne's first objective, where they made a last desperate stand. For a precious half hour they blocked Browne's entrance into Velletri, buying time with their lives so that the King of Naples could escape.[2]

Colonel MacDonald and over forty Irish officers were killed in this battle, while hundreds of red-coated Irish corpses were piled high around the gates of the town. The King of Naples escaped this major disaster, supposedly having been led to safety by an Irishman called Maurice Lenihan.

This major disaster marked the last serious participation of the Hibernia Regiment in Europe. In 1748, 170 of them were captured by Algerians when returning to Spain and endured three years' captivity in Algiers.

In 1777 the Hibernia Regiment became an expeditionary force for the Spanish crown. Its first venture was to Brazil in that year when it embarked from Cadiz and captured the Island of Santa Catalina; it also helped in the seizure of San Gabriel across the River Plate from Buenos Aires. After these successes it returned to Spain but its respite was of short duration for it was sent to Cuba almost immediately. In April 1780 Spain allied herself with her old enemy France to support the American rebels against England; hence the Spanish activity in the West Indies. On 9 March 1780 General Bernardo Galvez prepared to attack the English base at Pensacola, Fort George. He had approximately 5,000 troops under his command, about 600 of whom were from the Hibernia Regiment. The latter was commanded by Colonel Arturo O'Neill who was born in Ireland about 1737 and had made his way, via the Irlanda Regiment, to this command. Later, in 1802, O'Neill became a Lieutenant-General in the Spanish Army.

Evidently the Spanish had maintained a steady recruitment for their Irish Brigade because at the siege of Pensacola, the captain of the attacking grenadiers was a Captain Hogan, another native Irishman. Captains Pedro O'Daly and William O'Kelly were also native sons, the latter becoming subsequently the commander of the regiment.

The British commander of the town was General Campbell, a tough opponent. After two weeks of siege, Galvez had made little impact on his enemy with the result that the English general took the initiative and made a midnight sortie against the besiegers. The attack was a complete success: he spiked six of the enemy's cannon, killed over thirty of the besiegers and captured a number of officers, two of whom were Captain Hugo O'Connor and Lieutenant Timothy O'Dunn. O'Dunn had lost an arm in the struggle and died very shortly after his capture. The English buried him with full military honours.

But despite this British success the end of the siege came quickly and unexpectedly: on the morning of 8 May a Spanish grenade lobbed straight down on the fort's powder magazine finished the defence of the town.

The next task assigned the Hibernians was the capture of Jamaica. However, when the war ended rather abruptly the regiment was split up for garrison duty in the Caribbean. Here their most lethal enemy was Mother Nature; many of the troops succumbed to the tropical diseases prevalent in the area.

Irishmen seem always to surround themselves with an aura of romance, and even in the Western Hemisphere, across an ocean from their homeland, they lived up to their tradition. Following the official recognition of American Independence, there were many American loyalists who refused to live under the Spaniards in Florida and collected around them pirates, smugglers, renegade Indians, runaway slaves, army deserters and other dare-devils and desperadoes. Vincente de Zespedes, Governor of Eastern Florida, a Spanish soldier of outstanding integrity, was given the task of either rounding up or limiting the activities of these recalcitrants. He selected a Captain Carlos Howard (who had a honeyed Irish tongue) from the Hibernia Regiment to precede him into Florida with a view to persuading the marauders to cease their operations. Apparently, de Zespedes hoped that Irish charm would succeed where military incursions into the Florida swamps might mean disaster. Zespedes himself with Captain Edward Nugent and Colonel William O'Kelly plus 460 men of the Hibernia Regiment landed at Saint Augustine on 27 June 1784 and shortly afterwards took possession of the Castillo de San Marcos. Even though the American Revolutionary War was fought on behalf of independence, Florida remained in appearance a Spanish colony. Despite the years of rancour and bitterness which were the by-products of war, the Irish and the remaining English officials and the civilians got on well together. The Irish, who spoke both English and Spanish, were particularly skillful diplomats in smoothing over difficulties and even had time to fall in love — a very serious business in any Irishman's life. But love, then as now, usually brings problems and the first sign of trouble was the discovery of a young Irishman named Lieutenant William Delaney stabbed to death outside the home of a Spanish señorita, Catalina Morain, on 20 November 1785. Apparently, the young man was in love with Catalina who had the reputation of being somewhat generous with her favours. The murderer was never charged but it is a fair assumption that Delaney was killed by another rival for her affections.

In the romantic area Zespedes' troubles were only beginning. With him to Florida he had brought his very attractive daughter, Dominga, whose tempestuous nature and romantic notions found ready response in the heart of Lieutenant Juan O'Donovan. One night when her father was entertaining at dinner Dominga and Juan eloped and found an equally romantic regimental Catholic chaplain, Father Michael O'Reilly, only too happy to marry them. The priest, whether knowingly or otherwise, had been summoned on a false sick call but apparently married the young couple without very much hesitation, then conveyed the news to the Governor. Zespedes was so enraged that he arrested O'Donovan, but demanded at the same time a second and more formal wedding. At the time some obscure relationship existed between canon and military law so that it took many months before the Spanish courts recognized the marriage. In the meantime, the bridegroom was banished to Havana and was not reunited with his wife until almost three years later in 1787. Perhaps the length of the name they chose for their first son is an indication of the happiness with which they welcomed his birth : he was Juan Vincente Maria Barbardo Domingo Benigro O'Donovan.

The historical records of the regiment in Florida during that period betray the fact that the torrid heat of Florida swamps, Spanish blood, and the charm of the boys from Erin all conspired with Cupid to cause many other complications until 1791 when the regiment was sent again to Oran to defend it against the Moors. Here there was no time for romance and, regrettably, little chance for glory.

In battles at Masdeu, Argeles and Thuir it suffered many casualties until finally it was sent to the Port of Toulon as an army of occupation. Later it tangled with the famed Napoleonic Marshal Ney — a clash which ended in disastrous defeat. With that quick about-face of loyalties so prevalent in the period the regiment was now an ally of its old enemy the British. In after years as part of the Spanish Army it helped to throw the French Sixth Army out of Galicia. The Irishmen particularly distinguished themselves against some 6,000 French cavalry whose repeated attacks failed to move the Hibernians.

But the end of the Irish Brigade in Spain was in sight. Possibly the European conscience was being pricked by the truth that on too many battlefields the Irish faced their own countrymen. The Irish Legion, which was part of Napoleon's army, opposed the Hibernian Regiment at the siege of Badajoz in 1811; it is probably fortunate that we have no details of the actual battle because they would repeat a story too old, too tragic and too discomfiting.

Although Irish military influence in Europe was waning rapidly there was to be one final flurry before the terrible bloodletting of the two world wars. It was caused by the formation and struggle of the Irish Battalion of St Patrick in 1860. Although this unit has often been referred to as the Papal Irish Brigade it never reached anything like brigade strength and never fought even as a single battalion but as two separate units, each comprising about seven hundred men.

The reasons for the formation of the force are of considerable interest especially since it was the first — and, indeed, the only time — that Ireland sent a force for the express purpose of serving the Papacy. Following the defeat of Napoleon at Waterloo, there came a new and vital upsurge of Italian nationalism, so much so that the old ideal of loyalty to the ancient States and to the Papacy itself was challenged. Led by Garibaldi, the Italian nationalists demanded in 1859 that Pope Pius IX should surrender the northern papal provinces of Romagna, Umbria and the Marches. This the Pope refused to do despite the fact that Romagna had voted itself into the Nationalist Northern Italy State. Based on the Congress of Vienna of 1815, the Pope considered this voluntary annexation as a direct affront to the Church, especially since the Congress had guaranteed the sovereignty of the Church over all the Papal lands. Consequently, not only did he excommunicate the National leaders but, for good measure, he included King Victor Emmanuel himself in the papal decree. But when even excommunication appeared to have little terror for the religious rebels, the Pope appealed to all Catholic countries to come to his assistance; in 1860 he sent emissaries to most of the Western

European countries to request men and arms for a Catholic campaign.

Naturally, as a country with a devout adherence to Catholicism and one with an outstanding military tradition in Europe, Ireland was singled out as a ready supporter of the Papal cause; it rallied rapidly to Rome. The initiation scene was a dramatic one as told by Chaplain Cyril P. Crean:

On a certain morning in March 1860 the well-known editor of *The Nation,* A. M. Sullivan, sat in his office in Middle Abbey Street, Dublin when two visitors were announced — one was a friend of his whom he knew to be interested in the Pontifical Question; the other, Count Charles McDonnell of Vienna, trusted Attaché to Count Nugent, and a Chamberlain of the Holy Father, had come to see what Ireland would do, what aid she would contribute to the military defence of the Roman Patrimony. 'We know in Rome,' he said, 'that Garibaldi with the connivance and secret assistance of the Turin Government is organizing an aggressive expedition, but whether to strike at Naples or at us we cannot tell — in any case we shall be attacked this summer — what will Ireland do for us.?'[3]

Sullivan initially promised 10,000 men but then, words were cheap. However, in the spring of that year 1,400 men left Ireland for Vienna. They were a motley mixture without any military training before leaving the country. Some were from the Irish Constabulary and Irish Militia; there were lawyers and students and farmers, mostly from Tipperary and Kerry. The Constabulary sacrificed their pay and pensions and set out to fight for the Pope at a pay rate of one and half pennies a day. The reason given for the poor pay conditions was that the Papacy was most anxious that there should be no accusation of mercenary motives for its soldiers. After all, the possibility of martyrdom was always at the end of the road. The British, who were sympathetic to Italy, by offering a shilling a day to its recruits endeavoured to limit the Irish recruiting. It issued a proclamation from Dublin Castle 'reminding all persons concerned that, according to the Foreign Enlistment Act, any man entering a foreign service was guilty of misdemeanour punishable by fine and imprisonment, as was anyone helping him to do so, and that any master of a ship conveying such persons was liable to a fine of fifty pounds.'[4]

This action impeded the recruiting and was probably one of the reasons why the force was so limited in numbers. The surprise invasion of the Papal States in September of 1860 was another, for it neither gave time for proper training of the volunteers nor did it provide an opportunity to swell the ranks of the Irish who were finding their way either to Rome or Vienna via Hull and Antwerp. Originally, a Major Fitzgerald from the Austrian Army was appointed to command the Irish but because he held, already, a commission in the Austrian Army complications arose. The command then fell on Major Myles O'Reilly, a County Louth farmer who was also a militia officer. O'Reilly had a reputation for integrity and courage; later events proved that the confidence placed in him was fully justified.

The Papal Army was, indeed, a strange one; it was quite international and contained, as well as some of the most untrained soldiers in Europe, some of the finest officers ever to don a uniform. The over-all command was in the hands of the distinguished French General De La Moricière who was considered by many to be a second Napoleon; his Chief-of-Staff was an officer from the regular Austrian army, General Marquis Georges de Pimodan. Apparently, there were three official languages in the army: French, Italian and German. The Irish, who had been forbidden by their oppressors to speak their own language, had the choice of picking up one of these.

The major problems of the Papal force were those of money and supplies. The army totalled 18,000 men which, according to Crean, was made up as follows: '. . . 6,300 were garrison troops, leaving 12,000 available for the field. The entire force comprised about 16,000 infantry — of whom several thousands were untrained or only partially so — about 400 cavalry, and about 1,500 gunners, including garrison artillery. There were only five field batteries of six guns each with only four horses apiece. There was a frantic sense of having little time for anything but the barest essentials by way of training or arming the troops.'[5]

Enthusiasm was not lacking in the Irish troops but prior to O'Reilly's arrival they were more of an undisciplined rabble than an army. When he was finished with them they were referred to as 'a splendid battalion', which, naturally, was called the Irish Battalion of St Patrick. By the end of the summer of 1860 there were four companies of Irish at Ancona and four at Spoleto. Later the French commander removed two companies from Spoleto for service elsewhere, leaving less than 300 men at Spoleto under an inexperienced second Lieutenant named Darcy not seventeen years of age! Conditions of service at this time were quite appalling. O'Reilly came to the rescue again and assembled the whole Battalion at Spoleto in July and even though some 200 of the men returned to Ireland because of the almost unbelievable conditions of living, he inspired confidence in the others, improved their living conditions, and injected a new spirit of morale into the unit. The four Company Commanders at this period were Blackney, Coppinger, Boschan and Kirwan. At this stage the four previous companies were still at Spoleto; four others were at Ancona. Despite a serious shortage of weapons, 'discipline increased and improved beyond measure. The Company Commanders, Kirwan, Coppinger, Boscham and Blackney, got down to it — and it was drill morning, noon and night — with a will as they knew time was short.'[6] It is of interest that Coppinger later became a Brigadier in the U.S. Army.

(Another Irish officer with the Ancona contingent was Lieutenant Myles Walter Keogh who was born in 1840 at Orchard, Carlow. Keogh was awarded the *Pro petri sede* medal for his service in the Ancona campaign. After the papal struggle, he went to America where he was commissioned into the Federal army; his first assignment was as aide-de-camp, with the rank of Major, to General Stoneman. After the American Civil War, he was posted as a captain to the 7th U.S. Cavalry and was one of General Custer's command which was slaughtered to a man on the Little Big Horn, Missouri, in 1876. Some fifty other Irishmen were killed there with him. When Chief Sitting Bull died, the *Pro petri sede* medal was found on his body. The Sioux chief had taken it from around the neck of the fallen Keogh after the Battle of the Little Big Horn and had worn it as a tribute to the paleface warrior.)

On 15 September 1860 General Fanti, the Italian Commander-in-Chief, reached Foligno which was about twenty miles from Spoleto. The garrison of the latter had been augmented somewhat and had less than 700 men and about twenty-five officers; over half of this force consisted of Irishmen. Fanti approached the fortress with approximately 2,500 trained troops including over 400 of the famed Bersaglieri. Apparently, he considered that he would find the minimum of opposition and in a message told Garibaldi that he expected to occupy the town in a couple of hours.

Spoleto was an old walled city about sixty miles south of Florence and with a population of about 8,000 people; it was built on the side of a hill, which was topped by the old fort of Rocca built by the Spanish Cardinal Albornoz in the fourteenth century. O'Reilly was given the specific task of defending Rocca; the north side was safe because it was sheer precipice but on the south he had a real problem with a hill which would prove an easy task for the Bersaglieri. From the start O'Reilly realised that his undertaking was a hopeless one; in terms of manpower the odds were four to one while his armament was in the region of one to the enemy's twenty.

The Italians advanced on the night of the 16th and virtually surrounded the fortress. The Irish, according to a Dublin man called Dunne, tried 'to keep up cheerful' by songs and 'divarshun'[7] but all the time they were aware that the enemy were within yards of them on the other side of the walls. O'Reilly had another problem: the Italians fighting for the Pope were quite untrustworthy and he had to keep a watchful eye on them.

On the morning of the 17th Captain Brignone, who had been instructed by Fanti to take the town, sent his Chief of Staff under a flag of truce to offer surrender terms to the Irish Commander. He replied that as he was holding the citadel for Pope Pius IX he had no authority to surrender it. Captain Coppinger was, however, sent to Brignone to discuss the fate of the women in the fortress. The Italian general allowed O'Reilly's wife and other soldiers' wives to leave the fort for safe custody.

As soon as the women had departed the bombardment of the town started. It lasted for three hours but there was little sign that the determination of the garrison had weakened.

In fact, they had inflicted very severe casualties on the besiegers with their small arms.

On the instructions of Monsignor Arnaldi, the Bishop of Spoleto, the cease fire sounded while the aged Bishop consulted with Monsignor Pericoli, the Papal Nuncio, who was with O'Reilly. The two clerics, in the presence of O'Reilly, crossed theological swords: the Bishop argued that the Pope would not wish the bloodshed that was taking place while the Nuncio, while paying due deference to the old prelate, maintained that he had no power to tell a soldier what to do. The Bishop blessed them both an retired; almost immediately the barrage commenced with greater intensity. A soldier named Fleming from Killarney was killed while another Kerryman from the same town was shot through the throat, but some excellent surgery on the part of an Irish doctor saved him.

Brignone came to realize that mere bombardment was not the answer to his attack and that he must send his Bersaglieri to storm the fortress. Crean states: 'Santorelli describes what he calls the "gridi feroci", the ferocious shouts of the Irish on the walls as they stood up in their excitement, disdaining all cover, to pour shots into the advancing Bersaglieri.'[8] The fierce fighting lasted until eight o'clock in the evening when O'Reilly, with practically no ammunition left and the walls breached, decided to surrender. He sent Monsignor Pericoli to get the best possible terms — a mission that resulted in a personal visit by O'Reilly accompanied by Coppinger to the headquarters of Brignone who described O'Reilly as both honourable and brave. The garrison was allowed to march out as prisoners of war; the officers were permitted to wear their swords.

Despite the heavy bombardment and assault by the Bersaglieri the Irish losses were indeed small: only five were killed and twenty wounded. On the other side, the Italians had more than 300 killed and even a larger number wounded.

The Irish prisoners were returned in the following November to Cork in the steamer *Dee* having transhipped at three ports en route: Genoa, Marseilles and Le Havre. The Irish at Ancona did not have the same opportunity as those at Spoleto but they did distinguish themselves at Castelfidardo and Perugia. G. M. Trevelyan, the English historian, who is renowned in Irish circles for one pungent remark, 'Cromwell had planted the Pope's power firm and broad in Ireland, but Gregory XVI and Pio Nono had destroyed it in Italy',[9] wrote of the Irish Papal expedition as follows:

'French and Italian witnesses on both sides are unanimous as to the valour of the Irish. . . . For twelve hours of September 17 the North Italians bombarded the Rocca of Spoleto, and in the afternoon attempted to storm its gate. Almost all the small column of assault were killed or wounded. Both Irish and North Italians, here, as a few weeks later at Ancona, displayed the ferocious self-sacrifice of men fighting for ideals. The assault was repulsed for that day, but when night fell the castle was crumbling beneath the bombardment, the ammunition was running out, and the Swiss and Italian Papalists compelled Major O'Reilly and the boys to open the gates.'[10]

Visitors who go to view the Rocca ruins these days will find a carved stone on which is inscribed on a school wall: '17 September 1860 — a body of Italian soldiers led by the valorous Brignone, assaulting the Rocca, drove out of it the mercenaries of tyranny and liberated Spoleto. The bodies of the heroes who gave their lives lie in this temple, where the citizens, grateful until the last generation, will bring the everlasting tribute of prayers and tears.'

Thus is so much of history written.

1. Quoted by Thomas J. Mullen, jr, in *The Irish Sword,* vol. 8, p. 218.
2. *Ibid.,* p. 219.
3. *The Irish Sword,* vol. 4, p. 53
4. *Ibid.,* p. 54.
5. *Ibid.,* p. 56.
6. *Ibid.,* p. 59.
7. *Ibid.,* p. 101.
8. *Ibid.,* p. 103.
9. G. M. Trevelyan in *Garibaldi and the Making of Italy,* 1928 edition, p. 208.
10. *Ibid.,* p. 218 and p. 221.

CHAPTER XIII

Naval Action

Today, curiously but happily, the Adriatic is enjoying a profounder peace, with greater understanding from shore to shore, than ever since Rome fell. If, by their multitudinous colourful acts, all those Irish seamen have, by the accident of history, ultimately contributed to this end, I cannot think they would regret it.

— John de Courcy Ireland in
The Irish Sword

The Wild Geese winged their way many thousands of miles from home; most of them made history on land and against a panoply of battlefields and armour and conflict. But there were also some who sought adventure on the sea. Since there were no organized fighting units of sailors the stories of those who achieved fame and fortune must be read out of chronological sequence. What knowledge we do have of these mariners is due, to a great extent, to the Irish naval historian, John de Courcy Ireland.

Pride of place must go to Commodore John Barry who, though born in Ballysampson in County Wexford in 1745, went to Philadelphia at the age of fifteen. After serving as a cabin boy young Barry's first command was of a schooner trading from Philadelphia to the West Indies in 1766. In the following year he married Mary Clary of whom little is known. He remained on the West Indies run until 1774 when he was given command of the *Black Prince,* a transatlantic trader plying between Philadelphia and Great Britain. After two voyages Barry lost his command because she was sold to the Continental Navy and renamed the *Alfred.*

Although Barry was without a ship at the time the American Revolutionary War broke out, he became one of a three-man team entrusted with the task of preparing a Continental

Squadron for sea. Later he assisted in planning the defences of the Delaware River estuary.

In March 1776, the year America declared her independence from Great Britain, Barry, who has been dubbed the 'Father of the American Navy', was commissioned a Captain and given command of the *Lexington,* an official naval vessel of the Thirteen Colonies. Barry saw his first naval action against the British frigate *Roebuck* which, with two tenders, was blockading the Delaware. Barry attacked the *Edward,* one of the tenders, forced it to surrender, and sent it back to Philadelphia as a prize. History cites his gallantry, recording that most of Barry's men were almost untrained and that the *Edward's* complement were all experienced seamen. From that moment on he was the naval hero of the hour with the report of his action read in Congress. This was but the advent of a series of successful exploits which so impressed his commanders that in June 1776 he was nominated Captain of one of four frigates which the American government undertook to build.

While waiting for his ship Barry became part sailor — part soldier and was probably the equivalent of the present-day American marine. He was employed in Cadwalader's Brigade as a staff officer and fought with General Washington at Princeton. In 1777 he was performing a variety of duties, some naval and some military. In the meantime, his wife died and he married a Sarah Austin, daughter of a wealthy Tory family. This fact led, ultimately, to a series of domestic financial problems when the American government seized all Tory wealth including Mrs Barry's.

Barry's frigate never reached completion; when Philadelphia was captured by the British, the part of the warship that had been constructed had to be destroyed. However, in May of 1778 he was given command of a frigate *Raleigh* which he did not take to sea until the following September because of the difficulties of getting a ship ready in Boston. His first venture in her was something of a disaster; two days out of Boston he was attacked by two British ships and forced to beach his own on a deserted island. Unhappily, the *Raleigh,* which should have been destroyed, was captured by the British because a seaman failed to carry out the orders to burn her. Barry saved most of his crew and, following a court-martial, was himself acquitted honourably.

This misfortune, the problems about his wife's money, and a total lack of faith in the American ability to build a proper navy forced him to apply for leave. To add to his disillusionment he had had no pay for two years. The leave was granted and he undertook two highly profitable commercial ventures in the West Indies and added to the booty by capturing a British sloop. After a period as a special adviser he became the guardian of important official couriers on his ship, presided over the court-martial of a French Captain Landais, and became something of a 'factotum' for the Continental Navy. Barry was given command of the *Alliance* and once more took to the sea as a fighting sailor. His first challenge on this occasion was to engage two British ships, the *Atlanta* and the *Trepassey*. Barry came through this battle again the victor but at the cost of a severe wound to himself. When he returned to Boston in June of 1781, once again he was lionized for his achievements.

Two years later he was on the West Indies run again in his old ship, the *Alliance,* but this time carrying very valuable specie; he was also acting as escort to a French ship. He became involved in a scrap with the British frigate *Sybill* but as he observed two more warships coming to her aid he abandoned the fight and headed for home. This was his last battle against the British; when he came ashore he discovered that the war was over and that, according to the American leaders, there was no apparent need for a navy. After eight years of fighting he was on the beach.

Barry then entered politics, the interests of the ex-army and ex-navy personnel becoming his principal platform. Whether he was a political thorn in the side of the administration or just too valuable to keep at home it is hard to tell; at any rate, he was given command of a ship and was commissioned to open up trade between America and China.

Despite his fame, he was still waiting for his pay and expenses while he lived on his wife's money! There is little record of the outcome of the Chinese venture, but in the early days of the New World the Algerine pirates decided to 'make hay' before the new bright American sun started to shine. They became so daring in their marauding that America came to realize the hard way the need for a navy. Whereupon, in 1794, a squadron was formed and Barry was to be appointed Captain of it but had to wait until his own special frigate was built. Once again, this particular ship was never completed for Barry, despite the fact that he supervised it personally during its construction. Even President George Washington came to see it being built. But, in the meantime, peace was made with the Algerines and there appeared to be little necessity for speed in its completion. Three other ships were built and Barry was given command of one of them. On 22 February 1797 he was commissioned 'Captain of the Navy of the United States and Commander of the frigate called the *United States.*' Subsequently, he became commodore of a squadron consisting of his own ship and three smaller ones. His job at this time was more in the nature of training the early officers of the U.S. Navy rather than any participation in active conflict. It was for this reason that he has been called the 'Father of the U.S. Navy'.

Barry became Commander of the U.S. West Indies Squadron in 1798, a job he held for over a year during which time he became something of a socialite in international naval circles. But his ambition to become an admiral was denied him. He assumed shore duties in 1799 and served the Navy in an administrative capacity until September 1803 when he died.

At about the time Barry was in the region of the West Indies, another famous sailor was in the same waters and was involved in an incident with which Barry may have had some connection. The sailor was Nelson who, when in command of the *Boreas,* created a scene in St Kitts in 1785 because some 'vagabonds' had hoisted the Irish colours with thirteen stripes in them. There is little doubt that they were Irish sailors and that the colours referred to were those of the Thirteen colonies. But despite Nelson's problems with the Irish he still had many of them on his ships, either as impressed seamen or as volunteers. 'In H.M.S. *Temeraire,* the 98-gun ship of the line later immortalized by Turner's picture, no fewer than 220 Irishmen out of a total crew of 718 took part in the Battle of Trafalgar. The *Temeraire* which was astern of the *Victory* in the van of the British port column, was one of the ships most hotly engaged in the whole battle and had the sixth highest casualty list of the twenty-seven British line-of-battleships. Of the *Victory's* Trafalgar crew of 663 (excluding marines and boys) sixty-three are listed as Irish.'[1]

There is reason to believe that the bullet which killed Nelson was extracted by an Irish surgeon named Beatty; in fact, the latter's close friend, Lieutenant Ram, suffered the same fate as Nelson, that of being killed in the *Victory's* cockpit. One of Nelson's specially-selected aides was Rear-Admiral E. Galwey from County Cork, of whom he wrote in a letter to Admiral Lord St Vincent, dated 8 May 1798 : 'My First Lieutenant, Galwey, has no friends and is one of the best officers in my ship.' The reference to 'friends' is based on the practice of the times when most promotion was the result of having friends in influential positions. Apparently, Galwey achieved great success entirely on his own merit and, judging by his achievements, he deserved any promotion which came his way. During the Battle of the Nile in 1798 he was sent in charge of the only undamaged boat on the *Vanguard* to rescue the crew of the French ship *Orient*; at a later date he was sent with a party of marines to take possession of the *Spartiate*.

Galwey was made a commander in 1809 and then became Captain of the *Dryad* frigate. His successes included the capture of the French brigs *Ile Dieu* and the *Clorinde*. He was appointed Rear-Admiral in 1837 and served until 1840 when he died in County Cork having succeeded to the family estates.

A Limerick man who served with Nelson when he was captain in command of H.M.S. *Agamemnon* was Captain H. Compton. He fought with Nelson in the *Theseus* at Cape St Vincent and was promoted for gallantry.

Irish activity in the British navy at this time was not confined to fighting Imperial enemies; in the few mutinies in the British navy Irishmen predominated. Little wonder, too, for many of them who were impressed into it served under dreadful conditions.

George Thomas, the Irishman from Tipperary who became a rajah in India at the time of Lally, was one who suffered so very considerably. During his time the following rules applied :

'Anyone who shall kill another on board ship shall be tied to the dead body and cast into the sea with it.

'Anyone convicted of drawing a knife with intent to strike another with it or anyone who does so and draws blood shall lose his right hand.

'Anyone convicted of theft on board shall have his head shaved and boiling pitch thrown over him and feathers or down strewed upon him to distinguish him as a thief.'[2]

So, it is little wonder that de Courcy Ireland wrote: 'In fact, Irishmen were prominent in those few mutinies which actually resulted in ships of George III's fleets being sailed into French and Spanish ports, for example, H.M.S. *Hermione,* in which the mutiny was led in September, 1797, by surgeon's mate, Laurence Cronin. They also participated in the great mutinies of 1797 at Spithead and the Nore, when MacCarthy was mutineers' leader and delegate of H.M.S. *Inflexible* at the Nore, and Thomas MacCann of the *Sandwich,* also at the Nore was sentenced to transporation for life. Surgeon Mac-Murdy, at Spithead, was said to have been one of the chief United Irishmen agents "responsible" for a mutiny that the inhuman conditions prevailing would no doubt have caused in any fleet, Irishmen or no Irishmen.'[3]

On the other side of the picture activities of Irish naval enthusiasts were different. It was Richard Brinsley Sheridan, a former sympathizer with France, who after the Peace of Amiens opposed the cutting down of British naval strength; and William Marsden was secretary of the Board of the Admiralty while George Canning from Derry was treasurer of the Navy in 1805.

At the naval battle off Cape St Vinvent in 1797, the Irish fought on both sides, for on the Franco-Spanish side Don Enrique MacDonnell was a Commodore in the Spanish navy and was in command of the 100-gun Spanish ship *Rayo.* Mac-Donnell, who has been mentioned previously, served at one time in the Hibernia Regiment and was with it during the Florida campaign. Three other Irish officers also took part in the battle: Colonel Charles O'Neil, Lieutenant Connor, and Ensign Patrick MacSheehy.

About the same period in other waters and under a variety of flags Irishmen were adding lustre to naval history. The Third Earl of Granard was commander-in-chief of the first Austrian Imperial Navy, which was founded in 1720; he was partially responsible for the construction and development of the great naval port at Trieste. Forbes became a vice-admiral in 1736, having commanded H.M.S. *Canterbury* and *Cornwall,* and having held the appointment of British Minister to St Petersburg in 1733. His second son, John, born in 1714, was destined also for a very colourful career in the British Navy. He also became an admiral and one whose humanity and understanding were bywords in naval circles even if he was described by some as stubborn and unreasonable. His reputation for stubbornness was based on his refusal as the only member of the Board of Admiralty to sign the warrant for the execution of Admiral Byng who in 1757, after a disastrous attack on Fort Philip at Minorca, was court-martialled for cowardice, negligence and disaffection. Despite the fact that the court-martial acquitted him of cowardice and disaffection but found him guilty of dereliction of duty, he was sentenced to death. Forbes gave as his reasons for refusal to sign the death warrant his belief that a man acquitted of cowardice and disaffection could not be guilty of any negligence. He wrote in an official document outlining his reasons for refusal:

Admiral Byng's fate was referred to a court martial. His life and death were left to their opinions. The court martial condemn him to death, because, as they expressly say, they were under a necessity of doing so, by reason of the letter of the law, the severity of which they complain of, because it admits of no mitigation. The court martial expressly say, that for the sake of their conscience, as well as in justice to the prisoner, they must earnestly recommend him to his Majesty for mercy. It is evident then, that in the opinions and consciences of the judges, he was not deserving of death.[4]

Despite all the pleas, Byng was executed.

Judging by some of the tributes paid to Forbes after his death he must have been a fine sailor as well as a great humanitarian. The *European Magazine* of 1796 includes in its laudatory paragraphs the following: 'He was remarkable, above all other men, for his extensive and universal knowledge of naval affairs, having studied them, in all their branches, with a perseverance, and observed upon them with an acuteness and judgement altogether unparalleled.

'He attained such a summit of nautical skill, as rendered him the oracle of all those who were most eminent, whether in the direction of the fleets of this nation, or in the equally arduous task of superintending the civil departments of the different branches of the marine.

'In private life he continued, to his last breath, an example of the brightest virtues which can adorn the human character.'[5]

Apart from the Forbes family's considerable contribution to the British navy, it must be remembered that the tradition started on the Dalmatian Coast where many Irishmen remained instead of joining the British navy. Between the years 1797-1814 many Irish distinguished themselves at sea in the Napoleonic War. One of the most outstanding was Captain Henry Baillie, a commander of a frigate and later of a battleship, who was one of the greatest of the seamen fighting for the Russians. Not only did he drive the French Navy from the shores of Southern Italy but he also expelled the Austrians from Dalmatia. Here again history repeated itself for it was another Irishman, Count Nugent, who triumphantly recaptured Trieste in 1814.

There were many other Irish sailors serving in the Adriatic. At least four admirals fought in the British fleet there during the latter part of the eighteenth century and in the early part of the nineteenth. Rear-Admiral Daly served at one time in H.M.S. *Arrow* in the Adriatic and earned considerable distinction for entering a fortified port, cutting out and destroying a French privateer. Rear-Admiral Donal O'Brien made a hazardous and dramatic escape from the notorious French prisoner-of-war camp, at Bitsche, and walked some four hundred miles to Trieste where he managed to get a boat with the aid of the British Consul there. One of the more amusing aspects of the escape was that the British Consul turned out to be an Irishman named Donolan! O'Brien rowed out in his boat only to find himself in the middle of a battle being fought by the boats of H.M.S. *Amphion* and two French gunboats. Naturally he took a hand and later rejoined the *Amphion,* in which he had served previously. This was but one of a whole series of very important naval engagements in which he later proved his prowess. John Talbot's career was just as colourful as those of his fellow Irish sailors. As Captain of H.M.S. *Victorious* in February 1812, he captured the 74-gun *Rivoli* which had just been built at Venice. Apparently, had she been able to move freely in the Adriatic, she would have dominated it but Talbot intercepted her off Grado. He was severely wounded but because of his magnificent performance a special medal was struck in his honour.

The Wild Geese sailors as well as the soldiers were ubiquitous. Surgeon Barry O'Meara who was responsible for saving Talbot's eyesight after the Battle of Grado later accompanied Napoleon into exile. Interestingly enough, the naval espionage against Napoleon was conducted by another Irishman named Leard who was a cousin of Count Nugent. Then there were the Banfields, and Barrys, and O'Flanagans. The Barrys, from the naval viewpoint, were the most outstanding. Richard Barry, whose family was outlawed from Ireland for its activities in support of the Confederation of Kilkenny, was in the fleet that blockaded Venice during its revolt against Austria in 1848-1849. In the Franco-Austrian War of 1859 he commanded the battleship *Dandolo* defending Venice. In 1864 he conveyed the ill-fated Hapsburg Archduke Maximilian from Trieste to Mexico. Although Maximilian became Emperor of Mexico for a short while he was later executed in the frigate *Novara*.

Richard Barry's career was, however, not to be compared with that of his brother, Alfred, later called Ritter von Barry. De Courcy Ireland writes of him :

I estimate (that he was) the second greatest admiral the Austrian navy ever had. He became a legend in his lifetime, and the story of his behaviour at the great second battle of Vis or Lissa on 20 July 1866 is still spoken of along the Dalmatian coast. The battle was fought by a much inferior but energetically commanded Austrian fleet against the fleet of newly united Italy. The prize was ownership and control of Istria and Dalmatia, and the battle was probably the most decisive battle ever fought in the Adriatic. The Austrian fleet, in wedge formation, broke through the Italian battle line, and sank two large Italian ironclads, one by ramming. Barry's ship, *Prinz Eugen*, on the starboard flank of the wedge, passed through the enemy line under heavy fire, between the heavy ironclads *Maria Pia* and *Re di Portogallo*. The bridge of his ship (which was hit 21 times and fired more shots than any, save one, of her consorts), was wreathed in smoke, when Barry saw that he was within feet of *Maria Pia*. He was seen to raise his tall hat and bow ceremoniously to her captain, the Marchese del Carratto, after, according to the most widely current version of the story, first drawing his revolver to shoot him, and then thinking better of it and putting it way. Barry's abilities and conduct so impressed the Austrian commander-in-chief Tegetthof that, after the victory and the successful entry of the Austrian fleet into the harbour of Lissa which the enemy had been trying to seize, his *Prinz Eugen* was appointed to act as guardship on patrol outside the harbour all night. When Alfred Barry died in 1907 in Pula, where his grave can still be seen, the Austrian Navy was the eighth in the world and one of the most efficient, and Pula one of the world's finest naval bases — largely thanks to Barry.[6]

An Irish sailor, whose antecendents are unknown but who played an important part in Russian naval history, was Captain Peter Delap. In Russian official documents he is mentioned as having come from Ireland but the story of his arrival in Biorko Sound is more a matter for speculation than fact. The probability is that Delap was one of the Wild Geese who ended up either in England or Germany. At any rate he was probably on board one of a number of ships built for the Russians by these countries. He must have had education and experience beyond that of an ordinary seaman for on 18 May 1714 he was enrolled as a Lieutenant by the Russians and was very fortunate, because of his courage, to come to the notice of Peter the Great.

The Tsar joined part of his fleet at Helsingfors in 1714 and then sailed to Biörkö Sound. The Tsar went ahead of the main body to join his ship the *Katharina* and then ran into a fierce westerly gale. The gale, added to surging waters descending from the River Neva, created so dangerous a situation that a number of boats were lost. It became imperative for the Tsar to be put ashore to safeguard his life. Volunteers amongst the officers to undertake the responsibility in the face of such hazards were few but Peter Delap offered to try. The following excerpt from an official document tells the story: 'Upon a signal given a yawl was brought and, the Tsar getting in, Delap steered to Biörkö Island and set him safe ashore, receiving 100 roubles for his service, and out of which as was obliged to give the boat's crew 30. One ship lost her foremast and bowsprit; but the wind in time abating, the fleet proceeded to Kronslot.'[7]

Following this action, Delap became something of a protégé of Peter: he sent him on special missions, promoted him commander and posted him to the 64-gun ship *Ingermanland* and recommended him to the 'General Admiral' Apraksyn who commanded the Russian fleet. In 1718 Delap was given command of his own ship *Prince Alexander;* this was followed by a series of further commands. In one encounter with the Swedish Navy in 1719, Delap attacked the enemy flagship and compelled its commander to strike his colours. For this service he was promoted captain.

But in all his years of service, the mission most coloured by coincidence and irony was that of a raid on the Swedish coast in 1719. Six men-of-war, one of them Delap's (probably the *Yagudiel*), were ordered to cover a fleet of galleys conveying Russian troops to make an assault on the Swedish mainland. In charge of the Russian troops was the Irishman Major-General Peter Lacy. It would be interesting to know whether Delap and Lacy, united in a conflict so far from the green hills of Ireland, ever met or if they knew that their foe was another Irishman, General Hugh Hamilton from Fermanagh, who was commanding the Swedish Army! Hamilton prevented the landing and was, in fact, prepared to lead a Swedish army into Scotland to restore the Old Pretender had Charles XII, King of Sweden, lived.

Following the death of Peter the Great, Delap resigned from the Russian Navy and left Russia in 1729. After that date this fine sailor disappeared.

There were many other Irish sailors in the Rusian navy; in fact, there is some reason to believe that a David Butler actually founded it. Certainly Irishmen founded navies in four other countries: Argentina, Chile, Ecuador and Venezuela. Of these stories of adventure one of the more colourful is the tale of William Brown who was born in Foxford, County Mayo, and left Ireland with his family to go to America in 1786. When Brown's father died there leaving William destitute, he joined a merchantman as a cabin-boy, but in 1796, at the age of nineteen, he was impressed into the British Navy and served on a man-of-war. Little is known of his career with the British but it must have been a successful one for he married and settled down in the Argentine Republic in 1812. That he was well-known in Buenos Aires is a certainty, for after two years' residence there he was offered a naval command by the republic.

His first naval engagement was fought at the mouth of the Uruguay which was followed by a more decisive action off Montevideo. In this engagement he captured four Spanish ships and so encouraged the young republic that it gave him the title of Admiral and commissioned him to fit out a privateer. Brown and his privateer became the scourge of the Spaniards in the Pacific.

Brown retired again to his family in Buenos Aires as soon as peace was restored with the Spanish, but in 1825 Brazil declared war on the republic and he was called into service again. The Brazilians blockaded the River Plate, but Brown, although outnumbered in vessels by four to one, drove the enemy from the river mouth and in 1827 engaged a Brazilian squadron of some nineteen small vessels at the mouth of the Uruguay and completely destroyed the whole force. He then assembled a few brigs and once more sailed against the enemy. This time he took a severe beating and, though badly wounded himself, ran one of the brigs ashore and set fire to her. This defeat forced his government to the peace table where acceptable terms were hammered out.

In 1842 civil war broke out in the Argentine and Brown was summoned once more to take command of the fleet and blockade Montevideo. The English and the French resented the blockade, intervened in the struggle, and, in 1845, sent squadrons to seize Brown's ships, thereby rendering him ineffective. This forced Brown back into final retirement; he died in his beloved Buenos Aires in 1857.

Although long an exile, Brown kept in close touch with Ireland and its affairs. The following letter written by the

Admiral in 1843 and published in *The Southern Cross,* Buenos
Aires, in 1956 gives substantive proof of this :

> Gentlemen, I have to acknowledge the receipt of your letter
> of 29th ult. informing me of a meeting of our countrymen
> in Buenos Aires for the purpose of raising a subscription to
> be remitted to the general fund at home, having for its object
> the gaining by constitutional means the repeal of the union
> with England and soliciting my aid in furtherance thereof.
> I have to inform you that any measure tending to give peace,
> prosperity and contentment to the long-suffering people of
> Ireland must at all times meet my humble concurrence and
> aid, but more particularly at this moment though ever so far
> distant from that dear Erin my native land. The repeal of
> the Legislative Union (Ireland being governed by her own
> laws) will strike at once at the source of the evil so grievously
> felt and complained of, and cheer up a people too long
> accustomed to sufferings, to wrongs and to ills . . . please
> accept of five hundred paper dollars and would that it could
> be much more, with my hearty good wishes to accompany
> your subscription across the western ocean in favour of so
> just a cause, a cause which when gained must give fresh
> strength, command and vigour to her Majesty's councils, and
> command the respect among her enemies when knowing of
> the happy and disinterested union between the soon con-
> tented — please God — Erin and the lofty sovereign isle.
> Should you have to write to the great and good patriot, Mr
> Daniel O'Connell, don't forget to present my kind compli-
> ments as an admirer of his talents, constancy and persever-
> ance in advocating so ably the long injured Ireland's cause,
> for which may God reward him in this and the world to
> come. I am, gentlemen, your sincere obedient servant, W.
> Brown.[8]

The Wild Geese at sea deserve a volume of their own, especially when one considers that there is some evidence to support the theory that yet another Barry — John Barry, brother
of James Barry the Irish painter — in some remarkable way
is reputed to have founded the Japanese Navy !
  Why are the Irish not a great sea power ?

1. John de Courcy Ireland in *The Irish Sword*, vol. 4, p. 40.
2. A. B. Campbell, *Customs and Traditions of the Royal Navy*, (1956), p. 7. Quoted by Maurice Hennessy in *The Rajah from Tipperary*, pp. 9-10.
3. *The Irish Sword*, vol. 4, p. 41.
4. Quoted by John de Courcy Ireland in *The Irish Sword*, vol. 6, pp. 13-14.
5. *Ibid.*, p. 15.
6. *Ibid.*, pp. 78-79.
7. Obshchy Morskoy Spisok (General Naval List) published at St Petersburg in 1885, vol. I, p. 128.
8. *The Irish Sword*, vol. 2, pp. 297-298.

CHAPTER XIV

Fighting for America

Liberty is meaningless where the right to utter one's thoughts and opinions has ceased to exist. That, of all rights, is the dread of tyrants. It is the right which they first of all strike down. They know its power.

— Frederick Douglass

Although we still find descendants of the Wild Geese scattered throughout Europe in influential positions, their impact on that continent lessened during the second half of the eighteenth century. A number of them, under names changed either by marriage or mispronunciation, were guillotined during the French Revolution because as a result of military and social achievements they had been accepted into the French aristocracy and had to suffer the consequences. The Spanish possessions attracted many others; their story belongs to the New World and so it is there that we pick up the narrative again.

Irishmen had been going to America since the end of the Seventeenth century. As far back as 1680 there was a tract of land in Maryland known as 'New Ireland' County. There were various other areas settled by the Irish : a grant of 6,000 acres made to an Edmund O'Dwyer was called 'New Munster' and there were also 'New Connaught' and 'New Leinster'. By the beginning of the eighteenth century there were numerous Irish settlements on the Eastern seaboard of America and, very surprisingly, most of their inhabitants had lost not only their Catholic faith but also their identity. '. . . but, since Catholics were unwelcome in all of the colonies, except perhaps in Maryland and Pennsylvania, the Catholic Irish tended to conform at least outwardly to Protestant customs wherever they settled. As a result, whether for social or economic reasons, or simply because of the absence of priests, their descendants by the time of the Revolution for the most part had lost the old faith.'[1]

During the second decade of the eighteenth century an influx of Northern Ireland Protestants predominated in the Irish immigration picture in America; this did not mean that immigration from the other parts of Ireland ceased. By no stretch of the imagination could these newcomers be looked upon as Wild Geese of the old tradition, but later they became so closely involved with them that to understand the Wild Geese story in the New World it is important to have a clear picture of the Irish scene in America at the outbreak of the Revolutionary War in 1775. 'The Irish flocked into the country by the hundreds and thousands, helping with immigrants from France, Germany, Scotland, Switzerland and Africa to make the eighteenth century in British America "pre-eminently the century of the foreigner."[2] By 1760 the foreign born equalled one-third of the population of the colonies.'[3]

The outbreak of hostilities between Britain and America started in a flurry of recruitment in France. Louis XVI seized upon it as an ideal opportunity to strike at France's old enemy, the British. 'On February 6th, 1778, a treaty between France and the United States was signed, providing that France would aid the Americans on the winning of independence; and that should France and Great Britain become involved in war, the Americans would come to her assistance; and that neither party would make peace without the consent of the other. On May 1st, 1778, Washington received the news, and on May 5th informed the army.'[4]

Both sides had time to strengthen their armies for although the Boston Tea Party occurred in 1774 open hostilities did not start until a year later.

With so many Irish on the British side at this time it was obvious that America was to serve as yet another and broader battleground where the Irish would fight Irish. Nor was it a religious conflict this time. It would even be wrong to suggest that the Irish involvement was purely patriotic. Circumstances and individual interests were a predominant factor although on the Wild Geese side some semblance of patriotic fervour was expressed in a continued hatred of the British.

The Revolution had its origin in problems on the Eastern seaboard of America with Boston and New York as focal points. A realistic picture of the Irish situation can, therefore, be appreciated when one learns that an Irishman, Thomas Dongan, was the first Governor of New York.

Dongan was born at Castletown, County Kildare, in 1634 and joined the French Army. He rose to the rank of Colonel in the original Irish Brigade and, on restoration of the Stuarts and before the 1691 Flight of the Wild Geese, was sent by James, Duke of York, to act as Governor of the English province on the Hudson. There is an interesting story told of Dongan's arrival in New York in August of 1683. Apparently, some of his Irish brethren there were in doubt about his loyalty (and, indeed, about their own!) but, nonetheless, decided to give a banquet in his honour with an address of welcome. The perspicacious Dongan responded to the presentation in Gaelic, shattering his suspicious countrymen but at the same time inspiring them with confidence and loyalty. It was obvious that he knew his own people well. The news of the happenings at the banquet spread rapidly; Dongan was lionized and with good reason : he was a man of splendid integrity and achievement and was also a firm believer in education. In 1685 he gave permission to the Jews to open a synagogue in New York; he himself also founded the first classical school in New York City. Apparently, the teacher whom he appointed to head this institution was suspected of being a Jesuit spy — a fact which caused the Governor considerable embarrassment.

His own residence which was built by the renowned Peter Stuyvesant he called Whitehall. One of the major effects of Dongan's regime was that further Irish immigration into America was encouraged; he even wrote to the British authorities soliciting it. Records of Eastern seaboard settlements from Washington to Maine prior to the 1700s show many Irish family names. There is room for a separate volume on Dongan; later in his life he became the Earl of Limerick but died in England, one of the much travelled Wild Geese.

He was only one of many Irishmen who helped set the stage for Irish as well as American conflict. Before the Revolution Sir William Johnson, who was born in Meath in 1715, had established a large Irish settlement along the Mohawk River where he received a grant of 100,000 acres. He induced many of his countrymen to colonize there; so successful were his efforts that he formed a powerful Irish colony where 'for many years they regularly held St Patrick's Day festivals with athletic contests of all sorts after the manner of celebrating the day in Ireland. In 1747, they must have had a very gay celebration indeed, if we are to judge from Johnson's letter to the colonial governor, George Clinton, dated "Fort Johnson, March 18, 1747" wherein he said : "We kept St Patrick's yesterday and this day and drank your health and all friends in Albany, with so many other healths that I can scarce write." [5]

Johnson, always a staunch ally of the British, prevented the Six Nations of Indians from joining the French in 1745. When the French and Indian War broke out it was Johnson who trounced the French in 1755. Major Robert Rogers of 'Rogers' Rangers' fame, in his *Reminiscences of the French War*, describes how Johnson's men inflicted a further defeat on the French on 17 March 1757. It happened that on the night of the 16th the Irish troops under Johnson were given an extra rum ration to celebrate the advent of their National holiday. General Montcalm, the French commander at Ticonderoga, decided that this was the night for a surprise attack on the celebrants at Fort William Henry on Lake George. The outcome, however, was quite the opposite : Montcalm was met by an exhilarated Irish fighting force which, having mauled him severely, returned to 'drowning the shamrock'.

The Irish picture, therefore, at the commencement of hostilities was a confused one. There were a number of Irish organizations in the Thirteen Colonies and even now, after considerable research by scholars, it is difficult to understand or unravel their loyalties; the picture is a potpourri of inconsistencies. One organization which originated in Ireland about 1740 but spread to America before 1760 was 'The Ancient and Most Benevolent Order of the Friendly Brothers of St Patrick.' This was, supposedly, the society from which originated the Society of the Friendly Sons of St Patrick, but the historians of the latter group state in their work : 'All efforts to discover any formal connection between the Friendly Sons of St Patrick and the Friendly Brothers have met with no success.' [6] In all probability the Friendly Brothers had amongst its members many Irish officers serving with the British Army in Ireland, England and America, for after the Declaration of Independence and the withdrawal of the British troops from New York

F

in 1783 it seemed to disappear; the 'Friendly Sons' are still going strong.

And now the vital question : what happened at the outbreak of the war? Irish organizations as a whole did not appear to favour one side or the other and it must be remembered that Irish societies other than those mentioned existed outside New York. Murphy and Mannion in *The History of the Society of the Friendly Sons of Saint Patrick in the City of New York* sum up the situation very well : 'Though loyal to English interests their national characteristics asserted themselves, at least once a year, when they assembled round the festive board to celebrate the feast day of Ireland's Patron Saint. According to newspaper accounts of their banquets, the toast offered seem to us to be a peculiar mixture of inconsistencies. While on some occasions they drank to such sentiments as "The Memory of St. Patrick," and "Prosperity to Ireland" and condemned to "perdition" the "Enemies of Ireland", they also toasted the English King and Parliament as well as politicians of the time who ruled the people of Ireland with an iron hand.'[7]

George Washington joined the Friendly Sons in 1781 and attended three meetings. A copy of his acceptance letter follows :

To:
George Campbell, Esq.
President of the Society of
the Friendly Sons of St. Patrick
in the City of Philadelphia
Sir :

I accept with singular pleasure the Ensign of so worthy a Fraternity as that of the Sons of St Patrick in this City, a Society distinguished for the firm adherence of its Members to the glorious cause in which we are embarked.

Give me leave to assure you, Sir, that I shall never cast my eyes on the Badge with which I am honoured, but with a grateful remembrance of the polite and affectionate manner in which it was presented.

I am with respect and esteem, Sir

Your most obedient servant,
G. Washington.[8]

Many of his ablest supporters were also members.

Before turning to the military struggle of the Revolution and the part played by the Wild Geese, it is well to establish the position of New York in the conflict. At the outbreak of combat it ranked with Philadelphia and Boston as one of the three great commercial centres of the New World. It has a population of over 20,000 and during the wars was a permanent stronghold of the British forces. By the end of 1776 its population was reduced to 3,000 but, strangely enough, whatever commercial enterprise did remain in the city was in a large degree carried on by Irish merchants. Few of the Irish were open loyalists but they did do business with the English authorities.

The task of following the individual fortunes of the Wild Geese who fought in the American Revolution is a difficult one. Apart from those who came to the Americas via the West Indies, it is even a knotty problem to trace their regimental activities, despite the fact that Washington depended so much on Irishmen to lead his armies. Many of the Irish who were fighting with French units in the Americas returned to France, so that to outline specific areas of the conflict where the Irish alone fought the British is impossible.

In Chapter VI the formation of an 'Irish Officer Pool' in France was explained; apparently, this was also a useful source of leaders for the French forces helping the Americans. O'Callaghan states: 'The next year, 1777, we find officers of higher rank, or Colonel Conway of the Brigade, and Colonel Roche de Fermoy, in commands of note; the former, after an English allusion to him, as "a Colonel of the Irish Brigade", being further referred to, as "one of that numerous train of officers in the French service, who had taken an active part against Great Britain, in this unhappy civil war." When hostilities broke out between France and England, the Irish regiments in France, who considered themselves entitled to serve *before* other corps against the English — a claim more especially advanced, on this occasion, by the Regiment of Dillon — were not long left unemployed.'[9]

There is no further mention of de Fermoy's activities in America although there are numerous records of many other French officers.

Major-General Henry Knox, an ardent Irish Presbyterian, came to America from Derry in 1729; he was one of a family of ten. In his early years Knox worked in a bookshop in Boston where he became an avid reader of military history and particularly of the military genius of Marshal Maurice de Saxe of France who commanded at Fontenoy. When the Redcoats and the Bostonians began to come to grips Knox joined the Massachusetts Militia and because of his book knowledge of military lore was commissioned as an officer. By 1775 he was Colonel of Artillery in the Continental Army. This promotion was followed shortly afterwards by his appointment by Washington as Commander of Artillery of the American forces. There is a story told that on his appointment he asked Washington whether or not there *was* such a thing as the American Artillery; Washington is reputed to have replied that if there was he had better go and find it. And this is just what Knox did. He stole some of the British artillery at Ticonderoga and he routed the British from Boston and took 250 heavy pieces from them. During five years Knox really formed a formidable artillery but, what is more, became 'General Washington's General.'[10] He was, according to W. S. Murphy: '. . . the one officer in whom Washington could completely confide, one whose knowledge of military history and strategy surpassed his own, and one upon whom Washington could unfailingly rely for magnificent performance.'[11] For most of the war Knox was Washington's *alter ego* and was with him at Trenton, Princeton, Monmouth, Valley Forge and at Yorktown when, on 19 October 1781, the British surrendered. Knox's decisions were overruled only once: Rochambeau, the French General, selected Yorktown as the final battle area against the British.

The Marquis de Lafayette, who was commanding the French, 'said to Knox's aide: "You fire better than the French. Upon my honour, I speak the truth. And the progress of your artillery is regarded by everybody as one of the wonders of the Revolution. . . ." '[12]

Another French general — General Chastellux — in his *Travels in America in 1780-1782* paid him a further compliment: 'We cannot sufficiently admire the intelligence and activity with which Knox collected from different places and transported to the batteries cannon and mortars of large calibre for the siege. The English marvelled no less at the extraordinary progress of the American artillery and at the capacity and instructions of the officers.'[13]

Knox did not in any way fit the stereotype of the soldier; he was frequently referred to as 'pot-bellied John Knox' and his movements were described as 'lumbering rather than walking.' Nevertheless, his 250 pounds were as formidable as was his artillery. Knox became Commander-in-Chief of the American Army, a title he maintained until the Constitution vested the rank in the President of the United States. After his retirement from the army he lived in Boston until his death in October of 1806. Some historians claim that Knox was the founder of the United States Navy while others give that honour to Barry.

Another very colourful soldier who was also a commander of one of Washington's forces was 'Mad Anthony' Wayne who was also called 'Dandy' Wayne; he became a Major-General in the Continental Army and certainly belied the accepted connotation of the tag 'Dandy' by stopping a mutiny of his troops with threatening pistols and his bare fists. Wayne's grandfather fought for King William at the Boyne as a Captain of Dragoons; he came to Pennsylvania in 1722 with his four sons. In 1745 his grandson, the future General 'Mad Anthony', was born. The latter became a surveyor and one of the pioneers in clearing the Allegheny wilderness. He was selected by Benjamin Franklin to serve on the Committee of Safety, then making preparations for the coming conflict.

As soon as the fighting broke out, Wayne was given command of a battalion of Pennsylvania troops and had his first taste of battle in Canada. He distinguished himself at Three Rivers, Quebec, and then was recalled to defend Fort Ticonderoga on Lake Champlain. The hardships Wayne's troops suffered during the winter in the fort were appalling; their agonies were so severe that in February 1777 they mutinied. Their resistance was crushed immediately by the display of Wayne's personal gallantry. By this time he had become a Brigadier-General and three months after the mutiny he was appointed Commander of the Pennsylvania Line. The latter has been referred to by some historians, both Irish and American, as the 'Line of Ireland',[14] and 'Wayne's Irish Pennsylvanians'.[15] Both these statements are quite extravagant, for although there were many Irish in his command, there were English, Scottish, German and Dutch, all totalling some sixty per cent of the unit. This is confirmed in *The Pennsylvania Archives (Series 2)* which records the names and birthplaces of the members of the regiment. Obviously there were many Wild Geese from France and Germany amongst the Revolutionaries but these did not form a separate unit.

One of Wayne's major achievements was his defeat of a force of British and Hessians at Chadd's Ford; in a resounding victory over his enemies he virtually decimated them. Unhappily for him, this triumph was followed by a surprise attack at Paoli where his home was. He was severely criticized for possible negligence, the implication being that he was over confident and the proximity of his home had made him careless. Washington was one of his critics. This so angered Wayne that he demanded a court martial which afterwards exonerated him. In June 1778 Wayne was largely responsible for a victory at Monmouth; it was one 'which might well have been conclusive except for vacillation by Major-General Charles Lee, whom Washington called "a damned poltroon" for his behaviour there.'[16] A year later Washington gave him command of four crack regiments called the Light Corps.

His new command brought with it orders to undertake the most difficult assignment of the whole Revolutionary War: the capture of a fortress dominating the Hudson River at Stony Point known as 'Little Gibraltar'. It was 140 feet above the river and consisted of 100 acres of solid rock. Wayne was wounded in the head during the assault and was quite convinced that he was a dying man. With a flair for the dramatic he ordered that he be carried forward to the front line of battle and from there he commanded with such fervour that the fortress was captured. 'The people from Maine to Georgia congratulated themselves and General Wayne on so brilliant a proof of the country's glory.'[17] General Charles Lee wrote to him: '— your assault of Stony Point — is the most brilliant I am acquainted with in history; the assault of Schweidnitz by Marshal Laudon I think inferior to it.'[18]

Despite this spectacular achievement Wayne had another mutiny to face on New Year's Day, 1781. His troops, unpaid, hungry, ragged and weary, marched out of camp; it took the presence of Joseph Reed, President of the Continental Congress, Wayne, a Colonel Butler and a Colonel Stewart to persuade them to return. The promise of French assistance in the form of Irish Brigade troops from France was one of the contributing factors in their reconciliation.

Before the war ended Wayne received another bullet wound; just prior to the Battle of Yorktown one of his own zealous sentries wounded him in the thigh. This wound later proved to be the cause of his death but far from the scene of the Revolutionary War. It happened fifteen years after the victory at Yorktown when, still a soldier, he was battling Indians along the Ohio River Valley. Despite the triumphant conclusion of the American War of Independence, the Indians in that outpost were still helping the British and American Loyalists and were making scrappy forays to hold the western frontier of America at the Ohio River. 'Wayne's shattering triumph there was far more momentous for the future history of the United States — and of the world of today — than all his feats during the American Revolution'[19] But in November 1796 his old leg wound opened up and he died on 15 December of that year.

When Wayne took over command of the Pennsylvania Line he also took over as a subordinate officer one Richard Butler, who was born in Dublin on 1 April 1743. Butler's father, born in Wicklow of old Ormonde stock, emigrated to America in 1748 with his family. Young Richard became an Indian trader and later a fighter so that when war came his experience in the wilderness and his knowledge about survival there fitted him well for a commission in the Continental Army. His promotion was rapid and by 1776 he was a Lieutenant-Colonel. For the way in which he and his troops nipped at the heels of General Hoe's retreating army in 1778, Wayne said he displayed 'a large share of bravery and good conduct in driving the enemy from New Jersey.'[20] During the storming of Stony Point a year later, 'Dicky' Butler, as he was called, was in the forefront of the troops.

Like his commanding officer Wayne, after the war Butler fought against the Ohio Indians. He had the misfortune to be scalped although he managed to kill the Indian by a pistol shot before his death.

There were many Butlers among the Wild Geese who fought for James II. The family was descended from the Norman Conquerors of England; originally they were called 'Le Botiler', and this was changed to Butler. No fewer than twenty-five patents of nobility were granted to this family who are so well-known in Irish history as the House of Ormonde but who enjoyed such names as Dunboyne, Cahir, Mountgarret and Galmoy. Many of the Galmoys were Colonels in the French Irish Brigade. Others served at the Boyne and at Aughrim and were the special victims of Cromwellian treachery and the restored Stuart monachy. In the long history of Ireland few families have displayed such outstanding military chivalry and courage. It is amazing to find how strong and noble was their tradition in Europe for when Lafayette commanded French troops in America he is reputed to have said, when commenting on the Butlers in the American War of Independence, that 'Whenever (he) wanted anything well done (he) got a Butler to do it.' The Butlers were quite numerous in America. General Richard Butler (Dicky) had four other brothers fighting for independence in the same army. Like the Galmoy family, they took the name Pierce Butler as a favourite name; Brigadier-General Pierce Butler, one of the brothers, fought in the war of 1812, as did two sons of General Richard. Pierce Butler's son also served in the 1812 war; he became a Major-General. Altogether twelve of the Butlers fought in that war and later many were to fight in the American Civil War. Unhappily, they did not all fight on the same side.

To leave the Revolutionary War scene without reference to Major-General John Sullivan would be a serious omission. He was one of the more controversial friends and supporters of General Washington; it was of Sullivan that the First President once wrote that he had 'a little tincture of vanity' but along with it military 'genius'.[21]

Sullivan's links with the Wild Geese were very close; his grandfather fought as a Major with Sarsfield and went to France with him. Apparently, he too was a colourful character for he became engaged in a duel with a French officer and died in France as the result of an ulcer which developed from a wound received on that occasion. It is a pity that little is known of the circumstances of the quarrel, for General John seems to have inherited a share of his grandfather's inflammable spirit. Sullivan was typical of many wandering Irishmen who ended up in America although their parents had lived in Europe for a time as well as in Ireland. The General's father, Owen Sullivan, was brought up and educated in France but, disillusioned by the French treatment of the Wild Geese, he returned to Ireland first and then decided to go to America but not as a soldier; he was appointed on 20 May 1723 as one of two teachers of a school in Dover, New Hampshire. It was while the father was filling that appointment that the future Major-General John Sullivan was born.

The young man started his career as a lawyer before the Revolution and was a highly successful one. An ardent American he joined the New Hampshire Militia and at thirty-two was promoted to Major. He devoted much of his spare time to the study of military history and tactics, and in 1774 he became a Delegate to the First Continental Congress. In studying the careers of many of the Irishmen who fought during the Revolution, there was one interest that was common to many of them : they were students of military history and tactics. Biographies of many of the French generals as well as histories of the European wars were widely read. Their popularity seems rational from one viewpoint : the descendants of the Wild Geese, coming as they did from military families, probably had had engendered in them the idea that they should, wherever possible, continue that military tradition. There is no doubt whatever that no other nation had anything like their record of military achievement in so many and so widely separated parts of the world.

In 1774, at the instigation of Paul Revere, John Sullivan organized and armed a band of followers and captured the strategic Fort William and Mary, which dominated the entrance to Portsmouth, New Hampshire, harbour. It was Sullivan's seizure of this prize that provided much of the war matériel for Bunker Hill. The real significance of his coup, however, was that it was the very first *military action* of the American Revolution. History tends to give pride of place to Lexington and Concord but, in fact, John Sullivan's capture of the New Hampshire fort preceded the other two battles by months. Whitehall was particularly angry at Sullivan's success but, so typical of remote control and bureaucratic bungling, they did not attach to it the full significance that it deserved in terms of the consequences to British sieges.

During the actual war, Sullivan, one of the first twelve Brigadier-Generals of the American Army, had the task of defending Boston; this he did admirably. As soon as the British evacuated the city, Sullivan was appointed Commander of the American expedition against Canada. His military genius was displayed in his astute withdrawal of his forces from that ill-fated expedition; he did not leave one single sick or wounded man behind nor did he leave one piece of equipment for the enemy.

Coincident with his military skill, Sullivan had other less distinguished qualities; in fact, because of his impetuous temperament he became very much a thorn in Washington's side. At one stage he was ordered to hand over his command to a senior officer; his reaction was to submit his resignation to Congress. His friend, John Hancock, dissuaded him from doing so and Washington wrote to him: 'Do not, my dear General Sullivan, torment yourself any longer with imaginary slights. . . . No other officer of rank in the whole army has so often conceived himself neglected, slighted and ill-treated as you have done, and none I am sure has had less cause than yourself to entertain such ideas.'[22] This was only one of a number of letters written to him by Washington and all suggestive of unnecessary pique on Sullivan's part.

As his fellow-Irishmen Wayne and Butler had done, Sullivan also turned his military prowess against the Indians after the war. Here again is one of the strange paradoxes common in Irish history: Sullivan and Wayne and the Butlers all fought for liberty, yet not a single one of them ever believed that the Indians — the indigenous inhabitants of America — had any rights or claims to freedom. Admittedly, history is so full of whitewash that it may be unfair to single out the cause of the American Indians, but the fact does remain that throughout the days of the Wild Geese, the concept of freedom was in a very narrow mould. Today one is forced to face the question: what is freedom? But the careers of Lally, Eyre-Coote and many others all proved that in their day freedom was determined by the side one was on. The Sullivans played an important part in American history later. General Sullivan's father wrote the crimes of the British Government against the American colonists; the general's brother, James, was once a Justice of the Massachusetts Supreme Court and twice elected Governor of that state. Later in the Civil War, like so many other Irish, they fought each other, still shouting 'Freedom!' even before they had answered the question : what is it?

While it is impossible to delineate by actual units the extent of Irish influence on the American Revolutionary War, there is no dearth of information as to individual contributions and gallantry. We have indicated how important the military contribution of Irish leaders was but it would take many volumes to tell the story of the Wild Geese descendants and straightforward Irish immigrants in every other facet of the struggle for American independence. Biographies of many of these men have been written; their stories are well known in their particular spheres of activity.

Such a one was Stephen Moylan who came from Cork, where he was born in 1737, to America via Lisbon. His mother was Anne Doran; Stephen was educated in Paris with his brother Francis who was later consecrated Bishop of Cork. Two of his half-sisters became Ursulines. Stephen, however, turned to the more mundane profession of shipping. It was as a commercial entrepreneur that he came to America in 1768 and settled in Philadelphia where the Irish influence was strong; the old song 'I'm off to Philadelphia in the morning' is still one of the more popular of Irish ballads.

Moylan was an ardent revolutionary and as well as being Washington's secretary for a time he was also the Quartermaster-General of the Army. He became a fighting soldier for a while and commanded a regiment of Light Dragoons under the Polish patriot Count Pulaski, who dedicated himself to the cause of the American Revolution. Moylan did not like the Poles; the quarrel between the Irishman and Pulaski ended up with Moylan's being court-martialled and acquitted despite a formidable effort by Pulaski to get rid of his enemy by petitioning Washington against the Irishman.

One of the more fascinating aspects of Moylan's career was his marriage to Mary Van Horn whose father was a rich merchant. He must have had real astuteness as well, because he is known to have had General Lincoln of the American Army to dinner on the same day he had Lord Cornwallis to breakfast. He lived right in the heart of the war zone.

Moylan remained one of Washington's closest friends although his military efforts did not produce anything like the results of his fellow countrymen. His personal integrity and commercial honesty were his shining qualities; he repaid Washington twenty-five cents because he had been overpaid by that amount.

What a pity history does not record how he came to be overpaid when so many senior officers of the Revolutionary army got none at all, even when they went bankrupt from maintaining their own soldiers!

1. Richard C. Murphy and Lawrence J. Mannion, *The History of The Society of the Friendly Sons of Saint Patrick in the City of New York 1784-1955*, p. 1.
2. Curtis P. Nettels, *The Roots of American Civilization*, p. 383.
3. Murphy and Mannion, *Friendly Sons of Saint Patrick*, pp. 1-2.
4. *The American Revolution*, edited by Hugh Rankin, p. 177.
5. *Papers of Sir William Johnson*, edited by James Sullivan, vol. I, p. 82; quoted by Murphy and Mannion in *Friendly Sons of Saint Patrick*, pp. 11-12.
6. Murphy and Mannion, *Friendly Sons of Saint Patrick*, p. 38.
7. *Ibid.*, pp. 38-39.
8. *Ibid.*, p. 43.
9. John Cornelius O'Callaghan in *History of the Irish Brigades in the Service of France*, p. 616.
10. North Callahan, *Henry Knox, General Washington's General*.
11. Quoted in *The Irish Sword*, vol. 5, p. 164.
12. From *Knox Papers*, quoted by North Callahan in *Henry Knox, General Washington's General*.
13. Marquis de Chastellux, *Travels in America in 1780-1782*, vol. I, pp. 132-134.
14. Continental General Henry Lee, quoted by Michael O'Brien in *A Hidden Phase of American History*.
15. Thomas A. Boyd, *Mad Anthony Wayne*.
16. W. S. Murphy in *The Irish Sword*, vol. 5, p. 168.
17. Quoted by Thomas A. Boyd in *Mad Anthony Wayne*, p. 162.
18. *Ibid.*
19. W. S. Murphy in *The Irish Sword*, vol. 5, p. 169.
20. Quoted by C. W. Chancellor in 'The Five Butler Brothers of the

Pennsylvania Line' in the *Daughters of the American Revolution Magazine*, II, 1893.

21. Quoted by W. S. Murphy in *The Irish Sword*, vol. 5, p. 172.

22. *Letters and Papers of Major-General John Sullivan, Continental Army*, vol. I, p. 328.

CHAPTER XV

Federals and Confederates

Never at Fontenoy, Albuera, or at Waterloo was more undaunted courage displayed by the sons of Erin than during those six frantic dashes which they directed against the almost impregnable position of their foe. . . . The bodies which lie in dense masses within 40 yards of the muzzles of Colonel Walton's guns are the best evidence what manner of men they were who pressed on to death with the dauntlessness of a race which has gained glory on a thousand battlefields, and never more richly deserved it than at the foot of Marye's Heights on the 13th day of December, 1862.

— The Battle of Fredericksburg as
described by the London *Times*,
January 1863

Although America had won her independence it did not mean that all conflict between England and herself had ceased. It was natural that Britain should resent bitterly the loss of her Thirteen Colonies, and as a means of retaliation she imposed a blockade of American ships entering Canada and various ports in Europe and the Mediterranean. Ultimately, this devious attitude resulted in the War of 1812 — if it could be called a war — which was fought on the sea, along the Canadian border, and in places like New Orleans. Senior Irish officers were in the forefront of the conflict in all areas. 'In the end, the military significance of the war was trifling, and neither Great Britain nor the United States improved their historical images by one jot. Nevertheless, that war provided some fascinating military encounters and unleashed some gallant personalities.'[1]

There is one interesting aspect of the War of 1812 which helps to clarify the attitude of many of the Irish in Canada. An American army with a very small force made a somewhat

abortive attempt to struggle across the wilderness and attack
Canada. The very nature of the effort doomed it to failure,
but as a result of it '. . . of 25 who were originally in the fall of
1812 chosen to be charged for bearing arms against the British,
21 were originally Irish. This group was sent to Britain but
their trials never took place.'[2]

The War of 1812, the increased immigration of soldiers
of Irish origin from France, and the immigration from Ireland
itself all helped to set the scene for the conflict of the American
Civil War. Historians maintain that more books have been
written about this war — the bitterest in American memory —
than any other in the history of the world. It is probably true.
Consequently, the fortunes and exploits of the Wild Geese can
only be traced in broad outline. One basic concept must be
held in mind : Irish history in particular tends to disregard
the many thousands of Irishmen who fought with the Army
of the Southern Confederacy.

In order to get a clear picture of the circumstances which
created the different loyalties, a number of images must be
brought into focus. Despite the efforts of the early settlers in
America to encourage the Irish to push West and settle on the
land, most of the immigrants gravitated towards the large
towns and particularly towards the Catholic cities of Boston,
New York and Philadelphia. It is one of the baffling realities
of Irish immigration that even though the most menial labour
awaited the Irish in these cities, they preferred it to the uncer-
tainty of the land. From a sociological viewpoint this apparent
paradox is not explained easily. The Irish had at all times
been renowned as an adventurous people, yet in many parts
of America their pioneer spirit seemed to be lacking. Possibly
their treatment at home — the fact that they were driven from
the land — caused them to distrust it; hence, their preference
for the tangible security of the city where Catholicism and
what were in essence Irish ghettos provided them with a feeling of stability.

The large increase of Irish Catholics in the cities was deeply
resented by those who might be called the 'Brahmins of the
eastern seaboard.' Their indignation found practical expression
in the creation of a party called the Know-Nothing Party. 'A
veritable flock of secret societies, all bitterly anti-Irish-Catholic'[3]

were formed and, unhappily, were inflicting serious embarrassment, both socially and economically, on the Irish. To add to all these complications the Irish themselves were not united. Most of them did belong to the Democratic Party but there were others who placed themselves in a category superior to their fellow countrymen. These, for the most part, were Republicans. However, so bitter became the attacks upon the Irish Catholics that the editor of the *Irish-American,* Patrick Lynch, wrote in 1854 in the *New York Times* :

> Fellow countrymen . . . You have at present opposed to you a bitter, inimical and powerful secret society called the Know-Nothings; opposed to you, to us Irish particularly, on the grounds that we are impudent and voracious cormorants of petty places under government; that we are ignorant, turbulent and brutal; that we are led by the nose and entirely controlled by our clergy; that we are willing subjects of a foreign prince, the Pope; that we are only lip-republicans; that we are not worthy of the franchise; that by the largeness of our vote and the clannishness of our habits and dispositions we rule or aspire to rule in America; that we heap taxes on industrious and sober and thrifty citizens; and that for these and other reasons we should be deposed from our citizenship, and in fact rooted out of this American nation as a body by every fair and foul means.[4]

In the southern states the picture was entirely different. The Spaniards had at one time occupied New Orleans and Savannah, and their military leaders in these cities included many Irishmen from the three Spanish Irish regiments and from some of the other Irish regiments of Europe. Previously we learned that many Irishmen who served in the American War of Independence gravitated towards the south where there was an abundance of land and where many of the old Irish clans were to be found.

There were many Irishmen also in America who managed to remain neutral throughout the Civil War. It is interesting to note that in the city of New York a number of Irish family businesses remained strictly neutral. Another unusual aspect of the Civil War was that many Irish soldiers were already in the Far West and were joined after the Civil War by many more. Mention has already been made of Captain (Brevet Lieutenant-Colonel) Myles Walter Keogh who fought with the Irish in the Battalion of St Patrick at Spoleto, with the Union Army at Gettysburg and in the raid on Atlanta, and whose career as a soldier came to an end in the Sioux massacre at the Little Big Horn. There were others like him who drifted from Europe to the United States to offer their swords to the warring sides.

On 20 September 1860, when the state of South Carolina passed by a unanimous vote its historic ordinance of secession, politicians on both sides had already laid plans carefully for recruiting these Irishmen. It is on record that when the fateful attack on Fort Sumter took place on 12 April, there were Irishmen actually in the fort.

John Thompson from Coleraine was a private in Company E of the 1st United States Artillery. He describes the opening of the American Civil War:

On the afternoon of the 11th (April, 1861) about 4 o'clock, three officers from the rebel army made their appearance under a flag of truce, and formally summoned our gallant Major to surrender. This of course he refused to do. About 1 o'clock on the morning of the 12th another messenger notified us that General Beauregard, the rebel commander, would open fire on us immediately. This message found our little garrison, only 71, enjoying their usual repose, but they had taken the precaution of moving their blankets under the bombproofs in anticipation of a bloody melee before morning. The word was quietly circulated through the men that it was time to be up and get ready. At 3 o'clock we hoisted our colours the glorious 'Star Spangled Banner' and quietly awaited the enemies fire. Long before daylight, at $4\frac{1}{2}$ a.m. the first shell came hissing through the air and burst right over our heads.[5]

It must be remembered that in the twenty years preceding the Civil War over 2,000,000 Irishmen had left their homeland for America. It was natural that since the majority had congregated in the cities in the north, when the war began to accelerate far more Irish joined the Union Army than the Southern Confederates. This does not mean that the southern cause lacked sympathy among the many Irish leaders in cities such as New York and Boston; for one thing, a large number of southern leaders had attacked the Know-Nothing Party.

After the attack on Fort Sumter President Lincoln called for volunteers. The Irish response is best illustrated by the official figures of the Union Army : over 144,000 of its muster roll were either Irish or of Irish descent. As part of Lincoln's recruiting campaign came the reappointment of Colonel Michael Corcoran to the command of the famous 'Fighting 69th' Regiment of New York. (During the visit of the Prince of Wales to New York in October 1860, it was Corcoran who had refused to parade his troops.)

It was around the 'Fighting 69th' Regiment that the famous Meagher's Irish Brigade was formed in New York. Placards appeared in practically every street corner headed 'Corcoran's Irish Legion'. They promised $100 from the U.S., $50 from the city, $50 from the state, $13 one month's pay in advance. In rather small print they said : 'Irishmen, you are now training to meet your English enemies,' while in large letters on the posters there appeared : 'Remember Fontenoy!' The logic which inspired this appeal must be a source of considerable amusement for many, especially when one considers that it was the Mansfield Judgement in England which had abolished slavery. Corcoran was captured at Bull Run.

The Irish Brigade drew men from all walks of life and from every part of the world; Hungarians, Russians, anyone who had Irish ancestry rallied to the cause. Paul Jones in his story entitled *The Irish Brigade* writes : 'There were veterans, too, of the British army in India, mingled with schoolboys and family men from the five boroughs. There were men who had served at Balaclava and Inkermann, and men who hastened to the colors from the Irish Brigade that fought for the Pope in '60 and '61 at Spoleto and Ancona. The chaplains came from nearby Fordham and far-off Notre Dame, and the whole was bound together by an ardent desire to vindicate Ireland's ancient reputation for valor and loyalty.'[6]

By New Year's Day 1862, the New York Irish Brigade consisting of the 69th, 88th and 63rd New York Volunteers was at its zenith. On their regimental banners were an Irish harp and a wreath of shamrocks embroidered in gold on a field of rich emerald silk. The leader of the Brigade, Meagher of the Sword, was one of the most colourful Irish warriors of all time. He had been a leader of the Irish revolutionary movement in 1848; he was arrested after the abortive Rising and transported to Tasmania from which he escaped to America in 1852. Later he became one of the most brilliant orators in New York. It has been said of Meagher that he was probably the finest type of Irishman who ever emigrated to America, yet he was as much denounced by his own people in the years before the Civil War as he had been by the British before leaving Ireland. He was called anti-papal and anti-clerical, yet his courage, though somewhat flamboyant, was unquestionable.

The New York Irish Brigade was not the only Irish unit in the Civil War. The Western Irish Brigade was formed in 1861 and consisted of Irishmen of the early militia units in Chicago. These included the Montgomery Guards, the Emmet Guards, the Jackson Guards, and the Shields Guards. These came under the command of Colonel James A. Mulligan and paraded formally as a separate unit on 15 June 1861. Their first headquarters were known as 'Fontenoy Barracks', and they became a part of the 23rd Illinois Infantry.

In July of 1861, this Brigade was moved to Jefferson City, Missouri; the Commander of the Union troops in that area was a Colonel Jeff C. Davis but he was no relation of his namesake on the confederate side. By this time the unit was one of the best-equipped in the whole army and had amongst its 1,135 infantry some veterans of the European wars and the Mexican Wars. The adjutant was a Lieutenant James F. Cosgrove, who had served with the British Wiltshire Regiment in the Crimean War and wore the Sebastopol Medal. Many other officers and men wore medals of foreign service — a custom encouraged for its advantageous psychological effect on the younger recruits.

In August of that year, the new brigade was sent to Lexington, situated on the southern bank of the Missouri River, where Colonel Mulligan the Commander set up headquarters at the Masonic College.

All the activity and machinery for recruiting were not on the Union side. The Confederate Army was also doing its best to harness Irish manpower. Major-General Patrick Ronayne Cleburne was the senior ranking Irish officer in the Provisional Army of the Confederate States. He had been born in County Cork, where his family dated back to 1086, and had left for America in 1849 when he was 21. His pioneering spirit took him all the way to Arkansas. At the outbreak of the Civil War, he joined the Confederate service as a private and by 1862 was a Major-General. The study of military strategy was also his main hobby. His rise to fame verged on the meteoric principally because of his plan to capture the Union arsenal in Arkansas in March 1861. After many successful engagements he was killed at the Battle of Franklin in 1864. Cleburne became known as 'Stonewall of the West'; the American historian Fiske describes him as 'one of the ablest and boldest officers in the Confederate service.'[7]

There were four other famous generals on the Confederate side : Brigadier-Generals Finegan of Florida, Hagan of Alabama, Lane of Texas, and Moore of Virginia. As J. L. Garland points out in his article 'Irish Soldiers of the American Confederacy' : 'The tragedy of internecine warfare was emphasized by the case of the two Gwynn brothers, born in Ireland. Hugh was Major of the 23rd Tennessee Infantry, while James, from Pennsylvania, was Brevet Major-General in the United States Volunteers.'[8]

Of the actual Irish regiments in the Confederate Army one of the most famous was the Louisiana Tigers. This unit which had a bright zouave uniform was officially known as the 1st Louisiana Special Battalion and was raised by Major Roberdeau [sic] Chatham 'Bob' Wheat in New Orleans. At the beginning of the war, there were 24,398 Irish-born in the French-American city, as well as many descendants of the Wild Geese who had come from Spain, France, Poland and Austria. Originally, those actually born in Ireland were suspect in the South because of the predominant Irish element in the Union Army. There were, however, many instances of Irishmen changing their names in order to join the Confederate forces. This also accounted for the fact that although there were many Irish units in the southern army they were special companies rather than independent units and were attached to larger formations for security purposes. Altogether there were some 200,000 Irish-born in the southern states; apparently, there was little difficulty in filling the existent Irish units.

One southern unit is of particular interest. 'Meagher of the Sword' had toured throughout America forming Irish clubs and Irish military units. One of the latter was the 'Meagher Guards of Charleston, South Carolina.' When the war broke out and Meagher declared for the north, the unit he had formed in the south became known as the Emerald Light Infantry.

One other well-known southern unit was the Louisiana Irish Regiment commanded by a Colonel O'Brien. It had eight companies with such names as the O'Brien Light Infantry, the Loughlin Light Guards, and the Moore Guards.

As far west as Texas the Rio Grande Regiment had a majority of Irishmen in it; there was also a unit called Terry's Texas Rangers.

On both sides many volunteer militia units had been formed prior to the war. The men from these came mostly from fire brigade units which consisted mainly of Irishmen.

Encompassed within the sickening tragedy of the Civil War itself was a particular desperate poignancy for the Irish: on both sides green banners carrying the insignia of the harp and the shamrock and the slogans 'Erin-go-Bragh' and 'Faugh-a-Ballagh' were bespattered with Irish blood. The air of battle was often drowned with the shouts of Irish voices and the same Irish songs were sung on both sides.

One of the fiercest battles of the whole war was that of Fredericksburg; it was also the one which spawned the most bitter fighting between opposing Irish units. Meagher of the Sword with his Irish Brigade on that day wrote themselves forever into the annals of Irish courage and daring. In that panorama of human destruction General Robert E. Lee and his staff watched an Irish brigade advance to its slaughter in the face of his own merciless artillery. It was on that occasion that Lee is reputed to have said: 'It is well that war is so frightful. Otherwise, we should become too fond of it.'[9]

We have no record or description of the actual fighting soldiers on the southern side in the Battle of Fredericksburg, but it is known that some of Meagher's old brigade, as well as the many Irish from Virginia, took part in the grim struggle. There was, however, one incident which illustrates the kind of sentiment which existed in the opposing armies. Following the battle there ensued heavy firing from the rebel side and it happened that a man wearing the Confederate uniform staggered to the pickets of the Union Army. His voice identified him as an Irishman and he requested to be brought before General Meagher for a private interview. He was Michael Sullivan from McMillan's regiment of the Georgia Brigade. On the opposing side from Meagher's troops, he had watched as they stormed Marye's Heights during battle and had seen a colour-bearer shot and the colour fall in the mud. That night he had crawled out from his own unit, collected the Irish colour, and determined to return the flag to the Irish regiment. After delivering it into the hands of the General, he asked to be allowed to return to his own unit. Meagher responded : 'You have earned the good will and esteem of the Brigade. You are welcome to stay with us, if you wish.'[10]

Sullivan saluted, stated that it was impossible, and promptly fell to the ground from loss of blood from the wound he had received while escaping from his own lines. Meagher communicated with the soldier's commander and while there is no record of the ultimate fate of Sullivan it is known that he returned to his regiment.

But admidst all the battling and the erstwhile glory, a tragic fate had befallen many of the Irish in New York City. The ravages of war demanded fresh blood for the Union Army; the need resulted in a Draft Law which stated that the names of those eligible for military duty would be drawn from a hat. The unlucky ones were compelled to do military service unless they could afford to pay $300 which bought deferment for a year. Or, if those who could afford it would pay for other men to take their place at an agreed price, they were spared military service.

The Irish in New York recoiled from this kind of military chicanery, but they did listen to politicians who filled their ears full of propaganda about risking their lives to save Negroes who would, in turn, take their jobs. Bruce Catton, probably the most authoritative Civil War historian, wrote : 'True understanding did not come easily. Respectability was appalled by the Irish precisely as the Irish were appalled by the freed Negro.'[11]

It followed that this social climate created an undercurrent of antagonism amongst the Irish in New York which simmered and then boiled over in acts of anger that were without glory and even elementary justice. They rioted and rampaged through the streets of New York. Catton said : 'The draft riots were based upon ignorance, misery, fear and the inability of one class of men to understand another class; upon the fact that there really were "classes of men" in classless American society.'[12]

The New York riots were a disgrace to humanity. Negroes were chased through the streets of the city, caught, beaten and lynched. Attempts by policemen to stop these appalling murders resulted only in death for police and civilians. George Templeton Strong wrote : 'The mobs were made up of the lowest Irish day labourers; they were homogeneous, every brute in the drove was pure Celtic hod-carrier or loafer.'[13]

In an attempt to control the terror and fear sweeping through the city, Archbishop John J. Hughes addressed a crowd of 5,000 Irishmen and said : 'Keep out of the crowd where immortal souls are launched into eternity . . . Ireland has been the mother of heroes and poets but never the mother of cowards.'[14]

So effective was this appeal by the Archbishop that the riots ceased. It did not, however, dispel either the fear or the disenchantment with the whole war. In the latter days of the struggle even the glory of Meagher failed to arouse the martial enthusiasm that had always been associated with the Irish soldiers. After such an illustrious career, Meagher had a dismal demise : in 1867 while acting governor of the new Montana Territory, he was drowned accidentally in the waters of the upper Missouri. His body was never recovered.

Many relics of his gallant service still remain. Two swords are preserved by the Waterford Corporation on one of which is inscribed : 'Presented to Thomas Francis O'Meagher by the Members of the Napper Tandy Light Artillery, as a small token of their high admiration of his sterling devotion to the cause of Ireland and Liberty.'[15]

On the other side of the Atlantic in Notre Dame University

is a dark green silk flag about five feet square bearing the inscription : 'Presented by Citizens of New York to the 63rd New York Volunteers (3rd Regiment of the Irish Brigade), Brigadier General Thomas Francis Meagher Commanding. In grateful appreciation of their gallant and brilliant conduct in the Battle Fields of Virginia and Maryland in the War to maintain the National Domain and the American Union. November 1862.'

In 1914, many years after the ceremony and pomp that coloured these relics, the then President of Notre Dame University, the Rev Charles L. O'Donnell, wrote a special poem entitled : 'A Hosting of the Gael.' Two stanzas of it depict the role of Ireland in the American Civil War more vividly than any other literary effort devoted to that subject :

> *We are the men and these our brothers*
> *Who held the heights and threw us back;*
> *Over them, too, these thousand others,*
> *A green flag waved through the war cloud black.*
> *And Fredericksburg is an open story,*
> *It was Irish blood both sides outpoured,*
> *For they too, followed honor and glory,*
> *A green flag theirs, but not our sword.*
> *And we are come from the peace of slumber,*
> *Nor North, nor South, by division sharp,*
> *But Irish all, of that world-wide number*
> *In all times mighty with sword and harp.*
> *To lift once more, from the dust, our voices,*
> *In one last cheer that may echo far —*
> *Fredericksburg in the grave rejoices,*
> *Now the Flag of Green weds the Sword of Meagher.*[16]

1. W. S. Murphy, *The Irish Sword*, vol. 6, p. 1.
2. Reginald Horsman, *The War of 1812*, p. 123.
3. Richard C. Murphy and Lawrence J. Mannion in *The History of The Society of the Friendly Sons of Saint Patrick in the City of New York 1784-1955*, p. 284.
4. *New York Times*, 30 August 1854.
5. Quoted by Brian Hutton in *The Irish Sword*, vol. 5, p. 181.

6. Page 103.
7. Fiske, *The Mississippi Valley in the Civil War*, p. 335.
8. *The Irish Sword*, vol. 1, pp. 174-175.
9. Quoted by Paul Jones in *The Irish Brigade*, p. 156.
10. *Ibid.*, p. 162.
11. *The Centennial History of the Civil War*, vol. 3, p. 216.
12. *Ibid.*, p. 214.
13. *Diary of the Civil War, 1860-1865*, quoted in *Harper's Weekly*, July 1863.
14. Bruce Catton, *The Centennial History of the Civil War*, vol. 3, p. 216.
15. *The Irish Sword*, vol. 1, p. 90.
16. *Ibid.*, pp. 92-93.

CHAPTER XVI

Bernardo O'Higgins

By the middle of the eighteenth century, not a few Irishmen had seized the opportunities which Spain offered them with spectacular success. In the 'fifties the post of Secretary of State for Foreign Affairs was held by Richard Wall, an Irishman who had served his adopted country for many years in the Navy, the Army, and the diplomatic service. A decade later it was an Irish officer, General Alexander O'Reilly, who commanded the loyal troops and suppressed the riots in a rebellious capital. Other Irishmen made their fortunes in commerce and established thriving businesses in Cadiz, engaging in the lucrative South American trade and sending their own representatives to the cities of Peru, Chile, La Plata, Venezuela, Mexico and all parts of Spain's extensive empire.

— Stephen Clissold, *Bernardo O'Higgins and the Independence of Chile*

The contribution of the Wild Geese and their kinsmen to the development of the United States, although turbulent at times, cannot be questioned. In the southern part of the American continent their accomplishments were just as solid and lasting, although devoid of the spectacular and oft-vaunted glory.

Spain and Portugal were both the exploiters and developers of Latin America, as well as the territory then called the Kingdom of New Spain. The latter at that time comprised Mexico, New Mexico, Southern California, parts of Colorado and Texas. Mexico City was also included. In fact, one of the most accurate histories of the kingdom was written by an Irishman, Pedro Alonso O'Crouley, in 1774.

Both Spain and Portugal could be said to be havens for the Wild Geese after the Two Flights. Undoubtedly, both countries were more receptive and more generous to the Wild

Geese than many of the other lands which were concerned only with their military prowess.

Even before the days of the Flight of the Earls and after the Treaty of 1691, Spain took special pains to provide schools and universities for the education of the sons of Irish immigrants. As far back as 1614, 2,000 crowns were paid by Spain annually for the education of Irish students at Douai in France. Similar action was taken by the Spanish government to provide for students at Louvain and Antwerp; in fact, Salamanca University had a special Irish college for the sons of the Wild Geese. The extent of the educational facilities and cutural generosity offered by Spain can be appreciated from a letter written in 1592 by Philip III :

To the Rector, Master of the Schools and Cloister of the University of Salamanca.

As the Irish people who have been living a kind of community in this city have resolved to avail themselves of the opportunities it affords for advancement in letters and languages, a house being prepared for them, in which they intend to live under the direction of the Fathers of the Society of Jesus, besides allowing them this letter to charge you, as I do, to regard them as highly recommended, so as not to allow them to be maltreated in any way but to favour and aid them as far as you can : that as they have left their own country and all they possessed in it, in the service of God our Lord, and for the preservation of the Catholic Faith, and make profession of returning to preach and suffer martyrdom in it, if necessary, they may get in that University the reception they are hoping for.

I am certain you will do this and become benefactor to them, so that with your subscription and with what I am sure the town will give — to the authorities of which I also write — they may be able to pursue their studies with content and freedom, and thereby attain the end they have in view.

Vallavoid, 2nd August, 1592.

YO EL REY (I, the King)[1]

Time, place and circumstance have changed the names of
the descendants of the many thousands of Irishmen who became an integral part of Spain and her colonies. As Seán Galvin
wrote in his introduction to the *Idea compendiosa del Reyno de
Nueva España* : 'Yet of all the European countries it was in
Spain that they achieved the most recognition. Not only did
they find themselves Catholics in a Catholic country; their
situation stemmed from the very correct belief that Ireland had
been settled by people of Iberian culture about 3,000 years
before Christ. Thus the "Wild Geese", as they were called,
settled themselves in Spain as Spaniards and were treated as
such.'[2]

It is impossible to trace most of the descendants of the Wild
Geese, particularly in the Spanish dominions, just as it is virtually impossible to trace those Spaniards at home now who
have considerable Irish blood in their veins. There are, of
course, some whose achievements have made them so outstanding that their names have survived. Pedro Alonso O'-
Crouley O'Donnell was such a one; his father and mother came
from Limerick and County Clare respectively, and had their
son educated at the expense of the Spanish government.
Alonso O'Crouley married a girl named Mariá Power. His
Description of the Kingdom of New Spain is one of the major
contributions to Spanish literature.

The most illustrious name in the history of the Spanish
dominions, however, was the O'Higgins family with all the
colour and glamour that are associated so frequently with
roving Irishmen. Stephen Clissold wrote of Bernardo O'Higgins : 'To him, more than to any other man, Chile owes her
independence. Nor is the debt Chile's alone. O'Higgins played
his part on the wider American stage, for he also bore arms
in the Argentine ranks and devoted himself, and the resources
of his country, to the emancipation of Peru.'[3]

According to himself Ambrosio O'Higgins was born in Ballinary, County Sligo, in 1720 and was a direct descendant of
a Baron of Ballinary. Irish records do not substantiate this
claim; more objective researchers believe he was born in County
Meath although his parents did originate in Sligo. O'Higgins
joined the British army which he left in 1751. It was easy
at that time to leave the British Continental Army and find
refuge in Spain; at any rate towards the end of 1751 O'Higgins

was working in a bank in Cadiz as a clerk. He remained at this post until 1756 when, either on a business visit for clients of the bank or to visit his brother who was in some kind of trouble, he went to South America. While there he spent over four years roaming in Buenos Aires, Chile and Peru before returning to Spain.

Almost immediately upon his return he applied to the Spanish Council of the Indies for permission to go to the Spanish territories in South America; his visit had shown the vast possibilities for a lucrative career in those territories. Also, being something of a rebel, he found that Spanish rule at home was becoming politically too restrictive for a man imbued with exalted ideas of liberty.

Through the good offices of a fellow countryman named Garland who had served in the Hibernia Regiment, Ambrosio O'Higgins secured a job as a draughtsman in Chile. He accepted the appointment merely for basic security but was determined to make a business career for himself, believing that his banking experience would benefit him considerably. Consequently, when he left Cadiz in 1763 he took with him to Chile a large consignment of merchandise which was only partially paid for. When he left Cadiz he formed a business partnership with John Power who was probably related to O'Crouley's wife. Power turned out to be something of a rascal with the result that the unhappy O'Higgins had to bear a burden of debt for many years. Although O'Higgins was supposed to join Garland in Chile, the latter stayed on in Buenos Aires where he fell in love with a young lady. In those days royal permission to marry in the colonies had to be sought but before it arrived Garland abandoned his romantic notions, left his fiancée, and joined O'Higgins.

Chile at this time was considered one of the most backward and neglected territories of Spain. It was ruled over by a Captain-General. The officials who occupied this post found it impossible to keep the Indians in subjection with the result that various fortifications had to be erected throughout the territory. Garland and O'Higgins were given the task of drawing up plans for a chain of forts around the Bay of Corral in order to prevent any invasion and at the same time to keep the Indians at bay.

Unobtrusively, O'Higgins began to make an impression on those about him and to his surprise he was commissioned a Captain of Dragoons and ordered to raise a body of cavalry that could withstand the fierce Araucanian horsemen. Instead of drawing his troops from Spanish or foreign settlers, O'Higgins formed a mounted force of Chilean herdsmen. His personality was such that he earned their loyalty from the beginning and his success with them can best be judged from the following quotation : 'So judicious and rapid were his movements that he succeeded in surprising and attacking separately all the scattered troops of Araucanians either killing or capturing them. These successes gave another aspect to war. The Spanish troops could leave their forts and sally out into the open.'⁴

Soon it became obvious that despite his previous dissatisfaction with a military career and his experience as a bank clerk, soldiering was to be the life for the Irishman.

O'Higgins had an extraordinary insight into the problems of Spanish South America but at the same time he knew full well that the financial potential of the territories was enormous. One of his major objectives during his early years in Chile was the building of communications which would link Chile with Mendoza and Buenos Aires. For many months of the year snow prevented any form of communication. O'Higgins, by his untiring efforts and the construction of special shelters, established in 1766 a postal service to be maintained across the mountain passes and to set up proper communications. He did not believe in doing 'something for nothing' so he appealed to the home government for a special reward and asked to be returned to Spain to discuss the matter. He succeeded in returning to his adopted home, Cadiz, where his salary was increased. This was accompanied by a request to write a special report on Chile.

On his return to Chile he started to look towards Peru and determined to set up communications with Lima which in those days was known as the City of the Kings. Peru at the time was also under the Spanish Crown and O'Higgins saw for himself an opportunity for further advancement, especially since Tupac Amaru's rebellion was at its height. Also he had ideas for the settlement of large areas with Irish immigrants;

he was not able to implement this notion because the American War of Independence broke out and the Irish found North America more accessible than Latin America.

By this time O'Higgins was the favourite of the Viceroy of Peru and was promoted to the rank of Lieutenant-Colonel. In appearance he was not very prepossessing; his stature and sturdy build and high complexion had brought on the nickname of 'el camarón' — the shrimp. Nevertheless, in 1777 in middle age, romance entered his life in the person of Isabel Riquelme who was the daughter of a respectable Creole landowner who had an estate near Los Angeles. Isabel's mother had died shortly after her daughter was born and the girl had been brought up by her father, Don Simón. Very little is known of the romance except that O'Higgins was nearly forty years her senior. The circumstances surrounding their liaison are unknown but on 20 August 1778 Bernardo O'Higgins was born. There is no record whatever of the boy's parents ever marrying.

In July of 1788 Ambrosio O'Higgins was made Governor of Chile. On his way to the capital at Santiago he visited his son who, for the first and last time, saw his own father. How long the child's parents remained lovers is a matter for pure speculation.

Young Bernardo was educated by the Jesuits in Peru in a school specially founded for sons of high Spanish officials. 'After four years in Lima, he was removed from school by Don Ignacio Blake, another Irish friend and an old business associate of O'Higgins, and put on board a ship for Spain. Thence he had instructions to proceed to England, where he was to complete his education. He must have arrived in London at the age of sixteen or seventeen, sometime in 1794 or 1795 — the year in which a royal decree elevated his father to the supreme office of Viceroy of Peru.'[5]

Little is known of the circumstances surrounding his education in England; there is considerable mystery shrouding the whole experience. That Bernardo was christened O'Higgins, there is no doubt whatever, as a record of his baptism on 20 January 1783 is to be found in Chile. Yet, when in England he signed his letters to his father in his mother's name, Bernardo Riquelme. Apparently, during his years in England young

Bernardo developed a strong love for his native Chile and a definite hatred against Spain by whom the Chileans were subjugated through the medium of his own father. At this time he was in receipt of three hundred pounds a year. Bernardo's political life was probably formulated at this time by a friend named Francisco Miranda. The latter was a native of Venezuela and believed that the whole of Latin America should be freed from Spain; he looked upon Bernardo as a means of serving his own ends.

All this time Ambrosio was so involved with the affairs of his own exalted office that he had little time for his son and certainly had little idea of the plotting that was going on in England. However, it was not long before Miranda's plot was discovered. Obviously, England was using Miranda and his Latin American followers as a means of hitting at the Spanish, so that when the Spanish authorities gained possession ultimately of all the documents relating to the intrigue, one of the first names on it was that of Bernardo Riquelme whom His Catholic Majesty in Spain recognized as the natural son of his Peruvian viceroy. Bernardo returned to Spain in 1799 and despite all efforts to contact his father for assistance, he received no help, although at one stage he was practically starving. Even his guardian, Don Nicolás de la Cruz, had little sympathy for his ward.

In 1801 Ambrosio O'Higgins died, still endeavouring, apparently, to preserve a secret about his illegitimate son that was already known to most people. He made a will in favour of Bernardo who promptly returned to Lima, took possession of his inheritance and set about the political intrigue that was ultimately to make Chile free.

As a result of his father's inheritance, Bernardo became a well-to-do landowner, but this did not save him from the suspicion and dislike of the Governor who was well aware of his previous participation in the English plot.

A crisis in the affairs of Chile arose about this time. The Governor was ousted, and a junta composed of Chileans which included O'Higgins took over the government of the country on 18 September 1810. The day is generally accepted as the beginning of Chilean independence.

At this stage of his career Bernardo realized that military

might was going to be necessary to withstand coming Spanish onslaughts. Consequently, Bernardo took it as his personal responsibility to arm the Creoles and to prepare them for war.

This decision caused a new problem for O'Higgins for his own knowledge of military matters was limited to some slight training in a cadet unit in England. His thoughts, therefore, turned to Juan Mackenna who had fought under his father and who, because he was Irish, was totally trusted by Bernardo. Mackenna had a considerable reputation as a soldier. Bernardo wrote to the Irishman asking him to join him, since he knew that his own hatred of and obsession with the injustice of Spanish rule were equalled by those of the Irishman.

Typical of human behaviour throughout history, there were within the country malcontents who were jealous of the junta. In this instance they were two brothers, José and Luis Carrera, who were the chief political agitators throughout the whole of O'Higgins' career. José Carrera was responsible for splitting the patriotic party in two and succeeded in taking over the government of Chile. This did not prevent O'Higgins from doing everything possible to effect a reconciliation among the patriotic factions, knowing full well that the time was not far distant when the might of Spain would be hurled against them. This is exactly what did happen for the Spaniards had a strong foothold in nearby Peru. One of the results of the Spanish attack was that O'Higgins had to seek asylum in the Argentine and later in Peru.

Much has been written of O'Higgins' feats as a soldier; he became as able and courageous a leader as his father had been. He made good use of his time in the Argentine and in Peru and built up a force to reconquer his native Chile.

At Chacabuco with the assistance and advice of Mackenna, O'Higgins defeated the Spaniards and once more regained his country's freedom. This was in 1816; O'Higgins' army became known as the Army of the Andes. It was comprised of Argentinian and Peruvian patriots as well as Chileans and finally succeeded in restoring Chile to independent status.

On 15 February 1817, O'Higgins was appointed the Director Supremo of Chile but not before his old enemies, the Carreras, started a subversive campaign once more. In our day O'Higgins would have been described as an ardent social-

G

ist; he was the deadly enemy of the aristocrats and one of his first acts of legislation was to have all armorial markings on all houses in Chile removed. His personal history and illegitimacy as described by the church were permanent irritants also with the result that during his rule he showed little consideration for the Catholic Church's more power-drunk personalities.

Having established himself as the recognized and beloved leader of Chile, O'Higgins' obsession with the injustice of Spanish rule in other parts of Latin America caused him to turn his attention to freeing Peru. In that country there were already many patriots who were sympathetic to his ideas towards their Spanish overlords. His task was made easier by the fall of the Carreras which he brought about in 1817. José Miguel Carrera faced a firing squad in that year.

When O'Higgins arrived at the decision to invade Peru he made contact with his various friends there and in the Argentine. He was fully aware that, in order to achieve any success, he would need a navy and so, at the beginning of 1818, he sent an envoy to England with a view to enlisting the services of Lord Cochrane whose reputation as a sailor was world-renowned. Promised a large sum of money, Cochrane agreed to join him. The former's enthusiasm for the task was encouraged by the fact that about this time the British government made a loan of one million pounds to Chile and the British Admiral had no qualms about acquiring some of it.

O'Higgins set about building up an expeditionary force as well, to work in conjunction with the navy. To do this he enlisted the services of a soldier named O'Brien to whom he gave specific instructions to enlist Irishmen whenever he could.

Cochrane proved a success; he started the nucleus of the Chilean navy while O'Higgins mustered a force of nearly 8,000 men. The army still retained the title of the Army of the Andes. He was counting considerably on support from the Argentine, but because of diplomatic intrigue many of the Argentinian troops were withdrawn — the first serious blow to O'Higgins' plans.

In 1820 the Chilean fleet sailed from Valparaiso after surmounting problems too many to enumerate. O'Higgins himself supervised the revictualling of the ships — a fact which caused considerable irritation to Cochrane who believed that his personal authority was threatened. The English admiral decided to resign but O'Higgins knew when to give way, with the result that a plan for a combined operation formulated by Cochrane ended up with the capture of Valdivia.

Despite this success, the leader of the Argentinian group, San Martín, withdrew his support although many Argentinian officers still remained with the Army of the Andes.

The vicissitudes of the Peruvian campaign were aggravated further by intrigue within Peru itself. Notwithstanding the most heroic sacrifices of O'Higgins, his ambition to free that country came to nothing, and as a result his popularity with his own people diminished. The Royalists in Chile seized this opportunity to discredit O'Higgins so that in 1823 he left his country and went into voluntary exile. His venue of exile was, strangely enough, Peru but his real ambition was, expressed in his own words, '(I am) desirous of proceeding to Ireland to reside there sometime in the bosom of my family.'[6]

He never reached Ireland, for the internal strife in Chile that resulted from his departure as well as the intrigue within the country itself caused him to return home to act as advisor. As he himself rationalized it, he had sacrificed his youth, his health, and his fortune for the independence of Chile; therefore, in her hour of need he could not abandon her.

His years of peace and quiet were few for just at the time when he should have enjoyed a retirement from political strife he watched the bitter struggle which Simon Bolívar was making to free Peru. On 9 July 1824, accompanied by a fellow Irishman, John Thomas, O'Higgins set out to join Bolívar's army. He met and talked with the famed Liberator; both believed the struggle was hopeless but due to the brilliance of a General Sucre, unexpected victory was attained.

Shortly after his return from exile fighting broke out between Chile and Peru, and O'Higgins had to watch the bloodshed between two armies which he had done so much during his life to weld as one. For a while he turned his thoughts away from the military scene and once peace had been restored to his own country he had brilliant notions of settling parts of Chile with large numbers of Irishmen. He sought the aid of an Englishman and an Irishman — Sir Thomas Hardy and Sir John Doyle, respectively — to accomplish this. He visualized a Latin American federation controlled by England and Chile, a country in which there would be truth and justice and religious morality. Unhappily, he did not live to see the fulfilment of many of his dreams; the only vision that did become a reality was the independence of Chile. If he did not see Peru and the Argentine and various other Latin American countries independent, it was not for lack of inspiration. Undoubtedly, his noble leadership pointed the way for many of them to achieve their freedom.

1. Elliot O'Donnell, *The Irish Abroad,* p. 251.
2. Seán Galvin (editor) in the Introduction to *The Kingdom of New Spain,* p. vii.
3. Stephen Clissold, *Bernardo O'Higgins and the Independence of Chile,* p. 9.
4. Juan Mackenna in a Letter to Bernardo O'Higgins dated 20 February 1811, *Archivo O'Higgins,* vol. I, pp. 90-92.
5. Stephen Clissold, *Bernardo O'Higgins,* pp. 53-54.
6. *Ibid.,* p. 219.

CHAPTER XVII
Down Mexico Way

'*I cannot but highly esteem those gentlemen of Ireland who, with all the disadvantages of being exiles and strangers, have been able to distinguish themselves by their valour and conduct in so many parts of Europe, I think, above all other nations.*'

— Dean Swift, *The Works of Jonathan Swift*

The history of Mexico also felt the impact of the Wild Geese although their activities in that land are still shrouded in controversy awaiting the extensive research of historians.

The first major influx of Irish into Mexico started on 18 June 1768 when the second battalion of the Ultonia Regiment arrived in Vera Cruz from Cadiz. From there, accompanied by two other Spanish battalions, they marched to Mexico City in order to replace a demoralized regiment which was on garrison duty there. Apparently, Mexico City was one of those stations which had a very bad effect on the troops; drink and women were easily obtainable and as always these were the fomenters of perpetual quarreling. A viceroy in Mexico City in 1771 described the populace as '. . . composed of diverse races, is vicious, drunken, debauched, thieving.'[1] The people carried knives called Belduques and whenever possible used them on the occupying troops at night. As many as thirty troops in a month were knived and when the soldiers tried to defend themselves, the inhabitants threw stones at them.

As far as can be ascertained the Irish remained in Mexico City for three years during which time one of the principal officers was a Colonel Marcos Keating, who was born in Ireland in 1730. Keating joined the Ultonia Regiment in 1748, fought in the War of the Austrian Succession, was Adjutant to the famous Lacy at the siege of Gibraltar, and in 1784 became the commander of all artillery in New Spain. Keating

was undoubtedly one of the outstanding members of the Wild
Geese; he actually served forty-three years in the Spanish army.
Carlos Connely also joined the Ultonia Regiment in 1767 as
a cadet. He found his way into the Philippine Dragoons in
1771 where he spent eight years. He then joined the Dragoons
of Spain where he spent another thirteen years. And according
to military records he served as Captain but held the rank of
Lieutenant-Colonel.

Lucas Tracy was also in Mexico but the probability is that
his parents were actually born in Spain. He had joined the
Irlanda Regiment. At any rate by the time he arrived in Mexico
he had been thirty-four years in a Spanish Irish Regiment.
There were others also of note in Mexico about this time, some
of whom had fought in the Spanish-Portuguese campaign of
1762.

The second Irish military incursion into Mexico took place
in 1847 when America was at war with Mexico over Texas,
Arizona and California. [When Mexico won her independence
from Spain, she took over all the land that Spain had held.
This included not only what is now Mexico, but also what is
now Texas, Arizona, New Mexico and California.] Although
there were only a few scattered Mexican settlements in Texas
and California, the part of the United States next to Texas was
filling up rapidly with Americans. The dictator of Mexico at
the time was the notorious Santa Ana. He was as determined
to stop the hordes of Americans moving into Texas as America
was to keep the Mexicans out. These were the days when a
somewhat questionable glamour surrounded Sam Houston and
various other romantic figures of the southwest. However, on
28 February 1846 Texas was admitted to the Union and had,
therefore, a big brother behind her to help teach the Mexicans
a lesson.

General Zachary Taylor led an army against Santa Ana —
an army which included a large number of Irish soldiers.
Whether for idealistic reasons or in dereliction of duty because
of carousing and womanizing or because of false promises on
the part of the Mexicans, a large number of the Irish troops
deserted to the Mexican side. General Ampudía, in command
of the Mexican forces at Matamoras, urged the immigrants
from many European nations fighting with the American force

not 'to defend a robbery and usurpation which, be assured, the civilized nations of Europe look upon with the utmost indignation.'[2]

There is enormous controversy as to how many deserters there were, and possibly in the future historians may uncover some more accurate records than exist at the moment. A William M. Sweeny in the *Journal of the American Irish Historical Society*[3] states that there were only seventy or eighty deserters. In a journal with that title one would naturally expect that the dishonour of the Irish might be underplayed. But reason would seem to indicate that, in fact, the number was larger. More recent theses on the subject indicate official American acknowledgement of a much greater number. The deserters were formed into what was known as the San Patricio Battalion which was known by the Mexicans as Legión de Estrangeros. Deserters were offered a reward by the Mexican commander General Arista of 320 acres of good land; in fact, General Taylor commanding the American force stated himself that 'efforts are continually being made to entice our men to desert, and I regret to say, have met with considerable success.'[4]

The Mexican clergy, being almost totally Catholic, were reputed to be deeply involved in the Irish seduction and influenced the Irish Catholics by assuring them that it was their religious duty to defend Mexico.

The Irish Mexican battalion first came to prominence in the Battle of Buena Vista where it fought as a battery of artillery of 18 and 24-pounders. The Irish were, in fact, highly praised for their special ability to move these guns speedily over very difficult terrain. The next mention of them is made in the Battle of Churubusco. In this battle the Mexicans were defeated and many of the Irish, including their commanding officer one John Riley, were captured. Some idea of the disagreement over numbers of deserters can be gathered from Professor Richard Blaine McCornack's statement that: 'In the Battle of Churubusco, some 85 of the 200 men who formed the battalion were taken prisoner.'[5]

McCornack's figure of 200 certainly conflicts with Sweeny's of '70 or 80'. All the prisoners were tried by court-martial, one of which was presided over, strangely enough, by a Colonel

Bennet Riley. Fifty of the prisoners were hanged; sixteen others were sentenced 'to receive fifty lashes well laid on with a raw hide on his bare back : to forfeit all pay and allowances that are or may become due him : to be indelibly marked on the right hip, with the letter "D", two inches in length : to wear an iron yoke weighing eight pounds with three prongs, each one foot in length, around his neck : to be confined at hard labor, in charge of the guard during the time the Army remains in Mexico : and then to have his head shaved and be drummed out of the service.'[6]

Whether because he had the same surname as the President of the court martial or for some other more acceptable reason, John Riley was one of the captured soldiers who was flogged instead of hanged. Various writers give different accounts of his later life. Some say he married a rich Mexican lady and became a Colonel in the Mexican army. Others trace him to some peculiar damnation of their own imagining. A few facts, however, stand out : all who have written on the subject agree that the ferocity of the battle was due entirely to fact that the Irish were fighting Irish and that after the defeat of the Mexican side 'the Irishmen in our army, who had remained true to their colors, were the most clamorous for their execution.'[7]

It is well to realize that this incident highlights the maudlin sentiment and emotionalism that have frequently obliterated truth in recounting the adventures of the Wild Geese. They were not, by any means, all swans.

In an extract from the First Recorded Efficiency Report in the files of the United States War Department, dated 15 August 1813, we find the following :

Lower Seneca Town
August 15, 1813

Sir,

I forward a list of the officers of the 27th Regt. of Infantry arranged agreeable to rank. Annexed thereto you will find all the observations I deem necessary to make.

Respectfully,
I am, Sir
Your Obt. Servt.
LEWIS CASS
27th Regt. Infantry

1st Lieut. Wm. Perrin	Low vulgar men, with the
„ „ Danl. Scott	exception of Perrin. Irish
„ „ Jas. Ryan	and from the meanest
„ „ Robt. McElwrath	walks of life — possessing
	nothing of the character of
	officers and gentlemen.
2nd Lieut. Oliver Vance	All Irish, promoted from
„ „ Royal Geer	the ranks, low vulgar men
„ „ Miars „	without any one qualifica-
„ „ Crawford	tion to recommend them —
„ „ Clifford	more fit to carry the hod
	than the epaulette.[8]

This denigrating report can be counter-balanced by reference to a hundred histories. One short letter written by the Commander in Chief of the American Army in Mexico, General Winfield Scott, to a U.S. Congressman [William E. Robinson, a famous journalist who was elected to Congress as a Representative from New York in 1866] in New York provides a shining example of the other side of the picture : 'Truth obliges me to say that, of our Irish soldiers save a few who deserted from General Taylor, and who had never taken the naturalization oath — not one ever turned his back upon the enemy or faltered in advancing to the charge.'[9]

Because of the fine reputation of the Spanish Wild Geese, a special Irish unit found its way to Brazil but with results that were far from glorious. In 1826 Colonel Cotter, an Irish officer in the Brazilian service, was sent to Ireland by the Brazilian government to recruit soldiers to fight the Argentinians. Once again they were the victims of lavish promises : each man was to receive a shilling a day, one pound of beef and one pound of bread as rations, and was to be employed four hours each day in learning military exercises. A promise was made to them that they would not be sent out of the province of Rio unless in time of war or invasion. At the end of five years each soldier was to be given fifty acres of land suitable for farming. Cotter's recruiting expedition was highly successful; he was inundated with applications and 2,400 men, women and children sailed from Ireland in sturdy well-provisioned ships.

The Irish suffered another bitter lesson. On their arrival

G*

in Brazil no arrangements had been made for them; the then Brazilian Minister of War Barbozo, who had only just taken up the appointment, hated the idea of foreign soldiers and was determined to make life as miserable as possible for the new recruits. He was highly successful : the Irish received only less than half the promised pay; they were frequently left without rations and bedding and in a very short time were riddled with disease. No medicines were available to help them. For some reason the people in Rio de Janeiro, particularly those of Negro descent, despised the Irish whom they rated as slaves like themselves. Barbozo forbade the Irish to be armed when off duty; consequently, the 'escravos brancos' (white slaves) as they were called were easy victims for their enemies. The police deliberately refrained from interfering and, as far as the Irish were concerned, were unjust to the point of the ridiculous.

German troops had been recruited also, before Barbozo had become minister. They too received the cold shoulder but neither they nor the Irish intended to put up with the treatment they were receiving. They joined forces and on the night of 12 June 1828 mutinied in Rio, attacked the Negroes, and, to use an oft-repeated but accurate cliché, the streets ran red with blood.

Barbozo realized that he had gone too far so in July of that year four ships including the *Morro Castle* and *The Highlander* brought most of them home. Some 220 were invited to form a colony at Bahia; some years later a few of them were found languishing in Brazilian jails.

Despite all of their troubles some of their descendants are remembered for feats in Brazilian history, for in 1890 the Brazilian government bestowed the Order of Aviz of the class of Chevalier on Anthony Shaw, Albert O'Connell, Alfred McGuinness, and Alfonsis Martins.

---

1. Quoted by W. S. Murphy in *The Irish Sword,* vol. 2, p. 260.
2. 30 Congress, I Session, *House Executive Document No. 60,* pp. 303-304.
3. Vol. 26, 1927, p. 255.
4. 30 Congress, I Session, *House Executive Document No. 60,* p. 133.
5. *The Americas,* vol. VIII, no. 2, October 1951, pp. 131-142.

6. General Order 283, 11 September 1847, U.S. Archives, A U.S., Office of the Adj. Gen., Mexican War, Army of Occupation, Miscellaneous Papers, R.G. 94, Box 7.

7. Quoted by Raphael Semmes in *The Campaign of General Scott in the Valley of Mexico,* p. 316.

8. E. H. O'Toole in *The Irish Sword,* vol. 6, pp. 56-57.

9. Quoted by William M. Sweeny in *Journal of the American Irish Historical Society,* vol. 26, 1927, p. 256.

CHAPTER XVIII

The Last of The Wild Geese

Oh Mother of the Wounded Breast
Oh Mother of the tears,
The sons you loved and trusted best
Have grasped their battle-spears.
From Shannon, Lagan, Liffey, Lee,
On Afric's soil to-day
We strike for Ireland, brave old Ireland,
Ireland far away.

— Arthur Griffith

It is not an exaggeration to state that for the past three hundred years the Wild Geese have taken their armies to every part of the globe and have settled down on every continent save Antarctica. This survey cannot end without a look at the indentation they made on the African continent. It was there that two Irish Brigades were formed in the tradition of the Wild Geese.

Reference has been made already to an Irish Brigade operating in Spanish North Africa in the eighteenth century; nearly two hundred years later two special Irish Brigades were formed to help the Boers in South Africa. The first was formed by Mr John MacBride from County Mayo who was an employee of the Rand mines. A leading authority on the Irish participation in the Boer War, Walter McGrath, wrote :

From the start they were a patriot band. The original idea to form the Brigade actually arose out of the very active '98 Centenary Committees which were functioning in Johannesburg and Pretoria from 1896 to 1898, and which included many Fenians. In the latter year huge rallies were held in both cities at which many thousands paid honour to the memory of Wolfe Tone and his associates. One of their most active organizers was a South African baker named Sol

Gillingham, (who had no Irish blood in his veins but was greatly devoted to Ireland's cause), and he travelled to Dublin in '98 to represent the South African Irish at the home celebrations. MacBride, who at that time was resident in South Africa as a mine assayer, was one of the leading lights in the activities there, and as it became more and more obvious that war between the Boers and the British was inevitable, he suggested the idea of an armed Brigade to his committee. His suggestion was received with enthusiasm.

Many Irishmen had emigrated to the Transvaal so that when he made an appeal for Irishmen to fight on the side of the Boers he found a ready response in those who were reminded constantly of the many infamies against their own country by the British. Consultation with the Boers resulted in the decision to form a special corps. It was commanded by John Franklin Blake, an ex-West Point graduate from the U.S. who had seen service in the U.S. Cavalry in Arizona. Perhaps the following passage will illustrate the extraordinary attitude to freedom which was rampant at the time : 'He was attracted to Rhodesia after the grabbing of that country from the Matabele, and the subsequent press laudation of its alleged mines and resources by Mr Cecil Rhodes' various booming agencies.'[1]

Blake had fought the Indians, had given no thought to their freedom; the unfortunate Matabele moved him not but he still 'loved freedom.' The probability that anyone who was not Christian, with the possible exception of the Jews, was at that time ranked as a savage and not entitled to any form of human consideration, far less being given the liberty which was the right of white people.

It was at Dundee that the Brigade members received their 'baptism of fire'. They reached the place in drenching torrents of rain which did little to dampen their enthusiasm. It must have been a greater cause of concern to them to find that, assigned as they were to the artillery of Commandant Trichardt, they were opposed by Colonel Moller and his Royal Irish Fusiliers. In the subsequent engagement many of the fusiliers were driven into a cattle-kraal and forced to surrender, and some of the Brigade recognized and spoke to former school-fellows of theirs, whose humiliation and shame must have been a cause of great sadness to them. The retreat of the British at Dundee was later referred to in the English papers as the 'glorious British victory of Dundee'.

As long as the South African war is remembered in history, the long-drawn out Siege of Ladysmith, in which Boer bravery was negatived by bad leadership and which ended in a great victory for the enemy, will be spoken of. It was specially in honour of the Irish Brigade while camped on the slopes around the town that Griffith wrote the anthem of which some lines are quoted at the commencement of this chapter. The Irish were everywhere in the thick of the bursting shells around Pepworth Hill, and in his memoirs MacBride related that one morning as the Irish flag waved opposite the British fortifications a comrade-in-arms recited for him the words of a little-known verse on Fontenoy :

> '*We looked upon that Banner*
> *And our memories sadly rose*
> *Of our homes and perished kindred*
> *Where the Lee and Shannon flows*
> *We looked upon that Banner*
> *And we swore to God on high*
> *To smite to-day the Saxon might*
> *To conquer or to die.*'[2]

One of Blake's men, O'Reilly, distinguished himself on this occasion with that audacious courage associated with the Irish Brigades wherever they were. When MacBride's horse fell and threw him, O'Reilly placed himself between MacBride and the English guns while his superior remounted his horse.

In 1900 a second Irish brigade was formed by an Irish Australian who had gone to the Transvaal as a war correspondent for a Paris newspaper. Arthur Lynch was his name and he, like so many descendants of the Wild Geese who had made their way to Australia, became enamoured of the Boer cause. Apparently, the brigade formed by Lynch was known as the Second Irish Brigade of the Boer War. Michael Davitt, in his history of the Boer War, when referring to Lynch states : 'He was elected to the post of colonel, and being an able linguist, speaking French and German with fluency, he succeeded in enlisting about 150 "Irishmen" from several European nationalities, not hitherto reckoned as subordinate members of the Celtic racial family. Colonel Lynch soon earned such a reputation for capacity and for looking carefully after the comforts of his men that numbers of volunteers from other commandoes were induced to join the Second "Irish" Brigade.'[3]

In this war also there was a small contingent of Chicago Irish-American volunteers who were under the command of a Captain O'Connor. This particular group brought with them a number of Irish doctors who were of very considerable help to the Boers. It was in the Battle of Colenso that part of Blake's Irish Brigade dragged to the fore once again the extraordinary and unfortunate custom — now almost on the brink of becoming tradition — of Irish fighting Irish. Botha was commanding the Boer Army; one of the English divisions on the opposite side was General Hart's which was composed of three crack Anglo-Irish regiments and the Border Regiment. The Irish were the Dublin Fusiliers, the Connaught Rangers, and the Inniskillings. The very first shell of the battle exploded in the midst of the Dublin Fusiliers before they had time to deploy. The surprise was so shattering that the English force took a severe mauling.

As Davitt wrote: 'They had all lost their heads early in the fight, and Mr Thomas Atkins is not trained or expected to act independently of his superiors in any emergency. In this instance the troops were mainly Anglo-Irish and whatever initiative and courage was shown by the groups or companies of the Dublin Fusiliers or Connaughts who rushed for the river bank in face of the Mauser fire was exhibited in the spirit of desperate men who saw themselves helplessly led and hopelessly beaten.'[4]

With the exception of the Irishmen who fought at the Battle of Fontenoy there seems to be no record of feelings of abhorrence about their butchery of their fellowmen on the opposite side. One man who returned home from South Africa had cause to remember later in the Irish Civil War the bitterness that sours the air when brother fights brother. He was Arthur Griffith, the chief architect of the struggle that was to end in the Irish Treaty of 1922.

Arthur Griffith was back in Ireland when the Boer War broke out but his knowledge of South Africa had taught him how Boer guerilla warfare had enabled the Dutchmen to carry their unswerving determination for independence to a satisfactory conclusion. It was Griffith who realized that what could be done in South Africa could be done in Ireland. He picked the man to do it — Michael Collins.

And that dark cloud that had hung over the Wild Geese so often hung over the Irish scene in 1922 when, ten days after Griffith's own death, an Irish bullet fired by a brother Irishman killed Michael Collins — this time in different circumstances from so many past vicissitudes of the Wild Geese — on Irish soil. The need for the Wild Geese was practically over; the dank air remained and, at the time of writing this, still pollutes the Irish sky.

1. Michael Davitt, *The Boer Fight for Freedom*, p. 318.
2. Walter McGrath in the *Evening Echo*, 30 May 1956.
3. Michael Davitt, *The Boer Fight*, p. 322.
4. *Ibid.*, p. 265.

Conclusion

'Those who have chosen a voluntary exile, to get rid of oppression, have given themselves, with great gaiety of spirit, to the slaughter, in foreign and ungrateful service, to the number of above 120,000 men, within these forty years. They have shown a great deal of gallantry in the defence of foreign states and princes with very little advantages to themselves but that of being free; and without half the outward marks of distinction they deserved.'

— Sir Charles Wogan's reply to the
letter written by Dean Swift and
quoted at the beginning of Chapter XVII,
The Works of Jonathan Swift

If the Wild Geese are to be assessed in terms of brilliant and courageous achievement, they have won their place in the history of the nations. Unhappily, both at home and in places abroad, they have been glamorized to a degree that tends to detract rather than to enhance their contribution to humanity. If history is to be really valuable, then it must be devoid of sentiment. The scholar will ask immediately : how can history be written in such fashion? Certainly there is much better chance of objectivity the greater the margin of time between the event and its recording. At least, in such circumstances, time has had opportunity to modify emotion and melt some of the sentimentality.

Much has been written of Irish heroism. An honest effort has been made here to dispel the idea that the record of the Wild Geese was all glory.

The Irish who have stayed at home tend to display an enormous pride in the achievements of their fellow countrymen in other lands. It is justified but it raises a vital issue : did the circumstances of the Wild Geese emigration in the beginning create in them the concept that they were a nation especially fitted for mercenary adventure? Or did the Wild Geese record create in the Irish at home the urge to emulate the exiles in order to further national pride? The fact does remain that those who remained at home developed the idea that most emigrants should have in them the urge to gravitate to fighting and armies.

History forced them to leave their homeland as warriors. At the time of their departure few of them had any other skill and when they were betrayed by those whom they had left to serve, there was little else they could turn to. Dire necessity forced them to become adventurers. But from the nineteenth century onwards many of them have given evidence that they are capable of other things. Their literary and cultural contributions to the world have been great, and still, hidden away in the countries of Europe — in fact, in most parts of the world — are unknown men of Irish descent who are benefiting humanity in every area. This is not to say that they do not still produce military leaders in the world. Unhappily, up to the last war, this military genius was harnessed so that one Irishman always fought another. It was also exploited by other nations; probably the strangest of all of Ireland's many paradoxes is that in the last World War, for the first time in their history, those Irishmen who fought, fought together. Hence, in every theatre of war, on a proportionate basis they received probably more decorations than any other single people.

Ireland has now entered a new phase in its political and cultural life. Authors should not preach but they have the right to hope. The hope of this one is expressed in the words of John Boyle O'Reilly when he addressed the 150th Anniversary of the Irish Charitable Society, Boston, 17 March 1887:

> *Exile is God's alchemy! Nations he forms like metals —*
> *Mixing their strength and their tenderness;*
> *Tempering pride with shame and victory with affliction;*
> *Timing their genesis to the world's needs!*

That hope could be fulfilled if in the years to come the Irish people will listen to another of their poets:

> *Stay, countrymen! — e'en yet there's time —*
> *we'll settle all your score —*

*We cannot spare such honoured men — 'twould grieve
  our hearts too sore;
Things will go smooth — why quit the scene a
  thousand things made dear.
That wealth may deck ye in the spoils torn from
  affection here?**

*Digby Pilot Starkey, M.R.I.A., 'The Emigrants' edited by J. H.
O'Kelly, published by M. H. Gill & Sons, Ltd., Dublin, 1905, p. 200.

Military Chronology

War of the League of Augsburg, 1686-1697
A defensive league formed in 1686 against France. Its chief architect was William of Orange (later William III England) and its members included Spain, Sweden, Saxony, the Palatinate, the German area of Swabia, Franconia, Upper Saxony, Bavaria and the United Provinces. Pope Innocent XI gave his secret support to the League. In 1687 it was joined by the Duke of Savoy and the Elector of Bavaria. In 1689 it became known as the Grand Alliance of Europe against Louis XIV. It ended with the Treaty of Ryswick in 1697.

The Declaration of Rights, England 1688
Officially deposed James II from the English throne and secured the Protestant succession in England by vesting the English monarchy in William, Prince of Orange, and his wife, Mary. Mary was James II's daughter by his first marriage. James II, aided by Louis XIV, endeavoured to take back the crown by using Ireland as a base for his military operations. William defeated his father-in-law at the Battle of the Boyne thereby establishing himself firmly on the English throne.

Great Northern War, 1699-1721
Peter I joined Denmark and Poland to stop Swedish expansion under Charles XII. Ended with the Peace of Nystadt, 1721, after which Sweden ceased to be a great power.

War of the Spanish Succession, 1701-1713
This was a military line-up with almost the same combatants as the Grand Alliance except that Spain joined France as an ally. The war was caused by Louis XIV's attempt, with the connivanse of Philip V of Spain, to unite France and Spain.

It was fought in Italy to secure the Milanese; in the Netherlands for the Barrier Fortresses; in Germany for the control of the Danube; in Spain for the Crown.

The Turkish War, 1736-1739
Fought partly because of Russian traditional hatred of the Turks, the successors of the Tartars, and partly because of Russia's desire to expand to the south and south-east.

War of the Austrian Succession, 1740-1748
In 1740 Charles VI of Austria died and by a will, known as 'The Pragmatic Sanction', bequeathed his dominions to his daughter, Maria Therese, in preference to the sons of his brother, Joseph I. The English upheld the Pragmatic Sanction; the French allied themselves to Frederick II of Prussia and the resultant war between them was known as the War of the Austrian Succession. Fontenoy was one of the battles.

Seven Years War, 1756-1763
Maria Therese of Austria and Elizabeth of Russia attacked Frederick II of Prussia with a view to dismembering Prussia and dividing it between them.

Bibliography

Amiable Renegade. The Memoirs of Captain Peter Drake, 1671-1753, Stanford, California and London, 1960

Archivo General, Simancas (A.G.S.) Estado, legajo 2751

Archivo General, Simancas (A.G.S.) Estado, legajo 1881

Archivo General, Simancas (A.G.S.) Estado, legajo 1865

Archivo del Regimiento Infanteria Morteros 120 — Ultonia No. 59

Archivo Histórico Nacional (A.H.N.) Madrid, Calatrava, Expediente, 1830

'Bonaventura' A Spanish Bishop, Cork Historical and Archaeological Society, 1961

Boyd, Thomas A., *Mad Anthony Wayne,* New York, 1929

Callahan, North, *Henry Knox, General Washington's General,* New York, 1958

The Cambridge Modern History, (vol. VI — The Eighteenth Century) Cambridge, 1934

Carty, James, *Ireland From the Flight of the Earls to Grattan's Parliament (1607-1782),* Dublin, 1949

Catton, Bruce, *The Centennial History of the Civil War,* vol. 3, London, 1966

The Celt (Dublin, John O'Daly), nos 19, 20; 5, 12 December 1857

de Chastellux, Marquis, *Travels in America in 1780-1782,* London, 1787

Cianáin, Tadhg Ó, *The Flight of the Earls,* (edited from the author's manuscript, with translation and notes by the Rev. Paul Walsh, M.A.), Record Society, St Patrick's College, Maynooth; Dublin, 1916

Clissold, Stephen, *Bernardo O'Higgins and the Independence of Chile,* London, 1968

Coleman, Terry, *Passage to America,* London, 1972.

Corkery, Daniel, *The Hidden Ireland,* Dublin, 1967

Coxe, *Life of Marlborough,* vol. I

Davitt, Michael, *The Boer Fight for Freedom,* New York and London, 1902

Duffy, Christopher, *The Wild Goose and the Eagle, A Life of Marshal von Browne, 1705-1757,* London, 1964

Erlanger, Philippe, *Louis XIV* (translation), London, 1970

Fisher, H. A. L., *A History of Europe,* London, 1936.

Fiske, *The Mississippi Valley in the Civil War,* New York

Gibson, John S., *Ships of the '45*, London, 1967

Grant, James, *The Cavaliers of Fortune*, London, 1858

Harcourt, Felice (ed. and trans.), *Memoirs of Madame de la Tour du Pin*, London, 1969

Hayden, Mary and Moonan, George A., *A Short History of the Irish People* (Part I — From the Earliest Times to 1603), Dublin and Cork

Hayes, Richard, *Biographical Dictionary of Irishmen in France*, Dublin, 1949

Hennessy, Maurice, *The Rajah from Tipperary*, London, 1971

Horsman, Reginald, *The War of 1812*, London, 1969

The Irish Sword (The Journal of the Military History Society of Ireland) vols. I, II, III, IV, V, VI, VII, VIII, IX, X

Jennings O. F. M., D.Litt., M.R.I.A., Brendan, *Wild Geese in Spanish Flanders, 1582-1700*, (Documents, Relating Chiefly to Irish Regiments, From the Archives Générales Du Royaume, Brussels, and Other Sources); Dublin: Stationery Office for the Irish Manuscripts Commission, 1964

Johnson, Gerald W., *America Grows Up*, New York, 1960

Jones, Paul, *The Irish Brigade*, Washington, New York, 1969

The Journal of the American Irish Historical Society, vols. XXI, XXV, XXVI, XXVII, XXIX, XXXI; Published by the Society, New York

de Lally-Tollendal, Marquis, *Plaidoyer du Comte de Lally-Tollendal*, Rouen, 1780

Lawless, Emily, *With the Wild Geese*, London, 1902

Letters and Papers of Major-General John Sullivan, Continental Army, 3 vols., New Hampshire, 1930

The London Irish at War (A History of the Battalions of the London Irish Rifles in World War II); published on behalf of the London Irish Rifles Old Comrades' Association, Duke of York Headquarters, Chelsea, S.W.3

Mac Manus, Francis, *After the Flight*, Dublin, 1938

Manuscript 12161 in the Fonds Français of the Bibliothèque Nationale, Paris

Morris, William O'Connor, *Memoirs of Gerald O'Connor*, 1903

Murphy, M.A., John A., *Justin MacCarthy, Lord Mountcashel, Commander of the First Irish Brigade in France*, Cork, 1959

Murphy, Richard C. and Mannion, Lawrence J., *The History of the Society of the Friendly Sons of Saint Patrick, In the City of New York, 1784-1955*, New York, 1962

Négociations de M. Le Comte d'Avaux en Irlande 1689-90, Irish Manuscripts Commission, Dublin, 1934

Nettels, Curtis P., *The Roots of American Civilization*, New York, 1939

O'Brien, Michael J., *A Hidden Phase of American History*, New York, 1919

O'Brien, R. Barrie (ed.), *The Autobiography of Theobald Wolfe Tone 1763-1798*, London, 1893

O'Cahan, T. S., *Owen Roe O'Neill*, London, 1968

O'Callaghan, John Cornelius, *History of the Irish Brigades in the Service of France,* Shannon, 1969

O'Connor, Frank, *A Book of Ireland,* London, 1959

O'Conor, Matthew, *Military History of the Irish Nation,* Dublin, 1845

O'Crouley, Pedro Alonso, *The Kingdom of New Spain,* translated and edited by Seán Galvin, Dublin, 1972

O'Donnell, Elliot, *The Irish Abroad* (A Record of the Achievements of Wanderers from Ireland), London, 1915

O'Faoláin, Seán, *King of the Beggars* (A Life of Daniel O'Connell, The Irish Liberator, in a Study of the Rise of the Modern Irish Democracy 1775-1847), London, 1938

O'Kelly, J. J. (ed.), *Gill's Irish Reciter,* Dublin, 1905

O'Mahony, B.D., B.C.L., Rev. D., *Irish Footprints on the Continent,* London, 1927

Petrie, Bart., Sir Charles, *The Jacobite Movement — The Last Phase 1716-1807,* London, 1950

Plowden, Francis, *An Historical Review of the State of Ireland,* vol. I, London, 1803

Rankin, Hugh (ed.), *The American Revolution,* London, 1964

Russell, Diarmuid (ed.), *The Portable Irish Reader,* New York, 1946

Semmes, Raphael, *The Campaign of General Scott in the Valley of Mexico,* Cincinnati, 1852

Smith, Lewis Ferdinand, *A Sketch of the Rise, Progress and Termination of the Regular Corps Formed and Commanded by Europeans in the Service of the Native Princes of India,* Calcutta, 1805

Stephens, James, *Collected Poems,* London, 1954

Strong, George Templeton, *Diary of the Civil War, 1860-1865*

Sullivan, James (ed.), *Papers of Sir William Johnson,* 10 vols., New York, 1921-35

Thomas, Hugh, *The Spanish Civil War,* London, 1961

Thorpe's Catalogue for 1834 of the Southwell Mss.

Todhunter, John, *The Life of Patrick Sarsfield (Earl of Lucan),* London, 1895

Trevelyan, G. M., *Garibaldi and the Making of Italy,* London, 1928 edition

Voltaire, *Fragments sur L'Inde, sur le Général Lalli, etc.,* Paris, 1773

Walsh, Micheline (ed.), *Spanish Knights of Irish Origin (Documents from Continental Archives)* vols. II and III, Irish Manuscripts Commission, 1965 and 1970

White, Jon Manchip, *The Life and Times of Maurice Comte de Saxe, 1696-1750,* London, 1962

Index